THE GREAT

BASEBALL

REVOLT

THE GREAT

BASEBALL

REVOLT

The Rise and Fall of the 1890 Players League

ROBERT B. ROSS

University of Nebraska Press | Lincoln and London

© 2016 by Robert B. Ross. Portions of chapters 1, 2, 3, and 7 were published in Robert Ross, "Contradictions of Cultural Production and the Geographies That (Mostly) Resolve Them: 19th-Century Baseball and the Rise of the 1890 Players League," in *Environment and Planning D: Society and Space* 26, no. 6 (2008): 983–1000. Portions of chapter 5 were published in "Scales and Skills of Monopoly Power: Labor Geographies of the 1890–1891 Chicago Carpenters' Strike," in *Antipode* 43, no. 4 (2011): 1281–1304.

Library of Congress Cataloging-in-Publication Data
Names: Ross, Robert B., 1976–
Title: The great baseball revolt: the rise and fall of the 1890 Players League / Robert B. Ross.
Description: Lincoln: University of Nebraska Press, [2016]
Includes bibliographical references and index.
Identifiers: LCCN 2015035768
ISBN 9780803249417 (cloth: alk. paper)
ISBN 9780803294783 (epub)
ISBN 9780803294790 (mobi)
ISBN 9780803294806 (pdf)
Subjects: LCSH: Players League (Baseball league)—History.
Baseball—United States—History—19th century.
Classification: LCC GV875.P55 .R67 2016 |
DDC 796.357/64097309034—dc23 LC record
available at http://lccn.loc.gov/2015035768

Set in Lyon Text by L. Auten.

This book is dedicated to the memory
of my father, Robert B. Ross Sr.
May he rest in peace and may the
Orioles win the World Series.

CONTENTS

ILLUSTRATIONS

ACKNOWLEDGMENTS

This book was ten years in the making. It traveled with me from Syracuse to Cooperstown, to Brooklyn, to Beirut, back to Syracuse, and finally to Pittsburgh. I am afraid it will be impossible to acknowledge everyone who contributed to its development and completion. But I will try.

The following institutions provided various resources that helped make this book possible: Syracuse University; the Syracuse University Graduate School; the Maxwell School for Citizenship and Public Affairs; the Syracuse University Department of Geography; the Roscoe Martin Fund; the Chicago Historical Museum; the National Baseball Hall of Fame Library in Cooperstown (particularly Tim Wiles and John Horne); Sunny's Bar; the New York Public Library; the Brooklyn Public Library; the Boston Public Library; New York University and the Tamiment Labor Archives; the Society for American Baseball Research; the Tri-State College of Acupuncture; the Brooklyn Artists Gym; Room 58; the Pioneer; the American University of Beirut and its Center for American Studies and Research; the University of Nebraska Press; the University of Pittsburgh; the Heinz History Center; the Pittsburgh chapter of Orioles club; Espresso a Mano; Point Park University, including its Office of Academic and Student Affairs, the School of Arts and Sciences, the Department of Humanities and Human Sciences (especially Kim Bell, Kris Julian, and Julie Russell), and the Global Cultural Studies Program. The librarians at Point Park deserve special mention. Liz Evans, Dev Albarelli, Lauren Irwin, Melanie Kirchartz, Margie Stampahar, Robert Stancampiano, and Mandee Williams, in particular, went above and beyond the call of duty to help me track down various sources and resources.

Several professors have instructed, inspired, and encouraged me over the past twenty years. They have all contributed, whether directly or indirectly, to *The Great Baseball Revolt*. At the top of this very long list are Don Mitchell, Richard Dennis, Paul Stoller, Tod Rutherford, Jamie Winders, John Mercer, Leigh Shaffer, Helen Berger, James Trotman, Joan Welch, James Kneale, Ann Varley, Linda McDowell, and Sudipta Sen.

My dissertation committee at Syracuse University played the most direct role in helping me develop and shape this book. Chief among them is Don Mitchell. I will forever be indebted to him for his extraordinarily helpful supervision and for the example he continues to set as a radical scholar and teacher. This book would never have gotten off the ground, however, if not also for the countless hours that Tod Rutherford, Jamie Winders, John Mercer, Mike Wasylenko, and Richard Dennis spent reading and responding to its various drafts. Their critiques and suggestions allowed me to see the work's weaknesses as well as its strengths, particularly in relation to the research process itself. Gavin Bridge and Anne Mosher played foundational roles in helping me get this research started in the first place.

The Society for American Baseball Research's Nineteenth Century Research group has served as a valuable resource for learning about the minutia and broader trends of early baseball. Three researchers among this group have been especially helpful: David Stevens, the author of *Baseball's Radical for All Seasons: A Biography of John Montgomery Ward*, Don Jensen, whose research on Helen Dauvray provided many important ideas related to John Ward, and John Thorn, official historian for Major League Baseball. More recently, Craig Britcher offered some excellent insight into Lou Bierbauer and the chaos that ensued after the Players League fell.

Brook Sloan got to know this book very well, and I am indebted to her for her feedback and friendship. Matt Huber, Jim Ketchum, and

Megan Ward have read more-recent parts of the book and offered much-needed suggestions and encouragement. I thank Rob Taylor, at the University of Nebraska Press, for taking on this project in the first place and for his helpful guidance throughout. Tish Fobben, Courtney Ochsner, Rosemary Vestal, Barbara Wojhoski, and Joeth Zucco, along with everyone else at the University of Nebraska Press, have also worked tirelessly to help me complete this project.

My health and well-being, which needed a bit of maintenance over the past ten years in order to write this book, owe a lot to the work of Mary Hart, Betty Lerer, Moriah Ella Mason, Tyler Phan, and Anne-Francois Potterat.

A number of students have played vital roles in the development of my thinking, research, and writing, including, especially, Sara Ajlyakin, Abrar Al Mubarak, Ana Bird, Jewell Bohlinger, Karen Bullock, Mert Chapulcu, Kelly Cline, Lindsay Dill, Hannah Gerbe, Hind Ghandour, Holden Holden, Ian Horne, Rachel Johnson, Lamis Jamil, Bella LaQuatra, Samey Lee, Mallory Locante, Sean McKeag, Alex Munroe, Eric Probola, Lisa Rectenwald, Glen Keith Richards, Julia Richards, Robyn Roux, Tyler Shoaf, Hannah Simon, Casy Stelitano, Ian Sulkowski, Maddy Toy, Hana Valle, and Ben Zebrasky, among countless others.

I am fortunate to have a growing group of colleagues and friends at each of the institutions where I have worked and studied and across the broader academy. I am deeply grateful for their support, both personally and professionally. These folks are often the intellectual and emotional fuel that keeps me moving: Jeremy Braverman, Bill Breslove, Carrie Breitbach, Lisa Bhungalia, Elizabeth Campbell, Tracy Carty, Jason Cross, Karen Dwyer, Jamey Essex, Cindy Franklin, Dwight Hines, Matt Huber, Laam Hae, Euan Hague, Kirstin Hanley, Sami Hermez, Matt Hidek, Matt Himley, Noel Ignatiev, Jim Ketchum, Marisa Lerer, Jenna Loyd, Patrick McGreevy, Alyson Newquist, Tony Novosel, Reecia Orzeck, Sarah Perrier, Bill Purcell, Jehnie Reis, Clayton Rosati, Sarah Schulz, Ron Smith, Tom Slater, Joaquin Villanueva, Patrick Vitale, Megan Ward, Kristine Weatherston, Katie Wells, and Erica Lorraine Williams.

My friends outside the academy have equally fueled the inspiration for and execution of this book. I am thankful, especially, to Alaa Aqra, Omar Abuhejleh, Jon Banuelos, Jon Barton, Rachel Bickel, Kyle Bostian, Katherine Cunningham, Kate Daher, Loubna El Abbadi, Jennifer Forester, Noushin Framke, Olivia Gleser, Aaron Hoke, Ryan Hoke, Scott Koerber, Matt Kresge, Dave Matlin, Matt McDermitt, Beth McMullen, John Miller, Alice Novosel, Mariana Padias, Mike Sandusky, Jason Sapp, and Rachael Simon.

I would not have written, much less finished, this book if not for the loving support and patience of my family. I am sad that I did not finish this book in time for my father, Bob Ross, my uncles, Tom Marecek and Corky Ross, and my grandparents, Martin and Gladys Marecek and Donald and Peggy Ross, to read it. Their influence on every page is nonetheless evident to me. I am thankful for the encouragement and interest expressed by my extended family, including the Allans: Britton, Sarah, Christian, Sonia, Kathy, and Michael; the Mareceks: Lori, Scott, and Katie; and the one and only, Cristy Waite. My biggest thanks, though, go out to Anne Ross, Becky Ross, and Ken Stroh. Everyone in these acknowledgments is a superstar, but you are Hall of Famers!

INTRODUCTION

The celebrity trial of the year began with great anticipation on the morning of January 9, 1890. At the Supreme Court of New York on Chambers Street in downtown Manhattan, hundreds of baseball fans and reporters crowded in and around the second courtroom. The New York Giants, of the National League, were suing their star shortstop, John Ward, for allegedly violating the so-called reserve clause of his contract. Ward was refusing to play for the Giants in the upcoming 1890 season, choosing instead to play for a new Brooklyn team, in a league that he and several other members of the Brotherhood of Professional Base Ball Players were forming themselves. The Players League, as it was to be called, would challenge the National League for dominance over the newly expanding markets for professional baseball. Unlike the National League, which featured an autocratic style of governance by team owners over their players, the Players League would be at least partially owned and controlled by the players themselves. Most significantly, the rival league would abolish the reserve rule, which inextricably bound nearly all players, not just Ward, to their respective clubs for the duration of their playing careers. "The movement," Ward had explained, "is an experiment on our part to have the men who do the work participate in the profits of the pastime."[1]

After Ward was seated, accompanied by his friend and fellow ballplayer Ned Hanlon and his lawyer, John Howland, the Giants' chief

Fig. 1. John Montgomery Ward. National Baseball
Hall of Fame Library, Cooperstown NY.

prosecutor, Charles Beaman, approached Judge Morgan O'Brien, who was presiding over the injunction hearing:

The New York Base Ball club . . . last year spent $40,000 for a new [ballpark] and have a large capital invested. [The plaintiffs'] business depends greatly upon the skill and reputation of their players. Mr. Ward is one of the best players in the country. The New York Club cannot fill his place at short stop [*sic*] by a man of equal ability. His services are in great demand, and I may remark in regard to all these good qualities that he is also a lawyer. . . . If Ward does not play with the club in 1890 his loss will be irreparable and will endanger part or the whole of the capital invested. Therefore we ask for a temporary injunction restraining him from playing with any other club.[2]

The crux of the matter was, indeed, that without "one of the best players in the country," the New York National League team would most likely fail. It was Ward's labor and reputation that brought so many fans to the Polo Grounds in Upper Manhattan to see the Giants play. In fact, although Ward was one of the best and most popular players of the time, each of the National League's eight teams had several recognizable superstars, without whom they would find it very difficult to attract many spectators to their games. These players, who were also threatening to join the Players League, were virtually irreplaceable. It is no wonder then that the Giants wished to use the reserve clause to hold Ward to their club.

But to the chagrin of the National League, Judge O'Brien ruled on January 29 in favor of the right-handed shortstop. The reserve clause, he argued, was not sufficiently clarified in the player's contract. Ward had not agreed to indefinitely play for the New York Giants. Upon leaving the courthouse that day, Ward commented to a reporter: "Now that the case has been practically settled, we will go to work and complete our task of organizing the strongest baseball association in the country. I don't know just what course our enemies will pursue, but it is safe to predict that the Brotherhood will come out on top. . . . [T]he men who have been brave enough to hold out in spite of the induce-ments offered in the shape of League gold will reap their reward, and they deserve it."[3]

With Ward's acquittal, along with three other similarly failed cases brought on by the National League, the Players League proceeded, full speed ahead. The players formed new clubs in eight cities: Boston, Brooklyn, Buffalo, Chicago, Cleveland, New York, Philadelphia, and Pittsburgh. They hired contractors to build new, ornate ballparks. And in March many of the players boarded trains or steamers on route to Alabama, Georgia, and Missouri for spring training.

This book explores the conditions that prefigured the rise of Ward's case and, more generally, the rise—and eventual fall—of the Players League. How and why, in other words, did professional baseball get to a point at which, one, it was a profitable investment, two, players like Ward were essential to this profitability, and three, these same men sought to revolt from the National League and form their own league? Furthermore, how did this revolt of baseball's labor force inter-sect with the broader labor movement of the time? And why did the Players League last only one year?

Successfully resisting the National League was no easy task. The league was baseball's only major league at the time, and by the mid-1880s, it had developed into an economic powerhouse. Although base-ball had been surging in popularity in the years after the Civil War, the National League was the first association of professional baseball clubs that became consistently profitable.

In order to become profitable, however, the National League had to resolve a problem fundamental to professional sports and the per-forming arts. As explained in chapter 1, baseball players were the source of the owners' greatest stream of revenue. But baseball's on-the-field labor force was also the source of its greatest cost. In most other indus-tries this contradiction has been resolved by introducing machinery, dividing the labor process into several discrete simple tasks, and imple-menting any other procedure that eliminates the need for specialized skills. De-skilling thus reduces wages and employee control over the workplace and work process. But in industries where the extraordinary skills of the workers set in motion is precisely what consumers pay to see, as is the case in professional baseball and the performing arts, de-skilling is impossible. De-skilling these workers, if it were possible at all, would cut labor costs but also destroy the means by which the industry attracts its customers.

The National League solved this problem through a series of strategies aimed at monopolizing its power over the markets for players and fans, as detailed in chapter 2. By the mid-1880s, with these strategies fully in place, the National League's owners managed to develop monopolies over the best talent and the highest-paying fans. There were still dozens of professional and semiprofessional baseball leagues, but only the National League was able to place professional clubs in the biggest cities and only the National League could sign and retain the game's best players. Between 1876 and 1889 twenty players who would later be inducted into the Hall of Fame played for National League clubs. Only three nineteenth-century Hall of Famers never played in the National League, and they were excluded only because they were black.

Most effective at keeping players and their salaries in check was the reserve rule, which prevented players from pitting teams in competition with one another for their services. But it was this rule, along with other draconian measures issued by the National League, that impelled John Ward and his New York Giants teammates to form the sport's first-ever labor union in 1885, the Brotherhood of Professional Base Ball Players. Membership quickly spread to the rest of the league. As chapter 3 reveals, several attempts over the following four years to negotiate with the National League failed to bear any fruit and, in fact, seemed to propel the league into further tightening the owners' control over the players' mobility, salaries, and behavior, both on and off the field. In November 1889 Ward announced that due to National League intransigence the brotherhood would be creating a new league, the Players National League of Professional Base Ball Clubs.

Ward, a Columbia University law school graduate and future Hall of Famer, had been one of the National League's star players since his debut in 1877. A pitcher-turned-shortstop, he threw an unparalleled curveball, was one of the game's fastest base runners, and among the league's sharpest infielders. But his intellect and gentlemanly demeanor earned him as much respect in the baseball world as his play on the field. His leadership of the clubs he played for and captained gained him especially high esteem among fellow players. Like his compatriots across the league, however, Ward was systematically exploited and mistreated by baseball's paternalistic owners. An intelligent leader on and off the field, and a disgruntled employee like any other, Ward thus made a fitting president of the brotherhood and de facto leader of the Players League.

The men who do the work on the field were not, however, able to start the league on their own. A significant amount of money was needed to incorporate the clubs, build the ballparks, and sign the players. Brotherhood leaders in each of the proposed new cities, therefore, found wealthy investors who would back the players' new scheme. These efforts to line up the necessary money, along with the search for appropriate locations for the ballparks and the players who still needed to sign contracts to play in them, are the subject of chapter 4.

Baseball players were not the only disgruntled employees in the 1880s. The industrialization of production was proceeding full speed ahead, and with it, came an ever expanding and thoroughly exploited working class. The movements among these workingmen to organize unions, form or integrate into political parties, and generally agitate for better working conditions, higher wages, and shorter workdays were reaching a crescendo in the 1880s. In 1886, a year after the brotherhood was formed, Chicago police officers shot to death a striking worker and wounded several others at the McCormick's Reaper Plant. This action triggered a protest rally in Haymarket Square the following evening, which ended in the firebombing and deaths of seven police officers and seven workers.[4] The backlash to the Haymarket incident among bosses and police across the country reversed many of the gains the labor movement had achieved. More than anything the Haymarket bombing enabled the enemies of workers to accuse all organized labor movements of secretly harboring an anarchist or otherwise radical ideology, one that would ultimately result in violence. But despite these setbacks, most labor movements marched on.

The emergence of the Players League within this climate was neither accidental nor inconsequential. The surrounding labor movements inspired and enabled baseball players to create their own campaigns. The workers they read about in the papers, who fell into their social circles, and alongside whom many had worked during the off seasons, fed these players with ideas and attitudes about their class positions, rights, privileges, and potential tactics. But the clubs of the Players League, insofar as they hired carpenters and bricklayers to build their ballparks, musical bands to perform at their games, and concession salesmen to satiate their fans, directly intersected with already-existing organizing campaigns, strikes, and boycotts of variously positioned workers. The movement to form and operate the Players League was thus not just one that coincided with other workers' movements of the late nineteenth century but one that at times collided with it as well. Chapter 5 discusses these connections and conflicts between the Players League and other workers' movements.

Ultimately, the Players League had to compete with the National League to provide the public with a more attractive product. Put simply "the men" had to play baseball and play it better than anyone else in the country. The two leagues scheduled most of their games at the same times, in the same cities. Fans in the eight major league cities, plus Cincinnati, where the National League had an additional club, were forced into choosing between baseball in a Players League ballpark or baseball in a National League ballpark. Channeling success on the field to success in the box office was never, in the history of baseball to that point, so intensely contested. The leagues' win-loss standings, or "championship record," as the newspapers put it, were often listed on the same page as the attendance standings.

During much of the 1890 season, it seemed that the Players League had a decided advantage. The majority of its players had played in the

National League in 1889, while most of the 1890 National League players had played in the lesser American Association or in other minor and amateur leagues in 1889. The new league's ballparks were generally more attractive and accommodating. And the league, in most places, had the support of organized labor. Chapter 6 reviews the 1890 season, including its many on- and off-the-field highlights.

As the title of this book reveals, the Players League lasted only one year. Despite its apparent advantages, it folded shortly after the 1890 season came to a close. The National League once again stood alone as the premier organization of professional baseball at the beginning of the 1891 season. Why did the Players League fall? How did a league with so much talent and so much public support fall apart as quickly as it was put together?

And finally, why does this matter anyway? Is the rise and fall of the Players League in any way relevant to labor movements within the contemporary sports industry? Chapters 7 and 8 attempt to answer these questions.

THE GREAT
BASEBALL
REVOLT

1

THE PROFESSIONALIZATION OF BASEBALL

Baseball transformed in the latter half of the nineteenth century from a recreational game into a professional sport. As a significant swath of Americans became wealthier, and players became better skilled at their craft, more people began paying money to see them play. In the process the sport established itself as a distinctly white, American, and manly pastime. But struggles over the class and cultural character of baseball—in terms of who could or should watch the game, who could play it, and how they would be compensated for their labor—became an integral part the sport for the remainder of the nineteenth century and well into the twentieth. Related to these struggles was a central contradiction between, on the one hand, increasing revenues from ticket sales and, on the other, increasing costs from the salaries of the players who generated those sales.

How did baseball come to this point? How did it become an embodiment of certain racial, national, and gendered values, a game that people paid money to watch other people play, and the grounds on which various class and cultural conflicts took place? In short the press, the Civil War, changes in the way that the sport was played, and attempts to shape the image of the game together made baseball into an increasingly expensive and culturally evocative commodity.

A key component of the professionalization of baseball was the existence of mass media that promoted and carefully analyzed the sport. References to baseball and to the games involving balls, bats, and bases, which preceded it, are peppered across a multilingual collection of mostly children's books that stretches back to the fifteenth century.[1] But it wasn't until the 1850s and 1860s that publications began to report on the game as it was played by organized teams of adults. The baseball publications of both eras promoted the game (whether intentionally or not), but not until the mid-nineteenth century did they begin to publicize the game as something people should watch (and eventually pay to watch), not just play. This shift in emphasis was necessary in order for the sport to develop into a profitable commodity. Promotion, though, was not conducted without the attachment of certain ideas and values, which associated the game with principally (but not exclusively) America, manliness, health, Victorian middle-class values, and more tacitly, whiteness. Put differently, in the alliterative recollection of Albert Spalding, baseball was "the exponent of American Courage, Confidence, Combativeness; American Dash, Discipline, Determination; American Energy, Eagerness, Enthusiasm; American Pluck, Persistency, Performance; American Spirit, Sagacity, Success; American Vim, Vigor, Virility."[2] That this description of baseball comes from Albert Spalding is relevant not only because he became thoroughly involved in the National League's confrontation with the Players League. It is relevant first because Spalding was deeply invested in the game of baseball as the owner of both an NL franchise and an international sporting-goods company. The promotion of baseball and the attribution of specific qualities to it carried, for Spalding at least, an economic incentive.

But baseball was not, as Spalding suggested, born in America. It originated in eighteenth-century England as a children's game involving a stick, ball, and bases.[3] When Puritan settlers arrived in New England, they brought the sport with them. Early baseball on American soil was thought to be a means by which Puritan culture could be retained and reinforced. Robert Burk explains: "If accommodated to Puritan priorities, ball games were ritual occasions for community and spiritual socialization, the display of fellowship and skill, and the acting out of life's tests of harmony and piety by sober, respectable men."[4]

ALBERT G. SPALDING.

Fig. 2. Albert Spalding. The Miriam and Ira D. Wallach Division of Art, Prints and Photographs: Photography Collection, The New York Public Library. "Al Spalding," New York Public Library Digital Collections.

Participation in baseball facilitated the reproduction of social life and, as the Puritan settlers began to integrate with other people, served as a defense against other, encroaching ways of life.

Soon, however, baseball's popularity spread beyond the settler communities and beyond Massachusetts. Still, the game's associations with morality, sobriety, gentlemanly behavior, and white-collar social cohesion remained. Boys and men alike continued to play baseball in increasing numbers, and in 1842 the first official baseball club was formed. The members of the Knickerbocker Base Ball Club of New York began playing organized games among themselves on a field at Twenty-Seventh Street and Fourth Avenue in New York. Three years later they secured permanent grounds at the Elysian Fields in Hoboken, a short ferry ride from Barclay Street in downtown Manhattan. The Knickerbockers were primarily an exclusive social club of white-collar Yankee men. "To the Knickerbockers," Harold Seymour explains, "a ball game was a vehicle for genteel amateur recreation and polite social intercourse rather than a hard-fought contest for victory. They were more expert with the knife and fork at post-game banquets than with bat and ball on the diamond. Their rules and regulations emphasized proper conduct, and the entire tone of their organization was more akin to the atmosphere surrounding cricket—a far cry from the ethic of modern professional baseball."[5] Baseball thus served as a social forum with which a certain identity could be expressed and maintained. Participation in the club allowed men to fend off increasing outside pressures that threatened the solidarity of their ethnic-, class-, and gender-based identities. Baseball then was seen to reinforce a particular social position.

Soon other baseball clubs formed under similar principles. But as baseball became more popular, the game began to express different values for different people. Burk explains:

As the number of teams [in the 1850s] and interclub matches expanded, so too did reports of on-field lapses of decorum and discipline within and between teams; such lapses ranged from swearing and fighting on the field to betting, indecent anecdotes and songs, and public drunkenness off it. The perceived loss of "order" in the game as well as its modest geographic and social spread in the urban Northeast were signals of a more fundamental, however subtle, shift in the game's focus for its participants. Traditionally, intraclub activities and fellowship had been emphasized, with the secondary aim of displaying, and verifying, to oneself and one's immediate brethren, a presupposed social and spiritual worth within a relatively stable local order. Now the players' emphasis was shifting toward ball-playing in interclub contests as a means to preserve a public status under siege or to accumulate a greater measure of outer worth, both materially and spiritually. The emerging ethic . . . was less communitarian, more competitive.[6]

A veiled class and culture war of sorts thus arose between the people who wished to secure baseball's traditional ideals and those who sought to undermine them. Importantly, as Burk later notes, those on the latter side of this conflict were increasingly of non-English descent and of the skilled working class.[7]

In response the traditionalists formed the National Association of Base Ball Players (NABBP) in 1858 in order to, as Burk puts it, "guard against a . . . subtle acceleration of baseball's social and moral declension and preserve avenues for its emerging 'reforming' and acquisitive roles."[8] Led by the Knickerbockers, the NABBP initially consisted of twenty-two baseball clubs, the vast majority of which played in New York City. Clubs could join the league with a five-dollar (and later, fifty-cent) admission fee. Payment for player services was prohibited, but many of the club officials foresaw opportunities for profit in the not-too-distant future. The NABBP delegates who controlled the association and represented the clubs were almost exclusively white-collar men of English descent even though some of the players were now of other European and skilled working-class backgrounds.

The birth of the NABBP and the game's concomitant popularity compelled newspapers in the Northeast to begin reporting on local games. In addition to descriptive game summaries, some of the papers printed box scores and commentaries on the direction of the sport. The vast majority of this coverage was limited to the New York papers. William Cauldwell, of the *New York Mercury*, became the first journalist to cover sports on a full-time basis. Outside the city the earliest known newspaper coverage of baseball can be found in the July 1 and 2, 1859, editions of the *Amherst Express, Extra*. Under the headline "Muscle and Mind!" are descriptions of baseball and chess competitions between Amherst and Williams Colleges.[9]

Offering more thorough and reliable coverage than the newspapers of the 1850s and 1860s, however, were a handful of weekly publications devoted to sports, literature, theater, and opera.

Chief among them, the *New York Clipper* began publishing news about theater and baseball, among other forms of entertainment, in 1853. But it wasn't until Henry Chadwick was called upon to write about baseball in 1856 that the paper covered that sport with some breadth, depth, and quality. Widely read by even the players of the ball field and the stage, the *Clipper* was the authority on all things dramatic and on the dramatic side of all things athletic. The paper reported on a number of different sporting events, but baseball was allotted the most space. In addition to the games of all "major leagues," the *Clipper* occasionally included box scores and detailed accounts of college, semiprofessional, regional, and minor league games. Chadwick, who emigrated from England as a boy in 1837, wrote so augustly and pro-lifically about baseball that he soon became known as "the father of baseball." Accordingly, he never shied from taking a position on base-ball disputes large and small.

In addition to writing for the *Clipper*, Chadwick wrote the annual *Beadle's Dime Base Ball Player*, a book-length guide to the game. The initial volume in 1860 included various sets of rules (the Massachu-setts, New York, and new NABBP rules, for example), playing instruc-tions, and a short history of the game. "In presenting this work to our readers," Chadwick wrote in the opening pages, "we claim for it the merit of being the first publication of its kind."[10] *Beadle's*, indeed, was the first of many annual baseball guides. It sold about fifty thousand copies each year between 1860 and 1866 until other guides entered the market and pushed down its sales.[11] The 1861 version featured the first comprehensive publication of player and team statistics, includ-ing all records of the 1860 NABBP season. The earliest use of batting average, a measure of player productivity that has remained central to baseball's numerical lexicon ever since, can be found in the 1864 volume.[12] *Beadle's* continued to serve the baseball world as an author-itatively informative and prescriptive guide until 1881.

The media notwithstanding, one of the most effective tools for expanding the popularity of baseball was the Civil War. Both Confed-erate and Union soldiers played the game among themselves and, in some situations where there were prisoners, with each other. The war also provided new terminology to describe the game, which baseball's scribes quickly and long thereafter employed. Pitchers and catchers, for example, became known as the "battery" and a pitchers' array of pitches as his "arsenal."[13] At the same time, however, the war drained the organized ranks of a good number of players. Although the NABBP saw the birth of clubs from nineteen new cities during the war, several more teams were not able to compete, and many had to fold. The better players may have enjoyed immunity from conscription, as their under-the-table salaries allowed them to buy their way out of the war. The result, after the war, was increased competition among fewer clubs for more talented players. The Civil War, thus, increased the popularity of baseball while decreasing the number of people who could play it; in turn, the heightened skill requirements further popularized the game. Despite the NABBP's prohibitions, teams began paying players and charging admission. The commodification of baseball had begun.

After the war, as the mounting interest in baseball created a voracious hunger for information about the game, the sport's media expanded and multiplied. *The Ball Player's Book of Reference* supplanted the primacy of Chadwick's guide, selling sixty-five thousand copies in 1867, its second year of publication.[14] Chadwick himself contributed to the multiplicity of baseball guides, as he continued writing *Beadle's* and joined Robert De Witt in 1868 to write *De Witt's Base-Ball Guide.*

Across these guides and in the weeklies and dailies, baseball's writers debated the vices and virtues of the increasing commercial element of the sport. Chadwick was an adamant proponent of a return to baseball's simpler, less commercial ways. Profiting from the game himself, Chadwick did not decry the financial aspect of the game per se as much as he scorned much of the behavior that came from it. Gambling surrounded and infiltrated the game to such an extent that many fans lost interest in what they perceived to be fixed contests. Violence, too, sprung up in both the grandstands and on the playing field. And players were paid by deceptive and even criminal means. When Albert Spalding was a young pitcher for the Chicago Excelsiors, he was nominally hired as a clerk for a grocery store associated with the team's owner. William Marcy "Boss" Tweed directed the New York Mutuals, and he kept his team competitive by secretly putting his players on the New York City municipal payroll. At one point, according to Seymour, Tweed's eleven players earned a combined $38,000 a year in salaries.[15] But while Chadwick (among others) was a vocal critic of these developments, he also helped popularize and refine baseball to an extent that it could scarcely escape commercialization.[16] In 1868, indeed, the NABBP saw no alternative but to legalize professionalism. It hoped that by bringing salaries out in the open, it could remove some of the seedier elements that under-the-table payments elicited.

But the NABBP, now with more than two thousand member clubs spread across the country, had little power to stop the sport's insidious vices. After the 1870 season the association folded.

Two new associations emerged in its wake. On the one hand, ten of the NABBP's top clubs formed the National Association of Professional Base Ball Players (NAPBBP), hoping to capitalize on the sport's increasing popularity. Baseball's Yankee traditionalists, on the other hand, created the National Association of Amateur Base Ball Players (NAABBP) in 1871 in order to reclaim baseball's virtuous and redemptive qualities. But the latter association still could not escape the commercial element of the game, nor its controversies. According to Seymour, "The professional virus had so infected them that they could not even agree among themselves about gate receipts. Some clubs threatened to resign if gate money was allowed. Others warned they would quit if it were not. They had to put off making the decision, but it was tacitly understood that gate receipts could be accepted by clubs when on tour or by those who owned enclosed grounds and needed to defray expenses of upkeep."[17]

The commodification of baseball, then, was not so much a virus as it was a drug. A traveling club simply could no longer exist without a direct source of income. But more than anything, Seymour contends, it was the coverage by the media that killed the NAABBP. Now informed of baseball games across the country by the daily press and sports weeklies, local fans were more interested in the far superior quality of play in the other new baseball association than they were in their own NAABBP clubs. Consequently, after four struggling years the NAABBP collapsed.

The NAPBBP lasted only five years. Although the new professional association featured the best players of the day, it suffered from three general problems: first, the association was considered a cesspool of out-of-control immorality, as gambling and all its related vices spread among the players, teams, and fans. As Seymour writes, "Its weak organization could not cope successfully with the cancerous evils of gambling, revolving, and hippodroming."[18] Put differently, the NAPBBP appealed to working-class fans, not the sort of customers many of baseball's self-appointed guardians wished to attract. Second, as discussed in further detail below, the open and unregulated competition for players' services led to high salaries, which often drove teams into financial ruin. Third, there was a significant lack of competitive balance among the teams, with some clubs enjoying the most gifted players in the country and others barely able to complete a lineup. This led to financial ruin for many of the both exceptionally good teams (for few others could compete with them enough to offer a compelling form of entertainment) and the bad (no one wanted to see a team that consistently lost). Unable to resolve these problems, the NAPBBP folded after the 1875 season.

The inauguration of the National League in 1876 was meant, among other things, to combine the most appealing elements of the three failed associations, while reversing their negative qualities. The National League (NL) advertised itself as a morally upright baseball league that would also become profitable through its presentation of the finest baseball in the world. William A. Hulbert, a member of the Chicago Board of Trade and the manager of the Chicago NAPBBP team, along with Albert Spalding, initiated the plans for the new league. The very language of the NL's constitution, in addition to some of its mandates, was meant to improve the image of professional baseball and thus separate it from its working-class associations. From the outset the document claimed that the league was going to make baseball "respectable and honorable" and return prestige to "our national game." Later, league spokesmen stated that "the National League was organized in 1876 as a necessity, to rescue the game from its slough of corruption and disgrace."[19] In addition to the language used to describe the new league, four rules solidified the NL's reputation as a virtuous (and not working-class) organization.

First, each club was required to charge a fifty-cent admission fee. Despite grumbling from the press, the public, and some clubs, the National League fixed ticket prices at fifty cents. For ten additional cents fans could sit on the bleachers. For seventy-five cents they could sit under the cover of the grandstand behind home plate. Ladies, when accompanied by a man, were admitted free. It is not clear whether women were admitted at all if unaccompanied. The ticket prices not only kept a good number of working-class people from league grounds (particularly wives and kids) but also offered an additional measure of class-based segregation for the particularly wealthy aficionados. Seymour recounts how a Syracuse newspaper advocated such a scheme: "Reminding their readers of the 'drunken rowdies, unwashed loafers, and arrant blacklegs' who went to the ball games, they decried any policy which prevented 'the wealthy and respected gentleman' from getting a seat apart from 'his social inferior' by paying a higher price. In this way social classes would be seated separately 'without injury to any one's feelings,' just as it was done in an opera house."[20] Indeed, other forms of mass entertainment in American cities at the time had comparable prices. The theater, operas, lectures, and the circus all charged anywhere from twenty-five to seventy-five cents for admission.

The second rule that the National League imposed was to ban the sale of alcohol on club grounds. Nevertheless, the Cincinnati NL club was particularly notorious for the—in some eyes excessive—sale and consumption of beer at its games. A large part of Cincinnati's economy during the 1870s and 1880s was served by the brewing industry. At least twenty-seven breweries existed in the city in 1879.[21] The club did acquiesce to certain concerns, going so far as banning the sale of alcohol in the grandstand "in deference to the ladies" while still making it available in other parts of the ballpark.[22] Other clubs attempted to sell alcohol as well but soon realized that it ran counter to the league's pronouncements of "respectability." By 1880 all of the league's clubs had united against Cincinnati and decided to ban both the sale of alcohol in ballparks and the use of the field for any sort of play on Sundays. Before even allowing Cincinnati to comply with the new rule, the league expelled the club for its past indulgences.

The National League's third rule to establish itself as a virtuous, middle-class organization was to prohibit Sunday baseball games. The league itself did not schedule any of its match-ups on Sunday, but some clubs, particularly Cincinnati, would rent out their grounds to local teams or engage in exhibition contests. Other clubs did not even have those options, as they lived under city ordinances that prohibited ball play of any kind on "the day of rest."

Fourth, gambling was expressly forbidden. Four Louisville players were expelled for life in 1877 after becoming implicated in a baseball betting pool. "The Louisville People have made me what I am to day [sic], a beggar," complained Jim Delvin, one of those expelled, to NL president William Hulbert.[23] Offering fifty dollars to him from his own pocket, Hulbert responded, "Delvin, that is what I think of you personally; but damn you, you have sold a game, you are dishonest, and this National League will not stand for it."[24] The expulsions, along with the stipulation that gambling houses could not be located adjacent to ballparks, set a lasting example, which to some extent kept the practice out of major league baseball.

Spalding, who was also the owner of the Chicago NL club, was granted exclusive rights to publish the *Official League Book*, which contained the league's constitution and rules. Though not initially given such monopoly power over the National League's "guide," the former pitcher took it upon himself to publish *Spalding's Official Base Ball Guide*, a compendium of rosters, statistics, history, and commentary, much in the style of Chadwick's books (in fact, Chadwick was a regular contributor and editor). *Spalding's Guide* was also a vehicle for the entrepreneur to advertise his fledgling Chicago-based sporting goods business, which would eventually, as discussed in chapter 2, outfit most professional (and amateur) baseball players across the country. The publication thus served to bolster the sales and esteem of Spalding's two budding businesses, while also creating additional revenue through the advertisements of other products on its pages and with the sale of the book itself. Soon, with the growing success of all three ventures, Spalding was inseparable in the public mind from baseball, and perhaps sport more generally.[25] By 1884, moreover, both *Beadle's* and *De Witt's* ceased publication and *The Spalding Guide* became the primary annual of the National League. Spalding took advantage of this dominant position to continue offering editorial declarations on exactly what and whom he thought professional baseball should include and exclude, and how and why the sport should do so. For example, the 1884 *Spalding Guide* posited: "Where the ladies congregate as spectators of sports, a refining influence is brought to bear which is valuable to the welfare of the game. Besides which, the patronage of ladies improves the character of the assemblages and helps to preserve the order without which first-class patronage cannot be obtained."[26] The presence of women, to put it differently, could transform the ballpark from a space of working-class masculinity to one of middle-class gentlemanliness.[27] Later, Spalding reemphasized the need to attract the "reputable class" to the ballpark, which, one might assume, included "the ladies."

There are two classes of the patrons of professional baseball grounds which club Presidents and Directors have their choice in catering to for each season, and these are, first, the reputable class, who prefer to see the game played scientifically and by gentlemanly exemplars of the beauties of the game, and second, the hoodlum element, who revel in noisy coaching, "dirty ball playing," kicking against the umpires, and exciting disputes and rows in every inning. The Chicago, Philadelphia and Boston Clubs in the League have laid out nearly $200,000 within the past two years in constructing their grounds for the express purpose of eliciting the very best patronage of their respective cities. The Brooklyn Club have [*sic*] excelled in this respect in the American Association by constructing their grounds for a similar class of patrons. But all of the clubs have not followed this example, the majority committing the blunder of considering only the tastes and requirements of the hoodlum class apparently in catering for patronage. This is a great financial mistake. Experience has shown conclusively that it pays best to cater solely for the best class of patronage.[28]

The dichotomy that Spalding draws here was not just a reflection of a simplified understanding of sociology. Spalding was tacitly referring to the fans who attended games of the American Association, which emerged as a rival to the NL between 1882 and 1891.

In many ways the American Association (AA) did cater to the "hoodlum element," as it allowed the sale of alcohol, games on Sunday, and charged only twenty-five cents for admission. The association catered to the market that the National League refused to accept. Supported by the working class, the AA quickly became known as the "Beer and Whiskey League."[29] Even black players were admitted, for a short while and in limited numbers, to some American Association teams. Still, the AA operated in ways similar to those of the NL. A new guide emerged shortly after the AA's genesis, this one also coming from a player-turned-sporting goods manufacturer. Al Reach, one of the first known professional players in the 1860s and the owner of a Philadelphia-based sporting-goods emporium, published *Reach's Official American Association Base Ball Guide* from 1883 to 1891. Just as Spalding did for the National League, Reach also provided the AA with its official ball, even though, by 1886, the "Reach" ball was owned by Spalding.

Daily newspapers across the country were devoting an unprecedented amount of space to baseball in the 1870s and 1880s, thus further deepening the sport's reach and popularity. The *Chicago Herald*, for one, guaranteed plenty of positive exposure for Spalding's White Stockings, as the paper's owner, John Walsh, was also a key investor in the ball club. Chadwick's presence on the staff of the *Brooklyn Daily Eagle* made that paper an often-syndicated source for stories on baseball. Nearly every city with a major league team included comprehensive, daily newspaper coverage of its home club and the league in which it played.

Additional sports weeklies came to life in the 1880s, most notably *Sporting Life* and the *Sporting News*. Never missing a job opportunity, Chadwick wrote for the former. Perhaps because of his presence, *Sporting Life* was the stronger of the two in terms of its baseball coverage (both also reported on other sports; *Sporting Life* included a section on the theater). Even in the off-season, *Sporting Life*, which was as long as a full-size newspaper, devoted about half its pages to detailed stories on baseball. It was often the first publication to break news on player sales, league and association developments, and general baseball gossip. Every league and association, no matter how small or large, professional or amateur, received due space on the pages of *Sporting Life*. "Chadwick's Chat," usually on page 3 or 6, offered the tireless "father of baseball" another space from which he could opine on the sport. The paper's editor, Francis Richter, entered the editorial fray with fresh perspectives on the "national pastime," often writing in the players' favor during their disputes with owners. His daily reports from Baseball's 1888–1889 "World Tour" (see chapter 3) are the most vivid accounts of the trip on record. Both the newspapers and the sports weeklies, additionally, allowed players, owners, and league officials to make public pronouncements on the game, whether as guest authors (eventual Players League leader John Ward, for example, wrote quite often in several different publications) or as interview subjects.

For baseball players of all skill levels, several instructional guides began appearing in newspaper advertisements and on newsstands. Spalding and Chadwick, again, led the way. Starting in 1885 Spalding's Library of American Sports offered a series of ten-cent instructional books on everything from baseball to bicycling, hunting, and fishing. Chadwick authored many of Spalding's baseball books, including, for example, *The Art of Base Ball Batting* and *How to Play Base Ball*, as well as an instruction manual of his own—*The American Game of Base Ball, How It Is Played; A Manual*. In all the Library promoted participation in more than three hundred recreational activities and encouraged the purchase of an ever-widening array of sporting goods that, according to the books, were necessary to appropriately partake in the fun. Spalding's close association with the National League lent legitimacy to the books and sporting goods, just as his merchandise enhanced the esteem of the game's premier league. Widespread youth participation in baseball, furthermore, guaranteed the continued and expanded reproduction of the sport's labor force and fan base.

John Ward used his instructional book in part to teach people "how to become a player," but also to bring forth three major editorial arguments regarding the game of baseball.[30] First, he espoused a jingoistic theory that baseball was entirely and originally American. Those who, erroneously, in his eyes, believed that baseball derived from the English game of rounders were deluded by their contention that "everything good and beautiful in the world had to be of English origin."[31] As for the actual origins of baseball, "I believe it," Ward concluded, "to be a fruit of the inventive genius of the American boy."[32] Baseball, to put it differently, is American simply because it is.[33] Second, like Spalding a few years earlier, Ward encouraged women to attend baseball games, although his "Theory of the Game: A Chapter for the Ladies" seems more intended for men than for their female companions: "Whoever has not experienced the pleasure of taking a young lady to her first game of ball should seize the first opportunity to do so. Her remarks about plays, her opinions of different players and the umpire, and the questions she will ask concerning the game, are all too funny to be missed."[34] Ward's condescending remarks reflect the desire, in at least two senses, for women's attendance at baseball games. On the one hand, as Ward indicates, a woman's ignorance of the game can be a great source of amusement and sense of superiority for her male companion. On the other hand, Ward's self-assigned duty to introduce, "concisely, and with the use of as few technical terms as possible, the first principles of the game" to "the ladies" can be aligned with Spalding's rationale.[35] The continued presence of women at baseball games would give the sport a valuable sense of middle-class gentility. Nonetheless, the discursive and actual inclusion of women in the ballpark opened a quasi-public space for women hitherto made inaccessible.[36] Finally, and of particular relevance to the Players League, Ward's instructional book offered a stinging condemnation of baseball's reserve clause.

Less formally, baseball appeared in popular songs, poetry, nonsporting magazines, and literature between the late 1850s and 1890, thus reflecting and reinforcing the demand for the sport.[37] Even the church, in at least one instance, sang baseball's praises. The Reverend C. H. Everett, in a sermon given in 1865, extolled baseball, "whose regulations are calculated to prevent the ill-feelings engendered by other games, and one, moreover, which serves to attract our young men from places of bad repute, and to supply in place thereof the right kind of recreation and exercise."[38]

In sum, baseball's media functioned not just to promote major league baseball as a superior form of entertainment worthy of relatively high admission fees but also to shape and modify that superior product as something particularly American, respectable, middle class, gentlemanly, and, as detailed later, white.

As the central component of this commodified cultural construction, the players themselves developed considerable value across the latter half of the nineteenth century, many earning salaries on par with the most famous celebrities of the time. The problem for owners, however, was the seeming inseparability of the players' value and the value of the game. In other words, the greater the popularity of the game, the greater the players demanded to be paid, for, after all, they were the principal reason for the popularity. So as revenue from ticket sales increased, so too did players' salaries. It was a contradiction that owners struggled to resolve.

One strategy was to alter the ways in which the game was played so as to alter the performance of the players. Just as other industries have long manipulated labor processes so as to wrest control and value from workers, baseball's nineteenth-century guardians continually tinkered with the sport's rules, equipment, scoring, and playing conditions in attempts (whether successful or not) to transform both the appeal of the sport and the perceived value of the players. Baseball's owners had the final say on rule changes, but members of the game's media frequently offered their proposals and commentaries on which alterations would "improve the game." As the commercialization of the sport increased, players' voices on the matter held less, and eventually no, power over the matter.

Robert Burk argues that, in general, when nineteenth-century baseball magnates wished to boost attendance, they altered the ways the game was played so as to favor batting and faster-paced contests.[39] When owners sought to fend off players' solicitations for higher wages, they emphasized pitching, defense, and "teamwork." A tilt toward pitching, in particular, served budget-cutting needs quite well, as teams usually held only one or two pitchers (compared with nine or ten hitters/fielders) about whose salaries owners had to worry. The growing development of baseball statistics by the sport's daily, weekly, and annual publications offered a means by which players' execution of their labor processes could be quantitatively evaluated and hence valued. When management wished to reduce someone's salary, they would refer to his decreased batting average, runs, or hits, which, they would argue, reflected a deterioration of the man's skills. Alternatively, if the numbers did not point in the right direction, they could emphasize the qualitative aspects of someone's play, or, quite often, his declining moral character as a basis for reducing his salary.

Most changes to the game instituted by the NABBP and the NAPBBP involved enhancing the required skills of players. Some of these changes were intended to simultaneously improve both the appeal of baseball to the public and the character of the men who played it. At the same time, the execution of baseball's labor processes began to steadily split from the control and management of the game. It was this tightening over control and management, by and in the hands of nonplaying team owners and league officials, which implemented most of the changes to the labor process. After years of debate the "flycatch" rule was instituted by the NABBP in 1864. The rule stipulated that a fielder must catch a batted ball in the air (rather than after one bounce) in order to record an out. Opponents of the rule charged that it would further usher the game away from its coveted past. Its supporters claimed that the rule would elicit and draw attention to the heightened fielding skills of some of the game's players. And in doing so, they also claimed, the fly-catch rule would make baseball appear more "manly" to its followers. Furthermore, on-the-fly catches would put American sport on an equal footing with that of England, as cricketers also employed a fly-catch rule.[40]

The abandonment of self-umpiring in 1858 signaled a specialization, but also degradation, of baseball players' labor processes. Until then two competing teams would each choose a member to serve as an "advocate" to judge and control the play on the field. The advocates would sit at a desk or table in foul territory on the third-base side of the infield from which they called balls, strikes, outs, fair balls, and foul balls. A third, independent umpire, seated alone and often clad in a dark suit, top hat, and walking cane, would issue a final ruling if the two advocates could not reach an agreement. The NABBP's desertion of the "two advocate" system separated the tasks of playing from umpiring, thus giving rise to both a more specialized playing force and a new occupation within the broader business.[41] Burk, furthermore, posits that the change signaled "the centralization of on-field administration of the rules governing contests and conduct in response to the declension of decorum and good faith by players and spectators alike."[42] The introduction of "independent" umpires, who were not at all independent from the association's (and later, league's) management, thus shifted the balance of control over the labor process away from the players and toward owners and officials. Moreover, by doing so, the NABBP sought to improve the "moral" atmosphere at games, thus refining baseball into a more appealing commodity. One can therein see how umpires, not just players, now contributed to the value of the product. But umpires were much more easily replaced, as the skills needed to call balls and strikes, fair and foul, out and safe, as well as the ability to control the behavior of the players, were more widely attainable. The cost savings garnered from such skill generalization, however, were, at best, minimal. Games utilized just one umpire, whose wages did not replace those of the advocates but rather were added to them. The salaries of players, meanwhile, continued to *climb* after (and perhaps irrespective of) the elimination of their umpiring duties.

Even without such rule and personnel changes, the increasing competition and financial stakes of baseball demanded an escalating quality of play. As early as 1860 players became specialized at particular positions. Those positions, in turn, became associated across the baseball world with specific physical—and social—characteristics. "Catchers," Burk contends,

even if they stood thirty feet behind the batter, still benefited from having a "barrel-chest" that could withstand the punishment of the position, as did third basemen also. Gangliness could become a positive virtue in a first basemen, as could straight-ahead running speed in an outfielder. Strength could certainly have its uses for a batter, particularly when wielding a mahogany bat up to forty-four inches long. Nonetheless, the players occupying infield positions— particularly those in the middle of the diamond that required refined hand-eye coordination, mental concentration, and physical dexterity—were still seen as the truest exemplars of the traditional baseballist idea. Lingering associations of ethnicity with physical and mental attributes in turn shaped patterns of positional specialization by ethnic group as well as physiology.[43]

By 1870, Burk continues,

The on-field performance of the journeyman professional ballplayer displayed ever-growing refinement, specialization, and sophistication. First basemen now "covered the bag" against base runners, who themselves more frequently employed sliding techniques to avoid tags. Clubs quickly learned the advantages of developing a left-handed fielder at the position. Fielding in general, despite the absence of gloves, already had grown so refined under the fly catch rule that batters were instructed to hit down on the ball. Pitchers, considered the "cleverest" of players, now bent the rules by subtly bending their arms during their underhand deliveries. . . . Pitchers also changed speeds to confuse the batter and spun the ball off their fingertips to create curves. . . . Catchers, forced to stand closer to the batter in order to thwart base runners, but more vulnerable to injury because of it, despite initial ridicule began to introduce "bird-cage" face masks. . . . By 1875, St. Louis first baseman Charles C. Waitt introduced the first "glove," a skin-tight bit of apparel for either hand with the fingertips cut out and no padding, so as to prevent blisters without impeding throwing.[44]

So the development of baseball's labor processes involved technical improvements to the ways players went through the motions of throwing, catching, fielding, running, and hitting. And while baseball's labor processes may not involve the transformation of raw materials into a qualitatively new product, they do, like labor processes more generally, entail alterations of the laboring bodies themselves.[45] All these qualitative changes, moreover, elicited a quantitative change in the ways that players and contests of baseball were priced.

As the competition for skilled players and profitable victories intensified during the 1860s and 1870s, teams (which numbered in the thousands) had to expand the geographic scale of the market on which they found and employed highly skilled players. Until Harry Wright in 1868 fielded a Cincinnati Red Stockings team entirely of out-of-town professionals (at the cost of $15,000), clubs primarily hired local players.[46] But steadily after Wright, and especially as the NABBP gave way to the NAPBBP, teams hired players from across the country. This geographically expanding but numerically shrinking labor market worked in the players' favor, as they could pit teams against one another in a bidding war for their services. Baseball players, most of whom now were in their early twenties and without families, were free to move from one city to the next, shopping themselves around, or in the parlance of the day, "revolving," for the best offer.[47] Early on in its existence, the NABBP tried to slow the pace of revolving by instituting a thirty-day "residency" requirement, which prohibited players from playing for another team until they had stayed with their current team for at least a month. Players and clubs alike readily ignored this rule, and with a weak and decentralized governing body, the association was unable to enforce it. Revolving only increased in the NAPBBP, as did, consequently, player salaries. Across the five-year history of the professional association, salaries averaged "in the $1,300–1,600 range," according to Burk, with star players earning as much as $3,000 per year.[48] The result was the complete lack of competitive balance among the NAPBBP's teams, where the wealthier teams would horde the most talented players and win a vast majority of the games.

But this lopsided playing field, so to speak, hurt financially strapped and well-heeled clubs alike. The Harlem Globetrotters notwithstanding, even the best teams will not attract many spectators if they cannot offer at least some unpredictability, and some struggle, over the outcome of the game. Indeed, the slippery creation of suspense—both within a game and across a season—would prove a valuable aspect of professional baseball.

The National League and subsequently the American Association were more ambitious in their attempts to change the sport's labor processes, but these measures were no more effective at solving the industry's central contradiction between high salaries and high revenues. Initially, the National League shaped its rules around a faster and less offensive (in both senses of the word) game. The league's official ball (not until 1880 a Spalding) was considerably "dead" by design so that it would not travel very far. Nine balls constituted a walk, but the event was equivalent to an out when calculating a hitter's batting average. For the first several years of the National League, pitchers still had to throw underhanded, but they were permitted in 1876 to snap their wrists and in 1877 to bend their arms. In the NAPBBP's waning years, Henry Chadwick successfully convinced the association to legalize "fair-foul" hits, batted balls that started in fair territory but ended up in foul territory. But the National League quickly reversed this decision, thus narrowing the field for batters. Although the pace of the games did quicken, fans complained that there was not enough offense. Not a single team earned a profit in 1876.[49] After the 1879 season, the NL reduced the number of balls required for a walk to eight. This alteration favored pitchers, as it gave the hitter, who could only strike out by swinging and missing, fewer opportunities to hit the ball. Batting averages, consequently, fell by ten points between 1879 and 1880. The following year, in a move to reignite the offense that fans so coveted, the league moved the pitcher's "box" from forty-five feet away from home plate to fifty feet. Batting averages climbed fifteen points.[50]

One way the National League in its initial years managed to relatively limit salaries was to prevent players from signing contracts with other teams while the season was still going on. A player could negotiate his contract with another team only after the season had completed. This measure at least slowed down the process by which players set teams against one another in an escalating bidding war. When the American Association was formed in 1882 as a viable rival to the National League, the bidding war continued at full speed. Salaries rose on average about $500 between 1882 and 1883, as players moved from league to league (in both directions) throughout the season.[51] The "National Agreement" between the AA, the NL, and the Western League, in which the leagues agreed to separate labor and consumer markets (see chapter 2), ended this bidding war in 1883, and the growth of salaries significantly declined.

To perhaps further curb the rate of salary growth, the National League implemented two rule changes before the 1884 season that gave pitchers a decided advantage. Now only six balls constituted a walk, thus granting hitters even fewer chances to hit safely. More significantly, however, pitchers could thenceforth throw overhand, a move that made batting a far more difficult task than ever before. Consequently, batting averages dropped fourteen points.[52] At the same time, however, another rival league entered the fray. The Union Association, like the American Association before it, increased the competition between teams of the three leagues for players' services. But although salaries did rise that year, most players were successfully persuaded by their National League owners that the new league would not last to see the dawn of 1885. They were correct, as the Union Association's complete lack of competitive balance produced a dull and unpopular version of the "national game."

The National League and the American Association continued over the next five years to tinker with rule and scoring changes to balance salaries with baseball's public appeal. The number of balls needed for a walk increased once and decreased twice to land at the henceforth permanent four-ball walk in 1889. A strike zone between the knees and the shoulders was introduced in 1887, and the number of strikes for an out changed from four in 1887 to three in 1888. In 1887 a walk was considered a hit; in 1888 it was not. Each of these changes effectively altered the relationship between hitting and pitching and, as a result, players' salary demands and spectators' attendance. But changing the rules was a zero-sum game: anything that increased the popularity of the sport also increased salaries; alterations that reduced salaries also diminished popularity.

There is an additional component to the commodification of baseball, as well as most other branches of the sports and entertainment industry, which, seemingly, does not involve any labor at all. Spectators may consume the celebrity of the performer, regardless of what the performer does on the field or stage, and regardless of whether she or he even is in the midst of performing. To a certain degree (which has varied across time, space, and facet of the industry), consumers buy tickets to performances, games, and matches simply because they want to see the performers in the flesh (or later, on the screen). Moreover, they are attracted to, say, baseball, because of the perceived gentlemanly character, docile personality, manly nature, white race—in a word, image—of the players. But while celebrities can be famous for simply being famous, this realm of cultural commodification at some point traces back to the productive labor (even if it is not the celebrity's own) that serves as the original source of their earning power. In other words, the work of the industry's media can go only so far; at some point, the work of hitting, catching, and throwing a baseball must take place. Moreover, there is perhaps a bit of labor involved in the production of a celebrity image (and I am not yet speaking of the *reproduction* of images in the form of mass-produced films, magazines, Wheaties boxes, and tobacco cards, among other varieties). Baseball players, for one, must eat, sleep, and exercise in a way that allows their bodies to develop, operate, and *appear* at full capacity. These processes are all the more important for baseball players and other professional athletes than they are for other workers, as sporting labor processes engage, rather than alienate, bodies to a much fuller extent than do industrial and postindustrial labor processes. That is not to say that one should understand bodily condition as irrelevant to other labor processes—everyone needs to cultivate reasonably good health in order to continue working—but tending to the condition of a body is of the utmost importance for those workers who must everyday test its limits. The image of players, of course, is also created and maintained to a considerable degree by baseball's media. But the important point here is that in addition to their performance, baseball players' images were contributing factors to the ways in which they were valued. But again, to the extent that fans bought into this latter correlation (and most evidence points to the fact that they did), the same contradiction remains: the improvement of players' images made the game more attractive to fans, but in doing so it also gave players greater leverage over their salaries.

This contradiction can be seen most readily in the exclusion of black players from the National Associations, National League, and later, Players League. The American Association allowed a few black players until 1896; some of baseball's "minor" leagues, including the International League and the Inter-State League, admitted a black player or two; and several independent, barnstorming clubs, most famously, the "Cuban" Giants, fielded entire teams of African Americans.[53] But the bulk of professional baseball, especially the National League and the Players League, was racially segregated.

At first glance it might seem that the inclusion of black players in the upper echelons of professional baseball would have enhanced the value of the game while also curbing the growth of salaries. The playing abilities of black players were by all accounts on par, if not greater than, the white major leagues. Their presence en masse would have made any baseball organization a more highly skilled league. They also would have broadened the labor pool and, because of the white players' racism, probably hindered any efforts toward collective action. But the color of their skin—regardless of their baseball skills—also mattered to the fans, who, NL officials feared, would lose interest in an integrated form of entertainment.

The construction of an exclusively white game was not openly expressed on the pages of the annual guides or sporting press. But aside from the obvious absence of black players, there is some documentary evidence that such a strategy was actively administered. A report of the NABBP's Nominating Committee in 1867, for instance, explicitly prohibits black players from any of the association's approximately two thousand clubs:

> It is not presumed by your Committee that any club who have applied are composed of persons of color, or any portion of them; and the recommendations of your Committee in this report are based upon this view, and they unanimously report against the admission of any club which may be composed of one or more colored persons. . . . If colored clubs were admitted there would be in all probability some division of feeling, whereas, by excluding them no injury could result to anybody, and the possibility of any rupture being created on political grounds would be avoided.[54]

That the Nominating Committee could completely disregard the humanity of black players by suggesting that "no injury could result to anybody" by their exclusion reflects the depth—beyond but certainly not mutually exclusive of mere economic calculation—of racism found here.

In 1884 the AA's Toledo club, which included the first, and at the time, only black "major league" player (Moses Fleetwood Walker), was scheduled to play the NL Chicago club in a preseason exhibition.[55] The Chicago franchise, led then by Spalding, refused to play Toledo if Walker was anywhere near the field. Spalding's secretary, Jonathan Brown, explained the team's decision in a letter to Toledo's manager, C. H. Morton: "The management of the Chicago Ball Club have no personal feeling about the matter. . . . The players do most decisively object and to preserve harmony in the club it is necessary that I have your assurance in writing [to keep your] colored man [off the field]."[56] That Spalding did not write the letter himself, or make any public statements about the matter, or (through his secretary) even place any blame on the club officials reveals a further contradiction: baseball may have needed (and wanted) to be racially exclusive, but it still could not appear, in the eyes of its genteel supporters, to express the language of racism. It was easier simply not to speak of the matter.

The exclusion of players notwithstanding, black men did find their way onto National League fields. Mascots in the 1880s were often black, and in one way or another, disabled men.[57] As the *Chicago Tribune* described in 1890, mascots were "chosen for some hideous peculiarity, such as a dwarfed figure, hump-back or cross eyes."[58] Included in this list of "hideous peculiarities" was "black" skin: "If a little Negro, black as the ace of spades, dwarfed in every limb, and with crossed eyes could have been secured, the ideal mascot would have been presented to the gaze of the base-ball world."[59] To a far more humiliating degree than the "ladies" that Ward described, the presence of black mascots provided entertainment and a sense of superiority for white spectators and players. And just as the attendance of women reinforced the game's manliness, the presentation of black mascots solidified baseball's whiteness.

After the Civil War baseball was the most popular sport in America, exceeding the attractiveness of old and new spectator sports such as horse racing, boxing, tennis, football, cricket, and billiards.[60] And the concurrent rise of other parts of the entertainment industry, such as theater and opera, seemed to contribute to the popularity of baseball rather than compete with it.[61] But the infancy of baseball and the smaller-scaled profits (relative to say, manufacturing industries), on top of the inherent contradiction whereby players were the source of the industry's greatest cost and revenue, still put the business in a precarious position. In fact, only 25 percent of all professional baseball teams during the nineteenth century lasted longer than two years.[62] Between 1871 and 1889 more teams outright folded than survived. Many that did survive were scarcely making a profit.

Still many survived and earned remarkable profits. How did (and does) baseball last as a viable realm of capitalist production? How did baseball's investors resolve the contradictions of the industry? The answers to these questions are the subject of the next chapter.

2

THE RISE OF THE NATIONAL LEAGUE

Until the early 1880s most nineteenth-century professional baseball teams did not enjoy financial success. The Chicago National League club finished the 1879 season with greater revenues than expenses, and three teams made a profit in 1880, but the majority of teams either folded or struggled to survive. The volatility of professional baseball during this time is reflected by the fact that seventeen different cities hosted a National League franchise at one time or another between 1876 and 1881, and only two of the original eight clubs (Boston and Chicago) survived the entire period.

But from 1883 onward professional baseball, particularly the National League, became an increasingly lucrative investment. Boston turned a $20,000 profit in 1883 and Chicago made $40,000 that year; only two of the eight NL teams did not finish the season in the black. In total National League teams reported close to $1 million in profits in the 1880s, with far fewer teams folding than in the National League's initial years.[1]

So the question remains: given the contradictions of the industry laid out in the previous chapter, how did professional baseball teams survive? How, in fact, did many of them flourish? Baseball, particularly under the governance of the National League, became generally profitable via the implementation of three strategies. One, the NL created artificial monopolies, in the form of "territorial rights," around each team's consumer market. This helped to reduce the competition for customers' allegiance. Two, the league multiplied the earning power of the sport by selling ballpark concessions, the ballpark itself, telegraphing rights, sporting goods, and other products related (if only by association) to baseball. Three, team owners took greater control over the players themselves by significantly restricting their behavior on and off the field, mobility from one team to another, and ability to contest these and other measures.

This chapter analyzes the ways in which the National League produced and controlled the arrangements necessary to stabilize its markets and thereby resolve the contradictions that would have otherwise led to its peril. But as the following chapters detail, these strategies elicited a tremendous backlash from the players, which ultimately led to the creation of the Players League.

Territorial Rights

Upon its inauguration the National League instituted a system of "territorial rights" that governed the locations of its franchises and established monopolies over the teams' consumer markets. "In no event," article 3 of the original 1876 constitution states, "shall there be more than one club from any city."[2] Article 5, section 2, details this territorial control: "Every club member of this League shall have exclusive control of the city in which it is located, and of the territory surrounding such city to the extent of five miles in every direction, and no visiting League club shall, under any circumstances—not even with the consent of the local League club—be allowed to play any club in such territory other than the League club therein located."[3] There are two very similar but distinct provisions within this clause. The first, that only one National League club can reside within or close to a single city, was meant to create an amalgamation of local fan allegiance for the team. The National League spread its teams apart from one another so that they could enjoy maximum fan support rather than compete against one another for paying customers. The second, which stipulated that no National League team could compete against any other team that was located in or around its home city, was meant to consolidate the earning power of National League baseball. Nonleague teams were thus excluded from earning any revenue by playing against the presumably vastly superior National League teams. Territorial rights were necessary, given the high cost of labor, to maximize the revenue earned on the game in a way that did not enhance the value of the players.

Two other measures further regulated the location of National League teams and solidified their territorial monopolies. On the one hand, the constitution stated that "no club shall be admitted from any city whose population is less than seventy-five thousand ... except by unanimous vote of the League."[4] On the other hand, although not articulated in the constitution, the league founders strategically located teams in order to take advantage of a growing East-West rivalry afoot in nineteenth-century American life. Thus National League teams were generally located in the country's largest markets, and the League itself stretched across a sizable portion of the United States, from a cluster of cities in the Northeast to Louisville in the South and Chicago in the West.[5] Territorial rights thus enabled professional baseball to market itself to sufficient numbers of people at a national scale while still making it rare enough at the urban scale that people would pay premium prices to see a game. To be sure, there are specific historical circumstances, coupled with the provision that a unanimous vote among league delegates could override the locational mandates, which altered these geographic configurations from time to time. Worcester, Massachusetts, for example, was home to a National League team between 1880 and 1882, despite the fact that its population was less than seventy-five thousand. The relatively diminutive Troy, New York, too, enjoyed a team for a short while, which like that in Worcester, gained admittance to the league only through personal connections. New York and Philadelphia, meanwhile, did not host teams between 1878 and 1882, despite their large sizes, because they were both expelled from the league in 1877 for failing to complete their schedules, as mandated by the constitution. League president William Hulbert justified the exclusion of New York and Philadelphia during these years by arguing that only a well-disciplined league—one in which each club fulfills its responsibilities according to the constitution—would survive.

That the reintroduction of these cities in 1883 coincided with the National League's newfound profitability led some commentators to conclude that the league depended on New York and Philadelphia for its survival. Looking back in 1915 on the history of the league, John Ward attributed the NL's success precisely to the return of New York as a major league city:

> The big commercial boom in base ball . . . came with the establishment of a New York Club in the National League for the season of 1883. Although the Mutuals in 1876 had a season in the metropolis, it was not until the reestablishment of big league base ball here in 1883 that the sport got firmly on its feet. Files of the newspapers will bear out the truth of my assertion that until 1883 scarcely any notice was taken of the efforts to popularize professional base ball. With the publication of details of base ball in New York there was country-wide interest in the sport and news agencies sent out reams of interesting matter from this city. That put the national sport on a foundation which has permitted many abuses of the game by those in control without the public for any extended period ever losing sight of the greatness of base ball.[6]

But Ward's contention that the national popularity of baseball depended on the presence of the sport in New York might be overstated. He argues that the dissemination of New York's baseball news by the city's press to the rest of the country popularized the sport to an unprecedented and unrelenting degree. But while the *Clipper* ran out of New York, it had been publishing there for thirty years before the city landed the Giants in 1883. *Sporting Life* operated out of Philadelphia and covered baseball across the country. Moreover, as discussed in chapter 1, local newspapers in each of the National League's cities (in addition to others) extensively covered baseball both before and after 1883. Baseball had been enjoying significant, nationwide popularity for some twenty years by that point. The revenues gained by placing a team in the country's most populous city certainly helped the league, but Boston and Chicago were still routinely the most profitable clubs throughout the 1880s. Finally, Ward concludes that the national "foundation" that New York baseball enabled the league to build opened the door for certain "abuses." But as detailed later in this chapter, it was the other way around: these "abuses" helped the sport become and remain profitable. Other factors, too, contributed to the growing profitability of National League baseball.

Multiplying the Earning Power of Baseball

Similarly to the merchandising of contemporary baseball, baseball's nineteenth-century capitalists used the images, performers, and placement of the game to sell mass quantities of cigars, tobacco, board games, scorecards, fruit, telegraphing rights, advertising space, sporting goods, and publications about baseball, among other things. Most of the investors involved in these markets were either directly tied to the National League or were forced to buy from individual teams the exclusive rights to sell their products.[7] The league thus managed to mass-produce additional commodities that were associated with baseball but whose production was historically and/or geographically separate from the actual performance and performers of baseball games. In other words, the players and their escalating salaries were not involved in the production of these related products. Indeed, the labor needed to produce baseball's secondary products, unlike that of the game itself, could be readily degraded and exploited, hidden away beyond recognition, so that the price of these commodities could far outweigh their costs. Young boys, for example, were employed to peddle concessions at the ballpark.[8] The reproduction of a ballgame in the form of telegraphed presentations in saloons or of a detailed description in a newspaper required far fewer skills than the playing of the game itself and could reach greater numbers of people.

The most profitable segment of this ancillary market in the nineteenth century was the mass production of sporting goods. As early as 1878 the market for baseball-related goods was booming, as the *New York Clipper* suggests: "Bats are being made by the 500,000, balls by the thousand gross; uniforms by the thousand, and baseball material of all kinds in the same ratio."[9] Although at the time the industry was still fairly competitive, it would soon become dominated by Spalding and Brothers' worldwide sporting-goods business. Albert Spalding and his brother, J. Walter Spalding, started selling baseball equipment in 1876 from a single storefront located two blocks from the Chicago team's ballpark. Soon afterward the Spaldings secured a contract with the National League's Board of Directors (of which Albert Spalding was a member) to be the sole provider of baseballs for the league's games. Thus Spalding could advertise that his company's baseballs were the "official balls" of the National League. By 1884 the Spalding brothers made the official baseballs not only of the National League but also of the Northwestern League, the American College Baseball Association, the Louisiana Amateur Baseball Association, and the Iron and Oil Association.[10]

Spalding's products were not universally praised. The National League awarded the entrepreneur a contract in 1882 to provide the uniforms for every National League team. This provided the opportunity for one of the Chicagoan's most embarrassing blunders. Spalding chose uniforms that were color-coded in a confusing, rainbow pattern dictated by both team affiliation and defensive position. All National League players wore white pants, belts, and ties. Fans could distinguish each team by the color of their stockings (the Chicago White Stockings wore, in fact, white stockings). But individual players on the same team wore different colored shirts and caps according to the position they played: pitchers wore baby blue; catchers were clad in scarlet; first basemen dressed in scarlet and white; second basemen donned orange and black; third basemen were in blue and white; shortstops, in maroon; left fielders, white; center fielders, red and black; and right fielders gray.[11] Baseball fans and the press alike ridiculed the plan. One writer commented that the ballplayers looked like "a Dutch bed of tulips."[12] The National League failed to renew the contract the following year. Nonetheless, Spalding was still able produce the uniforms of most other professional and amateur baseball teams, including his Chicago club and, occasionally, other National League teams as well.

Seven years after the sartorial snafu, Spalding seemed to have forgotten the matter: "During the past twelve years we have, as is generally known, made virtually all the fine uniforms, both professional and amateur, that have been worn on the ball fields of the United States, and we have yet to hear of the first complaint of either quality of goods, or perfectness of fit."[13] Spalding's selective memory here was yet another discursive strategy necessary to continue producing commodities that were perceived to be of an extraordinary quality. Indeed, his emphasis on the "quality of goods" was not altogether unlike his emphasis on the quality of National League baseball. The difference, however, was that despite the use of "skilled cutters, who can make a dress suit as easily as a flannel shirt," as the advertisement continued, garment manufacturing utilized a workforce with much more attainable skills than did professional baseball.[14] Labor, therefore, came at a cheaper price and was readily dispensable. Moreover, whether in the case of caps and ties or bats and balls, Spalding was able to take advantage of his association with the highest level of professional baseball—a commodity in and of itself whose production levels were relatively limited, despite territorial rights—to mass produce related commodities to a virtually unlimited number of consumers.

Spalding's business was not restricted to just baseball-related sporting goods. The plump midwesterner took full advantage of, and somewhat propelled, the bicycle craze of the late nineteenth century by widely producing and marketing bikes for both children and adults. He and his brother (and eventually, brother-in-law as well) also produced everything from hunting and fishing gear to trophies and basketballs. The press to support this market, then, was provided by Spalding in the form of the voluminous Library of American Sports and his constant promotion of the social, moral, and physical benefits of sport. By the turn of the century, Spalding was a millionaire. Spalding and

Brothers storefronts could be found in dozens of American cities and a handful of foreign ones. And although the Chicago team that he owned became, in the 1880s, quite profitable, most of Spalding's revenue derived from his sporting-goods company. But the money earned by Spalding and Brothers provided a buffer against which any financial loss on the baseball field, in Chicago, or anywhere else in the league, could be readily absorbed. The excess money generated from selling products related to professional baseball, in other words, could make up for the diminished stream of money coming from the direct sale of that relatively scarce commodity. The two processes were interdependent, however, as the profits gained on related products depended, in the first place, on an association with that original commodity.

Adding to, and securing, the value of professional baseball was the increasingly well-designed ballpark. Ballparks themselves were presented as attractive elements of the sport, whose architecture and amenities were intended to draw white-collar people to attend. In 1882, when Philadelphia was attempting to regain membership in the National League, its team owners, "at the cost of many thousand dollars, fitted [their new] park in first-class order to cater to respectable audiences."[15] Two years later the club spent an additional $2,000 on improvements such as carpeted seats, fresh paint, and colorful flags. Chicago's park underwent a $10,000 renovation at about the same time, when, among other things, eighteen private boxes, featuring glass windows, curtains, and comfortable lounge chairs, were installed. Spalding had his box fitted with a new telephone.[16]

Furthermore, the production and maintenance of ballparks, and likewise theaters, museums, and concert halls, could again take advantage of the historical separation between the production of the performance and the production of the facility within which the performance took place. The social relations, for instance, of the carpenters and bricklayers who actually built the structures are hidden within this built environment, perhaps even more so to the extent that spectators and critics alike consider only the players and performers as the workers of this industry. Those "off-the-field" workers who were visible to spectators—including, according to Seymour, in the case of Chicago's ballpark, "seven ushers, six policemen, four ticket-sellers, four gate-keepers, three 'field-men' (groundskeepers), three cushion renters, six refreshment boys, and eight musicians"—were nonetheless thoroughly degraded and dispensable and thus unable to collect more than a trifle of the value created by the game they were furnishing.[17]

Disciplining the Players

The third, and at the time, most successful, way in which the National League resolved the contradictions of professional baseball was to take greater control over players themselves. In a series of measures issued during the late 1870s and 1880s, the league restricted players' behavior both on and off the field, mobility from one team to another, and ability to contest these and other measures. In doing so the National League managed to significantly reduce player salaries without reducing the game's ticket prices, level of play, or popularity.

Starting in 1877 National League players were charged fifty cents per day on road trips to cover part of their travel expenses. They were also required to buy, clean, repair, and replace their own uniforms. Umpires and club owners were authorized to fine players up to twenty dollars for using profanity on the playing field.

In 1880 the league's owners issued an "Address to the Players," in which they warned of new penalties for behavior infractions. Club owners and the league board of directors could fine, suspend, or blacklist players "from play, and from pay," for "illness, insubordination, or misconduct of any kind," proclaimed the document.[18] These measures, the address continued, would "surround the player of morally weak tendencies with wholesome restraints."[19] Thus the league would "reach the pocket as well as the pride of the player who deliberately and systematically [fell] short of the honorable discharge of his obligations toward the club and the patrons of baseball."[20] While such discipline was ostensibly intended to improve the morality and image of the game (and thus explicitly market the game for the "respectable" classes), it was also a means to curb the growth of player salaries. Fines, suspensions, and expulsions allowed clubs, on the one hand, to simply withhold or extract additional money from the players. On the other hand, the mere threat of these measures induced enough fear in the players to usually keep them from negotiating for higher salaries. Perhaps to set an example, Boston's president, Arthur Soden, expelled and blacklisted Charlie Jones in 1880 for merely asking the club for the $378 in back pay that was owed to him.[21]

At the center of these new disciplinary concerns were the players' purported drinking habits. Second baseman John "Moose" Farrell, for example, was fined $200 by his Providence club in 1880 for making five errors in a game the day after he returned from a drunken escapade on the Atlantic shore. Albert Spalding required his players to sign an oath of sobriety, as he was convinced that intemperance was the root of poor financial and athletic performance. In order to enforce the ban on alcohol, Spalding hired Pinkerton spies to shadow his players during the evenings and off-seasons. In 1884 he urged all National League owners to submit to the league's board of directors weekly Pinkerton reports on players' personal habits.[22]

The prohibition against the use of alcohol, however, did not stop all players from drinking, nor was it universally enforced. Mike "King" Kelly, widely regarded as one of the greatest players of the nineteenth century, was a notorious alcoholic who often showed up for games drunk and incapacitated. Drinking was part of his daily routine, according to Kelly's autobiography. "A little sherry and egg before breakfast, or a bottle of ale, will do no harm."[23] Rarely, though, was he ever seriously punished for his infractions. On the final game of the 1889 season, for instance, with his Boston team needing a victory against Cleveland to win the pennant, Kelly was too drunk to take the field. As the *Boston Globe* described it, "Kelly was down on the card to play, but owing to a jollification during last night and this morning with several theatrical friends, [he] found his hand had lost its cunning and fly balls were a deep mystery to him."[24] As his team proceeded to lose the game and the pennant, Kelly, slouched on the bench in an overcoat, muttered profanities to the umpire and his teammates. "You never win . . . when I don't play. Kelly is king. I am king," he shouted.[25] When a close play at the plate was ruled in Cleveland's favor, Kelly stumbled toward the umpire and threatened to punch him in the face. Police officers rushed to the scene, grabbed Kelly by the neck, and ushered him out of the ballpark. "Lighting a cigarette," the *Chicago Tribune* noted, "[Kelly] strode into the street with the dejected air of Napoleon in exile."[26] But even as Kelly's intoxication, in this situation, clearly did cost his team the pennant, the speedy outfielder was not disciplined by his team or the league. In his case Kelly—when sober enough to play—was so much better than just about every other player that his skills were deemed more valuable than his image.

Imbued with alcohol or not, the health of players came under increasing scrutiny by team owners. Players were required to make and pay for regular visits with team-appointed doctors. Clubs often used these doctors to manufacture information about contracted players for whom they no longer had any use. For if the players were deemed too unhealthy or injured to play, the owners were not required to pay them (and could, additionally, fine them). At the same time, players would often continue playing with serious physical impairments for fear that if disclosed, their injuries could cost them their salary or career. One player claimed to have finished the final five innings of a game with a broken wrist because he knew that if he had asked his "captain" to be replaced, he may have lost his position on the team.[27]

Most effective, at both disciplining players and reducing salary costs, was the implementation of the reserve rule. In a secret meeting held toward the end of the 1879 season, the National League owners agreed to each set aside five of their eleven players as men who could not be signed by any other team the following year. "The said named players," the agreement read, "are to be considered and treated as members of their respective Clubs, meaning and intending hereby that the men above as assigned shall be treated in all respects as players engaged and under regular contracts for the season of 1880, to the Clubs to whom they are assigned above."[28]

Fig. 3. Mike "King" Kelly. National Baseball
Hall of Fame Library, Cooperstown NY.

A reserved player would find, upon testing the market for a better contract with a different team, that no club would even attempt to negotiate to sign him. Enforced by expulsion and blacklisting, the reserve rule would thus largely prevent the best players from moving to other teams and leagues, thereby reinforcing each club's territorial rights. It also encouraged a competitive balance within the league, as it prevented wealthier teams from raiding the poorer ones. The National League, thenceforth, became, in the words of League president William Hulbert, more of a "business coalition" than a collection of individually competitive franchises.[29]

The reserve rule was a "vital necessity," Hulbert claimed, if the league was to avoid paying what even Ward considered "extravagant" salaries.[30] Indeed, the comments of Ward and others led Hulbert to (perhaps erroneously) conclude that not only did players understand the need for the reserve clause; "they [were] all anxious to be reserved, and their only fear [was] that they [wouldn't] be."[31]

The reserve rule was expanded in 1883 to include eleven players and in 1885, fourteen players, thus enabling clubs to reserve their entire rosters and even additional unpaid players, who, for one reason or another, never played. Charles Foley, for instance, missed the entire 1883 season because of illness. Accordingly, the club for which he played in 1882—Buffalo—did not offer him a salary. When Foley recovered, toward the end of the 1884 season, he was prevented from signing with a different club, as Buffalo claimed that it had reserved him all along, despite the absence of a contract. To make matters worse for the young outfielder, Buffalo then refused to sign him, although still holding him in reserve. Whether contracted or not, players across the league were thus completely immobilized. Without the ability to pit teams in competition with one another for their labor, players could not effectively use the power they held in their extraordinarily skilled bodies to determine the price of their labor. They instead were forced to take the salaries that were offered to them while the National League owners reaped the growing revenues for themselves. Average salaries dropped from about $2,000 in 1877 to less than $1,500 in 1882, while, as discussed at the beginning of this chapter, club profits soared.[32] Control over the professional game had now shifted almost entirely to baseball's owners.

The National League and its supporters in the press justified the reserve rule as a necessary and fair clause on which the survival of baseball depended. The 1884 *Spalding Guide*, for example, argues that until the National League instituted the reserve rule, players were "paid for according to their real value to a club," which consequently led to the "reckless competition for [their] services."[33] With the implementation of the reserve clause, owners could, more appropriately, pay their employees "on the basis of the relation [a players' work bore] to that of any other occupation he [might] be competent to engage in as a means of livelihood."[34] Thus, concludes Spalding, "the reserve rule . . . simply places a barrier to the reckless competition for the services of men who, outside of the ball field, could not earn a tenth part of the sum they demand for baseball services."[35] What Spalding does not mention here is that those workingmen earning "a tenth part" of a baseball player's salary made such dire wages in part because their labor processes had been degraded and de-skilled to a point where they were in "reckless competition" with one another for scarce jobs.[36] With the requisite skill level for these positions relatively low, far more men were able to work as, say, carpenters, bricklayers, and fence painters (and exceedingly more as common laborers) than were able to play professional baseball. Individual workers in these other industries were therefore unable to use their skills or scarcity as a means of establishing anything close to monopoly power over their labor markets. They were forced, instead, to take the abysmal wages offered by their employers. As already discussed professional baseball was unable to reduce the skill level of baseball players. But the reserve rule, coupled with discourse like that of Spalding in this passage, functioned to replicate some of the *effects* of skill reduction on player wages and power. The reserve rule made individual baseball players nearly as unable to bargain for higher wages as were degraded individual tradesmen or laborers. It is important to note, however, that neither Spalding nor any other National League magnate ever argued for an equalization of wages between baseball players and the average workingman. While Spalding may have been right that players never would have made as much money in other industries, it was necessary for his industry's survival to offer these men salaries just high enough to discourage them from choosing another profession.

Threats to the National League

Alternatively, however, baseball players could, from time to time, choose another employer within the same profession, despite the reserve clause. All three of the National League's strategies were periodically threatened and in turn reshaped and reinforced by the emergence of rival leagues. The National League's profits, which were abetted by the absence of competition, ended up inducing a competitive market over those profits, which, consequently and temporarily, minimized, if not altogether eliminated, the NL's monopoly over baseball.

The International Association (IA) was the first outside threat to the National League. As the NL came to life in the mid-1870s, a disparate group of baseball clubs outside its membership competed with one another and, in occasional exhibition contests, against National League teams. Many of these independent clubs sought membership in the NL; some succeeded (Indianapolis, for example, in 1878). Several teams that did not initially gain entrance to the NL banded together to form the International Association of Professional Base Ball Players. In 1877, its first year of existence, the IA included twenty-three clubs, mostly in Upstate New York and Massachusetts, as well as London and Guelph, Ontario. Although no teams were located in National League cities, some, such as the one in Lynn, Massachusetts, were close enough to worry club owners. No matter where these teams were located, National League directors were also concerned with the possibility that their players would jump to the IA in search of greater salaries or better working conditions.

Upon the association's inception, therefore, the National League worked to attenuate the competitive pressure. Hulbert and Spalding, along with newly welcomed league executive A. G. Mills, immediately offered membership into a "League Alliance" to IA and other non-league clubs. Ostensibly, the alliance established new territorial rights for member clubs and prevented teams from poaching each other's contracted players. In reality the alliance was designed primarily to protect the National League's player and fan markets. Two delegates from each IA club were admitted to National League meetings, but they were not permitted to vote. The younger association was not permitted to locate teams in any of the National League's markets, thus leaving the IA in small to midsized cities such as Syracuse and Auburn, New York; Columbus, Ohio; and London, Ontario. NL teams promised not to compete against any nonalliance teams within a five-mile range of an alliance team's city. Non-NL alliance clubs offered all contract information to the NL so that the league could know when players' contracts expired (in order to "fairly" sign them to NL teams).

During the initial year of the agreement, NL and non-NL alliance teams occasionally competed against each other before and after the dominant league's season and on its off days (Mondays, Wednesdays, and Fridays, but not on Sundays). But the NL soon discovered that games against clubs outside its membership in NL parks generated very little revenue. Fewer games against only the best (i.e., NL) clubs would increase demand. As the *Chicago Tribune* put it, addressing the IA, "The truth is, gentlemen of the smaller cities, the League . . . finds that it doesn't want you on their grounds. . . . The League can make more money off thirty first-class games than they can off sixty . . . and they are going to play the thirty with the clubs they think most likely to interest their patrons."[37] The prohibition of IA teams from NL fields, in addition to the decision not to expand the National League to make room for additional IA clubs, functioned to reinforce the scarcity and superiority of National League baseball, particularly as it took place in National League ballparks.[38] The sanctity of the ballparks would not be sullied by an inferior form of the national pastime. By limiting the quantity of its products the National League protected its quality. At the same time, however, league executives did not stop National

League teams from continuing to play in non-NL alliance ballparks. Instead, the senior circuit forced the IA teams to guarantee visiting clubs at least $120 or half the gate receipts, far greater figures than allowed within the National League. All interleague games, furthermore, had to use the rules, official ball, and umpires of the NL.

Still, the presence of the IA initially hurt the finances of most National League teams. Average salaries increased from $1,750 to $2,000 between 1876 and 1877, as the yet-to-be-reserved National League players jumped, or threatened to jump, to the new association.[39] The operating budgets of NL clubs included a much higher portion devoted to salaries. Boston spent $19,000 of its $30,000 budget in 1876 on player salaries. The following year the club increased its spending to $22,420 on salaries and $34,443 in total. Boston's losses, accordingly, increased from about $800 in 1876 to more than $2,200 in 1877. Despite their success on the field, St. Louis lost $8,000 and Chicago fell $6,000 into the red. But with the alliance firmly in place and interleague player movement thus far less possible, average National League salaries fell back to their 1876 levels in 1878.[40]

The financial pressures created more lasting damage for the International Association. The IA sputtered along for a couple years before collapsing in 1880. Seymour attributes the association's demise to a "lack of solidarity," as the clubs failed to effectively band together to fight the National League's dominance.[41] Some of the IA's teams did not even agree to join the alliance. Also, Burk argues, the widespread geographic distribution of the IA's clubs created traveling expenses too great for most teams to meet.[42] Many of the clubs also lacked the initial capital necessary to construct ballparks and attract the best players. Finally, the National League's qualitative superiority, coupled with its clubs' locations in bigger cities, brought far more spectators to their contests than the IA games could attract.

The American Association, as suggested earlier, proved a more menacing threat. The National League's prohibition against alcohol, coupled with its absence from some of the largest urban markets, created opportunities for investment that a handful of beer barons and disgruntled National League exiles could not pass up. Investors in Cincinnati, whose club was expelled from the National League in 1880 for insisting on twenty-five-cent admissions and alcohol sales (one of the team owners held a stake in the J. G. Sohn & Company brewery), joined forces with men from New York, Philadelphia, St. Louis, Louisville, Pittsburgh, and Baltimore to form an association intended to realistically challenge the National League. Unlike the backers of the International Association, many of the AA's investors had both experience running a professional ball club, and, perhaps more importantly, other businesses that could support and be supported by professional baseball. Chris Von der Ahe owned a saloon and brewery on Grand Avenue in St. Louis, adjacent to Sportsmen's Park, where the independent St. Louis Brown Stockings played in 1880. "Finding the ball fans good customers at his bar," Seymour explains, quoting from Alfred Spink's (unidentified nineteenth-century) book on baseball, "Chris became interested in baseball 'as he might have become interested in pretzels, peanuts or any other incitant to thirst and beer drinking,' so he secured the refreshment privileges and eventually purchased the ball club."[43] Insofar as it served as a vehicle for the consumption of alcohol, baseball was a lot like pretzels and peanuts. But unlike these salty snacks, professional baseball's extraordinary qualities made it an extremely rare and sought-after commodity. Nevertheless, like the White Stockings for Spalding's sporting goods, the Brown Stockings served as a means for Von der Ahe to sell more beer. And the beer and sporting goods, in turn, functioned as a way to sell more baseball tickets. Each depended on the other.

Rather than force spectators to travel across the street to the local saloon, however, the AA's leadership agreed to allow the sale of alcohol within the ballparks. With the late addition of Baltimore brewer Harry Vonderhorst as a club owner and the election of Kentucky Malting Company executive J. H. Pank as vice president, the American Association was quickly dubbed "the beer and whiskey league" by its critics. In addition to the presence of beer and liquor, the AA would flout the National League's Victorian standards by scheduling games on Sunday and selling its tickets for twenty-five cents. The latter two measures, especially, would allow a much greater proportion of working-class fans to attend AA games, thus further diverting the circuit from NL ideals.

Much like the NL, however, the new association voraciously went after the best available (and ostensibly unavailable) players. First, the AA tried to secure the National League's expelled, suspended, and blacklisted players, signing thirteen for the 1882 season. Most of its players came from independent clubs, including some of the disbanded IA teams. Several more NL players accepted advances for agreeing to "optional agreements" for the 1883 season. But many of these players took their option money and returned to the NL in 1883. The AA blacklisted such jumpers and instituted its own reserve rule to secure those who did stay. The bidding war for players caused salaries to soar to unprecedented levels. Even cash-strapped Providence saw its salaries rise from an average of $1,279 in 1882 to $1,446 in 1883.[44]

In addition to what Spalding would later call (in the passage quoted above) the "reckless competition" for players, the presence of AA teams in more-populous locales stood to wreak havoc on the NL's finances. Five of the six association clubs in 1882 outdrew Chicago, the National League's most popular team that year. All six AA cities combined included one and a half times as many people as the eight NL cities. While most National League teams lost money in 1882, the American Association Philadelphia and St. Louis clubs claimed to have made profits of $200,000 and $70,000 respectively. Such figures were probably exaggerations, but the relative popularity of the AA most likely did bring with it some degree of financial success. And with these deepening pockets, the association was well positioned to lure additional National League players to its own teams.

A. G. Mills, the National League's new president, pushed through two developments that began to change these fortunes. First, he allowed for the readmittance into the National League of clubs from New York and Philadelphia. Supported by a group of wealthy industrialists willing to spend $40,000 in 1883 for the team's payroll, the

New York "Giants," as they were subsequently called, put the NL back in the country's most populous city. And while Philadelphia's reentry, despite the allowance of a twenty-five-cent admission price, was not as initially successful, the team soon landed on solid financial and competitive grounds and thenceforth remained a fixture in the National League well into the twenty-first century. Second, and more significantly, Mills persuaded the AA to enter into a new form of the League Alliance called the "National Agreement" or "Tripartite Pact." Along with the newly emerged Northwestern League, the NL and the AA agreed in March 1883 to respect each other's player markets and territorial rights. Philadelphia and New York would stand as exceptions, as the NL and the AA both kept their teams in these cities. But each circuit's reserve rule was rigidly respected, and it was from this mutual desire to end bidding wars and contract jumping that the reserve clause was expanded to include eleven players from each team. In 1884 the National Agreement was strengthened to protect its members from the short-lived Union Association. Any club that played a team outside the Tripartite Pact would be expelled from its league and the agreement. Having secured and reinforced their player and consumer markets, both the NL and the AA surged in popularity and profitability throughout the 1880s. But having reserved most of the best players upon the signing of the National Agreement, the National League stood head and shoulders above the American Association for the rest of the latter's ten-year history. As other leagues (such as the Eastern League, the New York State League, and the International League) entered the fray, they, too, were brought into the National Agreement, thus reinforcing the territorial rights and control over players held by the major league teams.

On their own professional sports, as well as most performing arts, face debilitating contradictions. But the production of certain arrangements, as this chapter has shown, enables the industry to resolve these contradictions. For professional baseball in the nineteenth century, the construction of territorial rights, the creation of additional revenue made possible by mass-producing products related to the sport, the control over players, and the creation of intracapital agreements to reinforce these measures provided the institutional framework necessary for sustained profitability.

With these arrangements in place, it seemed that the National League had fought off all the demons that plagued organized baseball up until the early 1880s. But, as the next chapter reveals, these measures, particularly those levied on player mobility and behavior, generated considerable resentment among the players. In response a group of National League players formed, in 1885, the Brotherhood of Professional Base Ball Players, the sport's first labor union.

3

THE BROTHERHOOD OF PROFESSIONAL
BASE BALL PLAYERS

The combination of the three strategies described in the preceding chapter, together with trade agreements with the American Association and a few other rival leagues, enabled National League clubs to firmly establish a monopoly over the baseball business and thus generate steadily increasing profits. As Ward recalled, "A one-league monopoly was always the ambition of the controlling spirits of the National League. To make it the central figure in the base ball world has been their aim for years, and to this end they have directed every effort. Once securely established as the supreme power in the direction of affairs they would dictate terms to all other leagues and associations and maintain a position that would make the National League the center of power and interest." But, Ward concluded, "the project was all but accomplished and miscarried only through the League's utter failure to consider the rights of its players."[1] Thus by apparently solving the contradictions of the professional baseball industry, the National League exacerbated the central contradiction of capitalist production more generally—that between capital and labor. And this contradiction, more than any other, nearly put the National League out of business.

The "miscarriage" of the National League's plans, as Ward viewed it in the spring of 1890, began in the summer of 1885. The results of an August 1885 meeting among National League representatives particularly irritated the players. In conjunction with the American Association, the league agreed to now allow each club to reserve twelve players (up from eleven) and to make the reserve rule perpetual, thus officially binding all players to their clubs for life. The delegates also decided on a $2,000 salary limit, which was to be universally applied the following season, regardless of players' previous salary figures. Together with the American Association's agreement to respect the National League's player and consumer markets, the new policies firmly solidified the league's ability to control the price of labor.

The Birth of the Brotherhood

Just two weeks after the details of the National League's 1885 meeting were published in the sporting press, a group of nine men from the New York club, seeking "mutual protection of the players," secretly formed the Brotherhood of Professional Base Ball Players.[2] The widely respected Ward, who had just graduated from Columbia Law School, was elected president. The purpose of the brotherhood, as stated in the preamble to its constitution, was, "to protect and benefit ourselves collectively and individually; to promote a high standard of professional conduct; [and] to foster and encourage the interests of the game of Base Ball."[3] In short, the brotherhood sought to reform the National League, not, initially at least, to radically transform it. That only about 10 percent of the league's players earned salaries greater than $2,000 (with Ward and a few of his teammates securely among them), and that the brotherhood only very marginally sought to unionize the players of the American Association, suggests that the brotherhood was primarily geared to "protect and benefit" the sport's best players. With the additional stipulations that the "conduct" of the players and the "interests" of the game were chief among their concerns (the brotherhood eventually issued fines for intemperance and other moral infractions), the brotherhood's politics were not significantly different from those of other skilled trade unions. Although by different means, both narrowly sought to protect their own position within the industry and their industry's position within the broader economy. What separated the brotherhood from other fraternal organizations and trade unions, aside from the players' considerably higher incomes, were the conditions they sought to create in order to "protect and benefit" themselves. While bricklayers, plumbers, and carpenters organized in order to reduce, if not altogether eliminate, competition among themselves for similarly paying available jobs, Ward and his brethren attempted to garner and exploit a free labor market so that the most skilled among them would earn the highest salaries. Moreover, labeling both National League baseball players and tradesmen as "skilled" is misleading. While most trades required certain skill sets that needed to be acquired over time, decades of skill degradation made such abilities relatively easy to attain. The standard deviation between the most highly skilled baseball players and the league average (not to mention the overall average, if all amateur and professional baseball players were included) was tremendously large compared to the variation of skill levels among, say, carpenters. The brotherhood's politics were aimed at exploiting this difference, while even the more conservative trade unions sought to minimize the effects of such intratrade disparities.

For these reasons it has been suspected by some baseball historians, and quite a few contemporaneous National League boosters, that the more ordinary players—who were not adversely affected by the league's salary caps and, in fact, benefited from the $1,000 minimum salary—did not always share Ward's interests.[4]

But in fact the brotherhood proved to be a magnet for nearly all National League players. By the end of the 1886 season, the organization had formed chapters in every National League city and gained the membership of more than one hundred players, close to 90 percent of the league. That most league players did join the brotherhood, despite the differences among them, can be attributed in part to the close social ties within the playing force. The National League was universally white and predominantly American born, with a majority of the athletes of English, Irish, or German descent.[5]

The players also came from a similar class background apart from their positions as professional baseball players. Between 1855 and 1870 the majority of ballplayers were either skilled craftsmen or proprietors of small businesses such as, in Burk's words, "newsstands, bars, billiard halls, haberdasheries, and sporting goods stores."[6] While comprehensive data on the 1885–89 brotherhood members' occupations outside baseball are not available, contextual and anecdotal evidence suggests that a significant proportion of these men worked as skilled craftsmen in addition to, or at least before, serving as baseball players. According to an 1887 *New York Clipper* survey, most players still identified themselves as "workers" and believed that they would forever be members of the working class.[7] Their identification as such had to do, in part, with their relationship with club owners and league management, but it also most likely reflected their prebaseball, off-season, and projected postcareer employment. Mike Kelly, for instance, spent his teenage years working in a mill for three dollars per week, "carrying baskets of coal from the basement to the top floor" as well as delivering newspapers between New York City and Patterson, New Jersey.[8] During the early years of Kelly's professional baseball career, when he played for the Patterson Keystones and the Columbus Buckeyes in the 1870s, he spent the off-seasons working in a silk-weaving factory.[9] "We didn't get big salaries in those days," Kelly wrote in his autobiography, "and a fellow was sometimes pretty lucky to get his salary."[10] When the seasons ended, "the ballplayer was without an occupation" and in need of work.[11] John Kerins worked as a boiler-maker in the off-season, and John Glasscock was a shipwright. Buck Ewing, one of the brotherhood's founders, was a teamster, earning ten dollars per week before he signed with the Troy club in 1880. John Clarkson learned the cigar-making trade in addition to playing professional baseball. Few baseball players attended college.[12]

On top of these shared demographics, baseball players spent countless hours together on trains, in hotels, at the theater, and, for some, in saloons, not to mention on the ball field. The social pressure to join an organization of which nine or ten of your (better performing, mind you) teammates were members must have been too difficult to elude. Those few men who did not join the brotherhood, such as Chicago captain Adrian "Cap" Anson, were generally, for one reason or another, sympathetic to management.[13]

The brotherhood's popularity among even the weakest players can also be credited to the fact that the organization did, to some extent, reach out to them. Sick or injured players, who as a rule were not paid by their club owners (if they were even still employed), could receive up to ten dollars per week from the brotherhood's "relief committee." Curry Foley, an outfielder and pitcher whose career-ending injury put him on hard economic times, was the recipient of a February 1886 benefit dinner organized by the New York chapter of the brotherhood. Ward made the first donation. Additionally, the brotherhood advocated on behalf of players who, in the organization's view, were unfairly disciplined. Ward convinced Washington owner John Gaffney, for example, to rescind a $100 fine that he imposed on Cliff Carroll for attending his own wedding instead of playing in the day's scheduled game. When a former player passed away during the 1887 season, the brotherhood sent a representative to his funeral.

Ward and his New York teammates were not the first people to attempt to organize professional baseball players. As early as 1880 the *New York Mercury* urged the National League's employees to "rise up in their manhood and rebel."[14] But neither that comment nor a more serious effort in 1885 by a Philadelphia sports writer, William Voltz, to establish a protective association that would have benefited sick and needy players caught on with the men on the field. Ward's near-universal reputation as one of the best, most intelligent, most honorable, and, indeed, manliest players—particularly compared to the outsider personas of journalists—must have been a strong factor in attracting such a high percentage of players to follow him.

The Labor-Organizing Education of John Ward

Just what influenced Ward is more difficult to discern. The president of the brotherhood grew up in Bellefonte, Pennsylvania, a small town just north of State College. Ward's parents struggled to maintain a middle-class existence. His father, James Ward, was a failed small-business owner, who declared bankruptcy shortly before dying of tuberculosis in 1871. Ward's mother, Ruth Ward, was a schoolteacher and was deeply admired by the two thousand or so residents of Bellefonte. By the time Ward was born, in 1860, Bellefonte was racially integrated, though not without its share of racism. An editorial in the *Bellefonte Democratic-Watchmen* nearly three weeks after Ward's birth, for example, warns that there is "no greater curse to a community than a large, idle, vicious population of Negroes," with which Bellefonte was "deeply afflicted."[15] Ward's later participation as the only white man in an 1892 game between two otherwise all-black teams suggests that he saw, at the very least, racial integration as a benefit rather than a curse.[16] At age fourteen Ward attended Penn State College, which at the time had minimal entrance requirements and was, according to a contemporary historian, "an academic dumping ground" for teenage boys who could not gain admission to the more prestigious Pennsylvania, Villanova, or Lafayette Colleges.[17] Ward never graduated (he and a few of his friends were expelled for stealing chickens from a neighboring farm), but he did play baseball and he played it well.[18]

Ward's labor politics, like those of the other members of the brotherhood, probably developed most directly from his experiences as a professional baseball player. From the beginning of his professional career in 1877 through his founding of the brotherhood in 1885, Ward had learned firsthand both the possibilities and the precariousness of professional baseball. As Ward commented years later on his first year as a professional player, "I had already seen that base-ball was lucrative only to players in the first class, and I concluded that if I could not get into that I would quit altogether."[19] At that time, in 1877, Ward's statement was doubly true: not only were the best players the only ones who were highly paid, but because of the free market on which they traded their ability to work, they could earn even more money than the top players would a decade later.[20] There were several thousand professional and amateur baseball players at any given time during the 1870s and 1880s; about one hundred of them played in the National League.

Faced with this slim chance of success, Ward prepared for other options. After his dismissal from Penn State, Ward took a job as a traveling salesman, which had him hawking nursery products ("strawberry plants and fancy shrubbery") across northern Pennsylvania.[21] A bit later he wrote to the president of Penn State College, asking for a "certificate of dismissal," which would have indicated to potential employers that Ward at least had attended college.[22] But Ward's job quickly left him broke and stuck in the middle of nowhere. By chance he hopped a train to Renovo, Pennsylvania, "determined to accept the first employment that offered a livelihood."[23] In Renovo, Ward indeed found employment, but this time as a pitcher for the minor league Renovo Resolutes. "I could pitch the 'curve,' at that time an effective novelty, and I had in consequence gained some local reputation," Ward remembered.[24] He earned ten dollars a month plus board. A few months into the season, Ward left Renovo for Williamsport, where he was offered a higher wage and the chance to play for a more popular team. Williamsport would prove more frustrating than it was worth, though, as "before [the first] pay-day came, the manager had left town, but neglected to leave his address," wrote Ward.[25] Later that summer Ward moved to Philadelphia, where again, he was promised more than he was paid. Thus, Ward lamented, "during my first ten weeks of professional play, including service with three clubs, I received only ten dollars."[26] Ward also played for clubs in Janesville, Wisconsin, and Buffalo, New York, that year. By the end of his first season, Ward found himself "high and dry upon the strand . . . again reduced to a hand-to-hand struggle with necessity."[27] Back in Janesville for the winter, Ward took a factory job, where his "principal duty was to keep up steam in a stationary engine." It is possible that the position was provided for him through a connection with the Janesville team and therefore cushier than Ward portrayed it ("ten hours a day all winter for my board"), as many off-season jobs for baseball players were at the time.[28] But given the fact that Ward did not end his 1877 season nor start his 1878 campaign in Janesville, it is more likely that he simply seized upon the best opportunity that was available to him in a place that was somewhat familiar. There is also a chance that Ward later inflated, or at least accentuated, his working-class credentials in an article published in *Lippincott's* in order to drum up support for the brotherhood, which was about to first publicize its existence when Ward's article appeared. Even if that were the case, Ward's work in Janesville, like that of some other ballplayers in other cities during the off-season, was real enough, however temporary.

Ward started the 1878 campaign in Binghamton, the home of a struggling International Association club. The Crickets, as they were called, foundered throughout the first two months of the season, but Ward pitched extremely well. During the second week of July, Binghamton's owners released all their players and folded the club. The *Binghamton Morning Republican* noted the following day, "Several of the nine [ballplayers] are secured for their pay, while others have from one to five weeks' wages due.... The latter offer to release the [owners from all salary claims] if it will pay their bills about town.... Most of the players can secure engagements elsewhere. Ward will probably go to Syracuse or Rochester."[29] It is not clear whether Ward was one of those men to whom wages were due, but regardless, another incident of owners unable or unwilling to compensate their players had left an imprint on his consciousness. But while some of the Crickets may have, indeed, ended up in other IA cities such as Syracuse and Rochester, Ward landed in the National League with the upstart Providence Grays.

Ward quickly became a star not just in Providence but across the National League. In just his second year, Ward threw a perfect game, only the second time that had happened in the history of Major League Baseball.[30] Behind Ward's stellar pitching and capable hitting, the Grays would go on to win the National League pennant that season.[31] Ward tested his abilities for both team leadership and entrepreneurship during his years with Providence. In addition to outplaying most of his teammates, the slender Pennsylvanian quickly emerged as a beacon of morality on the Grays. The Providence players were known for their excessive drinking, late-night carousing, and lax attitude toward physical fitness. Ward, having none of that, tried to convince his teammates that moderation, rest, and good health would help them perform better on the field. Management, keeping in line with the National League's attempts to project a Victorian image, was impressed and appointed Ward captain in June 1880. The rest of the Grays, however, were not yet ready to submit to Ward's stern discipline, and the pitcher resigned from his captaincy within a month.[32] Socially Ward thus found himself somewhere outside both the player fraternity and the realm of management.

Also while in Providence, in 1881, Ward opened a private business. Seeking to cash in on the growing market for sporting goods (see chapter 2), the left-hander bought a sporting goods and tobacco shop called the Baseball Emporium. Its first location, at 61 Dorrance Street, in downtown Providence, proved unsuccessful, so he moved the emporium to 75 Weybosset Street, a few blocks away. Within a year, however, Ward's business, like those of his father more than a decade ago, went under.[33]

Perhaps most important to his development as union organizer and president were the changes to the National League's labor relations, which Ward directly experienced and witnessed around him. Ward's salary figures are not available for 1878 and 1879, but in 1880 he earned $1,700 and was placed on the league's first reserve list.[34] Providence's team owners released all its players two weeks before the end of the 1880 season so that they did not have to give them their final paychecks. The team re-signed its reserved players, including Ward, at the beginning of the 1881 season. Worse than the deflated salaries brought on by the reserve rule, according to Ward, was the growing practice of buying and selling players against their will. In October 1882 Ward learned that he would play the following year for the new National League club in New York. Bryan Di Salvatore argues that Ward was thrilled with this move, and given his new salary—$3,100—he may very well have been.[35] But the fact remained that clubs controlled the movement of players from one team to another regardless of whether the players liked it. In his *Lippincott's* article, published three years after he had joined the New York club, Ward tacitly suggests that he was ready by 1886 to leave New York:

It seems that a man cannot, with any credit to himself, play in the same club beyond a definite time. Three years is in most cases the limit. The local public has seen him at his best, when, by a combination of good play and good luck, he has done particularly well. It makes this his standard, and expects it from him forever after. If he does that well he is doing only what he should, and if he does less he is playing poorly. . . . The interests of both clubs and players demand some scheme providing for a gradual change.[36]

If Ward or any other player did want to leave, this sort of thinly veiled sentiment seemed the only way forward. Fully reserved players could not just pick up and leave, as the free agents of today's era can do after their contracts expire. Nor could a player publicly express his desires for his club to sell him, lest he lose favor with his fans. Players who were sold and refused to go were blacklisted. So players' control over their mobility was limited to these sorts of allusions and nudges, which, of course, were rarely successful; Ward ended up staying in New York through the 1889 season. Moreover, while his $3,100 salary in 1883 was impressive, reservation ensured that he would make this much in a single year only three more times in his career. Ward's salary dropped to $3,000 in 1884 and to the league maximum, $2,000, in 1885, before rising to $3,100 again in 1888, 1889, and 1890.[37]

Ward's tenure in Manhattan was softened, and most likely made enjoyable, though, by several factors. First, after a couple of initial years teetering near the bottom of the league table, the New York club finished in third place or above in four out of the next five seasons. It won the pennant in 1888 and 1889. Despite a shoulder injury that prevented him from pitching much ever again, Ward quickly learned how to play center field, second base, and finally, shortstop. He became one of the best fielders, hitters, and base runners in the National League.

Second, Ward fell in love with a famous Broadway actress named Helen Dauvray near the beginning of the 1887 season. Each side of the celebrity couple enhanced the profile of the other and brought further attention to the New York theater and baseball worlds. Dauvray, for example, awash with money, donated a sterling silver cup to the National League in 1887.[38] The "Dauvray Cup" was to be awarded to each season's league champion. Gold medals, then, went to each of the winning team's players. Although most parties admired Dauvray's generosity, the National Police Gazette called the move an "advertising play": "What is wrong with Helen Dauvray? Is she not of sufficient importance in the theatrical world, that she is seeking notoriety and cheap advertising in baseball circles by offering a costly 'loving cup' as a trophy?"[39] There might have been some truth to the Gazette's assertion that the cup was self-serving. Actors, perhaps even more so than baseball players, depended on their public image in order to strengthen their market power. Informed by the gossipy theater press (which, as noted earlier, often doubled as the baseball press), audiences seemed just as likely to attend a dramatic performance because of an actress's skills as they were from an affection for her personality, good looks, and charm. And either way any sort of publicity was necessary for an actress or actor to establish popular name recognition. Moreover, baseball and theater crowds overlapped in the late nineteenth century. Dauvray's silver cup was a means by which she could make further inroads with that particular consumer market. Coupled with Ward, Dauvray could, in turn, deepen theatergoers' interest in baseball. She also seemed to be a genuine fan of the game, one who was attending contests at the Polo Grounds long before she met Ward.[40]

There is a chance, too, that Dauvray's role in Ward's life was more than mere lover (and eventually wife), emollient to his stressful career as a New York "base-ballist." Actors in the 1880s were also losing more and more of their market power to an increasingly monopolized cabal of capitalist financiers. A narrowing group of producers, theatrical booking agents, and theater owners—who, by 1896, would materialize into a six-man, all-powerful "syndicate"—was extracting a growing proportion of value from the actors they employed.[41] While calls for unionization among actors did not publicly emerge until later that decade, and an actual actors' union would not form until 1913, Dauvray and Ward must have felt some professional empathy for each other.[42]

Fig. 4. Helen Dauvray. The Miriam and Ira D. Wallach Division of Art, Prints
and Photographs: Photography Collection, The New York Public Library.
"Helen Ward, avec les amities de Helen Ward à M. Chadwick"
New York Public Library Digital Collections.

With Dauvray whispering in his ear, Ward probably understood the-ater's inverse relationship between its growing popularity and most actors' compensation. By most accounts the situation was worse for actors than it was for baseball players, but Ward had to have been aware that his sport could just as easily fall down that same path if he and his peers did not put up some sort of struggle.

Ward, however, had little respect for his wife's professional career. Once they married, he demanded that Dauvray give up acting. She "had to choose between me and the stage," Ward reportedly told a friend upon their separation in 1890, "She chose the stage."[43] But Dauvray insisted that her immediate return to acting was not the rea-son for their separation: "It is true that Mr. Ward and I are living apart. It is true that I am going back to the stage, but that our separation is caused by my uncontrollable desire to return to the stage is absolutely false. I do love my art, but I loved my husband more and the stage has never in the past or in the present moment possessed for me charms as attractive as those of a happy home."[44] If this is taken at face value, then why did the celebrity couple of New York permanently separate (and later divorce)?

Perhaps it had something to do with Jessie Dermot. Dermot was well known across New York as the stunningly beautiful and extraor-dinarily younger wife of prominent attorney and former Tammany Hall politician George McDermott, whom she married in 1884 at the age of sixteen. McDermott rented a room to Ward in his East Forty-Seventh Street building in 1887. Sometime before the end of the base-ball season, with her husband perpetually drunk and often gambling away their fortune at the racetrack, Dermot began sleeping with her new neighbor. In October, just a week before he married Dauvray, Ward was found by McDermott in his young wife's arms. A "severe tussle" ensued, which left Ward bloodied and bruised.[45] Ward moved out, married anyway, and continued his relationship with Dermot well into 1890, at which time Dermot was beginning her acting career. Ward and Dauvray's separation occurred just days after the ballplayer was caught by McDermott walking out of a downtown restaurant with Dermot on his arm. This time around Ward knocked out McDermott with one swift punch. It made the papers; Dauvray and Ward split; and Dermot, after a brief escape to Maine with Ward, moved to California.[46]

Suffice it to say that Ward became familiar with the theater business. And this exposure to somewhat parallel labor struggles probably affected the development of his labor politics and leadership capacities. Clearly, fidelity and feminism were not considered requisite characteristics. He could not have developed into the brotherhood's president, though, without other influences as well. After his first season in New York in 1883, Ward enrolled at Columbia College Law School, then located in Midtown Manhattan between Forty-Ninth and Fiftieth Streets and Madison and Fourth Avenues. Ward lived just a short walk away, at 139 East Forty-Eighth Street.[47] Unlike his years spent at Penn State, his law school education was rigorous:

> He was required to take the "regular" law school entrance exam, covering Greek, Roman, American, and English history; English composition, grammar, and rhetoric; and Caesar, Virgil, Cicero, or "other Latin authors deemed by the examiner to be equivalent to the above."
>
> Once in school, as one of 365 enrollees, he studied municipal law, constitutional history, political science, and international and constitutional law, and took part in moot courts. He read Blackstone's *Commentaries*, Perry on trusts, Washburn on real property, Fisher on mortgages, Stephen on pleading, Ortolan's Roman law, Wietersheim's *Geschichte der Völkerwanderung*, Maten's *Recueil des Traites de la Paix*, Calvo's *Droit International*, and many others.[48]

To put this into perspective, most baseball players did not attend college at all, much less an Ivy League law school. Because the majority of players were at least second- or third-generation immigrants—and most of these were of Irish or English descent—it was even rarer for a ballplayer to speak a second language, particularly French or Latin. Few baseball players came across in the papers as well spoken, much less able to pass entrance exams in composition, grammar, and rhetoric. But Ward not only engaged with this curriculum; he excelled at it. In 1885 Ward was awarded a fifty-dollar second prize for "distinction" in constitutional history and constitutional law.[49] He graduated that same year cum laude. Not fully satisfied, Ward then enrolled for a second degree in political science, which he received in June 1886.[50]

Ward attended law school in the first place in order to prepare himself for a career outside baseball. He briefly explained this decision in his 1886 *Lippincott's* article: "I have no immediate intention of retiring from the diamond; still, I want to be prepared for the future. Our occupation is an uncertain one. A broken limb to-morrow may be the end of it for me. Besides, a player's reputation lies with the public: he leans on popular favor, and that he may find at any time to be but a broken reed."[51] Ward thus dampened the insecurity of a professional baseball career with the possibility of a practice in law. It was an individualistic, self-preserving move. But it was one that would affect the whole of professional baseball.

Perhaps because of the cachet of the degree or from those skills and qualities gained along with it, Ward's time at Columbia helped him further develop his reputation within the baseball world as an intelligent, manly, and effective leader, one in particular who could represent the interests of players without ruffling the feathers of management. He was also now able to understand and articulate exactly how the reserve clause was not legally justifiable in a manner that (initially at least) did not seem like a threat to the National League. He was just another, albeit extraordinarily important and respected, part of baseball's cadre of scribes and commentators who had opinions on how the game of baseball could be improved. Beginning in 1885, three months before he graduated, the Ivy Leaguer started to publicly question the legality and utility of the reserve clause.

Ward wrote a letter to the *New York Clipper* in February 1885, rebuking the National League owners for blacklisting nine players who had jumped from the NL to the Union Association (UA) in 1884.[52] Some of these players had jumped after their contracts had expired, but because of their reservation status, they were expected to re-sign with the same National League team. Other players were in the middle of multiyear contracts (which were usually just two to three years) when they jumped. Ward argued that the league should "unconditionally" reinstate the former set of players and "conditionally" readmit the latter. In making this argument, Ward started to chip away at the legality of the reserve clause. While the rule served as a "protective measure," it functioned as "an *ex post facto* law . . . depending for its binding force upon the players solely on its intimidating effect."[53] Furthermore, those players who ignored their reserved status were merely breaking "a rule of the [league] to which they were not parties."[54] The target of Ward's attack in this instance, though, was not the rule itself but rather the way in which it was enforced. The only crime worth expulsion, Ward contended, was "crookedness" (in other words, the fixing of games). "To put the players who have violated the [reserve rule] in the same class with 'crooked' men," Ward argued, "is manifestly unreasonable and unjust."[55]

Perhaps because of his appreciation for contractual law, Ward held contract jumpers in less regard. The distinction between reservation and contraction was an important one for Ward, one that he would develop more fully in the coming years. Multiyear contracts, Ward suggested here, could provide ample security for club investors while still allowing for some player mobility and autonomy. After all, "men who invest their capital in baseball," Ward reasoned, "must have some assurance of its protection, or there will not be found men willing to go into the business at all."[56] But while contract breakers "have certainly done wrong," they deserved a lesser punishment than that which was given to them, perhaps "fines, suspension for a definite time—anything but expulsion. Let that be reserved for the one capital crime of 'crookedness.'"[57]

The UA jumpers should be reinstated, Ward continued, not only because their crimes did not fit the punishment, but also because the National League had already forgiven UA owners for virtually the same infractions. Henry Lucas, the president and chief investor in the Union Association, was allowed to join the National League as owner of his St. Louis club after the UA folded at the end of the 1884 season. But a year earlier Lucas had openly disregarded the reserve rule, calling it "the most arbitrary and unjust rule ever suggested" and urging that it "ought to be broken."[58] The league's inconsistency, Ward concluded, was "influenced by motives of revenge," not "wise and careful legislation."[59]

By April 1885 the National League had readmitted all nine of the UA jumpers. Ward's *Clipper* piece notwithstanding, it was a group of trade unions that protested most vociferously on behalf of the blacklisted players. Blacklisted players were "workingmen kept out of employment by a body of capitalists," they argued, threatening to boycott professional baseball until the players were reinstated.[60] While working-class men had long been interested in baseball as spectators and at varying levels as participants, such a statement is the first known endorsement by organized labor of players' struggles as workers. It is interesting to note that it was the unions that framed the problem as one between capital and labor, while Ward, at this point, characterized it only in terms of legal justice. There is no indication that Ward had had any association whatsoever with organized labor or the labor movement up to this point.[61] His working life outside baseball was too short and varied for him to have become deeply involved with any trade unions; his parents were not of the working class; and as a college student, baseball player, and devotee of the theater, he did not afford himself many chances to mingle with tradesmen. But perhaps the workingmen's voices in this instance, and the growing labor movement from which they came and which Ward as a knowledgeable New Yorker could not have ignored, prodded the ballplayer and his colleagues closer toward a political-economic understanding of their situation and closer toward unionization. If nothing else, the players might have gained new language with which to identify themselves and their cause.

In any event Ward's capacity to write clearly and knowledgeably about baseball and the law must have impressed his future brethren. Given these qualities, in addition to his considerable experience as a player, his manly demeanor, and his popular appeal, Ward made a suitable leader for the brotherhood. "He is a scholarly gentleman and a good fellow, and a great ball player," Mike Kelly wrote of Ward in 1888.[62] Even the otherwise detached *Clipper* noted in the introduction to Ward's 1885 letter, inadvertently foreshadowing the future, that he was "admirably qualified by intelligence and experience to speak as the representative of the professional fraternity."[63] Ward's writings were the first denunciations of the reserve clause written by a player himself. That no member of the brotherhood publicly disputed them suggests that either they generally agreed with and trusted him or he was the mouthpiece for what the organization had collectively decided to publicize. It was probably a combination of the two, although Ward's 1885 *Clipper* piece was published months before even the New York chapter of the brotherhood had formed. With that said, there is a danger in overemphasizing Ward's role in the brotherhood based simply on the availability of his writings vis-à-vis the lack of archival material related to other players' thoughts and actions. Ward was, by his title, the leader and spokesman of the brotherhood. But one should be careful to consider that there were most likely conflicting voices within the brotherhood, which for a variety of reasons never escaped the secrecy of the organization. And there were probably also public expressions from other members of the group, which have been lost within or outside the archives. The appearance and disappearance of Tim Keefe's brotherhood minutes—which, to be sure, do not seem to contradict anything that Ward had to say—stands as a reminder of the slippery and limited nature of historical data. Even Ward's own material has been greatly compromised by historical circumstance; an 1892 fire at his Brooklyn home is thought to have destroyed countless notebooks, scrapbooks, journals, and photographs.[64] Still the predominance of data related to Ward that have survived should not be attributed only to historical accident. Ward was by all available accounts the most capable, willing, and respected representative of the playing force.

Toward the end of the 1886 season, when the brotherhood had organized chapters in most National League cities but was still operating in secrecy, Ward published his "Notes of a Base-Ballist" in *Lippincott's*. The piece can be read as Ward's first attempt to establish professional baseball as a proper profession and the "base-ballist" as a legitimate worker. In addition to recounting his own biography, which, as I have noted, sent the Pennsylvanian-turned-New-Yorker from team to team, and job to job, in search of secure employment, Ward emphasized the "unpleasant" aspects of working as a ballplayer. For instance, the traveling was hard on the body and mind: "It is pleasant to travel when one has plenty of leisure and is at liberty to go or stay as his inclination directs. But it is anything but pleasant to travel as we do. We play every day, with just time enough between dates to reach the next city. The ride is usually made by night; and, what with the loss of sleep and the fatigue of the games, we lose all appreciation of the interesting and the beautiful. I am often so worn out in body and mind that my sensibilities are dulled."[65]

And certain fans just made it worse:

Picture, now, if you can, the agony of a man in this condition when pounced upon by that bane of the ball-player's life, the base-ball "fiend." You are just comfortably seated when you see him coming. . . . The vampire's scent is keen for his prey. You *feel* him coming down upon you, and every nerve tingles at his approach. He addresses you familiarly, and, though he has been present at the game, his first question usually is, "How did the game make out to-day?" Is there in any language any combination of words that can torture a man as those words have tortured me? Will there be base-ball fiends in the world to come? If so, Mr. Ingersoll's belief is a delusion and a snare.[66]

Ward thus positioned the baseball player as a worker who toils under adverse conditions not of his choosing. Although he walked a fine line by characterizing overzealous fans as bloodthirsty "fiends," the brotherhood president began to dispel the notion that ballplayers lived lives of luxury and leisure.

Moreover, the present institutions of baseball treated its employees unfairly, in some ways worse than any other. Again Ward acknowledged the benefits that the reserve rule had brought to the game: "Capital could now be invested in base-ball stock without the possibility of seeing it rendered valueless at the end of six months by the defection of a number of the best players."[67] And he praised the National League for ridding the sport of vice and immorality: "Under this new regime the character and deportment of players have improved and the game has grown steadily in popular favor."[68] But under the reserve rule, "an abuse . . . has sprung up: Clubs sometimes retain men for whom they have no possible use, simply for the purpose of selling them to some other club. In this way the player loses not only the benefits a free contract might give, but also the amount paid for his release. For it is fair to infer that if the club was willing to pay that amount for his release they would have been just as willing to pay it to the player in an increased salary."[69]

Although he ostensibly accepted the existence of the reserve rule, Ward's two bones of contention here are directly related to the nature of the clause. First, even with the reserve rule in place, teams would have lost considerable control over the players' mobility if the sale of players were prohibited. While the prereservation years featured players moving from one team to another more or less at will, full reservation without the ability to buy or sell players would have kept them in place but made it impossible for owners to control the flow of players from one team to another. The effects, in terms of the inability to change an unsuccessful team or sell off more-expensive players when times were tight, would have been nearly as debilitating as the free movement of players without reservation. So it was unlikely that owners would have prohibited player sales without also somehow altering the reserve clause.

Second, Ward's call for a "free contract" attacked, wittingly or not, the mechanism by which reservation was possible in the first place. The reserve rule was not, at this point, written into players' contracts (it was, instead, noted in the National League constitution, to whose rules the contracts vaguely referred). When a player signed a contract, he was not agreeing to reservation per se but rather to abide by whatever rules and regulations the National League constitution dictated. But given players' exclusion from not only writing and amending the constitution but also from knowing its precise contents, they had no freedom to negotiate the terms of their contracts beyond salary (and this, again, was limited by varying caps). Without "free" contracts reservation was thus made possible, but also, as Ward surely knew from his study of law, was standing on fragile legal grounds.

Above all Ward's *Lippincott's* article was part of a continuing effort to win over public support for the players. Part of that campaign involved the same kind of discursive work that the National League had already been engaging in for a decade now: changing the public perception that baseball players were, in Ward's words, "an improvident and even dissipated set."[70] On the contrary, Ward argued, "I believe that baseball players *as a class* to be as well behaved as any other in the community."[71] Additionally, "if honesty, generosity, courage, integrity, and true politeness, which is a kindly regard for the feelings of others,—if these, coupled with a full physical development, are manly attributes, then do I know some ball-players who may rank as representative men."[72] Within the media's discourse about baseball at least, the struggle for Ward and the brotherhood, then, was not just about class identity per se but about a particularly gendered class identity as well. It might seem easy to pry these two identifying factors from each other and predict that the players' working-class identity would become far more antagonistic to the National League than would their manly image. But on the one hand, identity does not break apart so neatly; baseball players could not have successfully identified themselves as workers—or at least the sorts of workers they wished to be portrayed as—without also projecting a manly image (and vice versa). And on the other hand, the players would, as will be seen with the Players League, distinguish their manliness from that of the National League in ways that were just as explosive as their depictions of class. The more appropriate distinction is not between different aspects within identity but rather between identity and material condition. In this instance Ward attempted, as he would more frequently in the following four years, to highlight certain aspects of the material conditions of players' lives in order to construct a manly, working-class identity. The success with which the players could discursively align identity with material condition in the eyes of the public would prove crucial to their ongoing struggle.

Ward racialized the players' struggle as well. In addition to the abuses and inequities already mentioned, the buying and selling of players, Ward contended, likened these men to slaves. In fact Ward noted that slaves were considered more valuable: "There is another feature in this live-stock transaction [i.e., the buying and selling of players] not at all flattering to us. In the old days an able-bodied slave sold for from twelve hundred to twenty-five hundred dollars, while the highest price I have yet heard of as being paid for a ball-player was one thousand dollars."[73] While it is doubtful that Ward actually believed that bought-and-sold baseball players suffered a lower status than black slaves, he is still using the historical imagery of race as a way to characterize the plight of his fellow performers. Nonetheless, the allusion to slavery serves two ends: one, it suggests that baseball players are treated in an absurdly denigrating manner; and two, by doing so, it implies that the loss of one's whiteness is as great an offense as the theft of a players' manliness and working freedom. But regardless of the language he used, Ward's principal contention was that baseball players—like livestock, like slaves—had lost all mobility and agency regarding their employment. They were merely commodities to be bought and sold, shipped here and there, employed by capital and consumed by spectators. Using the imagery of slavery and cattle in this way, though, allowed Ward to begin to associate this argument with larger racial and class struggles.

The Brotherhood Steps Up

Although rumors had persisted throughout the summer of 1886, the brotherhood did not publicize its existence until November 11, when it held its first "official" meeting. Francis Richter broke the story in the November 17 edition of *Sporting Life*.[74] The National League's initial response to the existence of the players' union was one of indifference. One league official went so far as to comment that the brotherhood would have a positive influence on the game. After all, Ward's leadership in the areas of player morality fit right in line with the league's larger project to improve the image of baseball. The National League even welcomed Ward's presence as the unofficial representative of the brotherhood on the playing-rules committee at the board of directors' meeting after the 1886 season (Ward successfully argued for new rules that would push the balance between pitching and hitting back toward the latter).

During the summer of 1887, however, relations between the brotherhood and the National League soured. On July 20, Ward published an open letter in *Sporting Life* to National League president Nick Young in which he excoriated the recent use of the reserve rule.[75] (A week later he published in *Lippincott's* the same letter under the headline "Is the Base Ball Player a Chattel?")[76] The reserve rule's initial effects, Ward conceded, "were clearly beneficial," as the "protective measure . . . gave stability to the game by preserving the playing strength of the teams, and it acted as a check on the increase of salaries."[77] But, Ward continued, "however satisfactory in its original application, I scarcely believe there will be any one found to justify it in the purposes to which it has been recently applied. Instead of an institution for good, it has become one for evil; instead of a measure of protection, it has been used as a handle for the manipulation of a traffic in players, a sort of speculation in live stock, by which they are bought, sold, and transferred like so many sheep."[78] Ward's equation of ballplayers with livestock, like that in his previous *Lippincott's* article, was another way of saying that team owners did not buy just a man's capacity to work for a given amount of time, but rather they bought the whole man as well. This expansion of the owners' authority was not only economically detrimental to Ward and his cohorts but dehumanizing as well.

The same week that Ward's letter ran, New York's owner, John B. Day, started a rumor that Ward's teammates did not like him and no longer trusted him. Ward had just relinquished his role as captain, and Day pounced on this as an indication of his failed leadership. "I am confident that there is hostile feeling toward Ward," Day said to a reporter while riding the Third Avenue elevated train downtown from the Polo Grounds. "And I think the change of captain a good one."[79] A New York club stockholder, Joseph Gordon, echoed Day's remarks: "Something must be done mighty quick," he said. "How do you expect a nine to play when three of the players will not even speak to the captain?"[80]

Ward quickly denied the rumor. He had tendered his resignation weeks ago, allowing his friend Buck Ewing to take on the role. Ward's departure from the position was itself an act of protest to ownership's extended control over the players. Ward wanted team captains to enjoy total control over players' behavior on and off the field, rather than share on-field directing with managers and cede off-the-field authority to owners and/or managers. The latter, Ward argued, should only be in charge of financial aspects of a team. Such a system, though described only in passing here, would form part of the management model for the Players League. As for the purported hostility toward him, Ward commented, "The statement that there are three men in the team who do not speak to me is entirely false. Indeed, I did not know I had an enemy in the team, and certainly there are none who could not command my friendly services at any time."[81] There is reason to believe Ward here. In addition to the fact that he continued to serve as brotherhood president for three more years, Ward was vindicated by teammate "Orator" Jim O'Rourke (perhaps the second most respected man in baseball), who denied all the allegations. Furthermore, an "ex-New York Correspondent 'Layman,'" who claimed (and, indeed, appeared) to have inside knowledge of the affair, likewise asserted that the rumors were "absolutely false."[82] Day and Gordon fell silent on the matter.

Meanwhile, other clubs were clamoring for Ward's services, in the hopes that the rumors were true. Pittsburgh offered New York $5,000 for the shortstop, and Washington and Boston also expressed interest. But Ward wasn't going anywhere, lest his New York club lose its best and most admired performer.

All this chattering reached a crescendo in August 1887, when Ward asked the National League to meet with a committee from the brotherhood to draw up a new, equitable contract. The National League, to this point, had yet to meet with the brotherhood on an official basis. While it publicly acknowledged the organization's existence, the League refused to recognize the brotherhood as a body able to negotiate on behalf of the players. Ward insisted in a *Sporting Life* column that "a new contract which [would] represent the equities of both parties and stand a legal test" could "be best secured by the League meeting a committee from the Brotherhood."[83] In particular, Ward argued, "a contract should be agreed upon which should itself determine all the relations which [were] to exist between the player and his club."[84] No longer, in other words, should contracts merely refer to the National League constitution and National Agreement in regard to the terms of employment. "If the player is willing to concede the right of reservation to the club," he continued, "let that be stated in the contract, and if there are any limitations on the right, let them also be stated."[85] The reserve rule should stay, but "it need[ed] modification." In particular reservation should not extend indefinitely across the lifetime of a player. Instead, "the time during which a club [might] reserve a player should be limited to, say three or five years and the number of reserved should possibly be reduced."[86] This could be accomplished by issuing "contracts [which would] be signed for one, two or five years."[87] That way "a player could ... take his family with him and feel secure of his stay for a definite time."[88] "At the termination of the contract," then, "the player [would go] free upon the market."[89] Finally, Ward concluded, "the new contract should be drawn in such a way as to do away entirely with the buying and selling of players."[90]

The modified reservation system, which Ward proposed here, would have served as a compromise between owner and player control over the latter's mobility. Clubs would reserve players only for the years specified in their contracts. What this would have meant, of course, is an end to the reserve rule as they knew it. There is little difference, in fact, between Ward's proposal and the system of free agency secured by the Major League Baseball Players Association in 1976, still enjoyed today.[91] Players would not have had the freedom to "revolve" from one team to another at will, as they did before reservation and particularly before the National League. But they would have been able, as baseball players currently are, to set in motion a bidding war among teams for their services after their contracts had expired. The owners could have still colluded against the players (as was the case with the reserve rule in the first instance), but so too could teams take advantage of the opportunity to sign better players. After all, the best team wins, and the winningest team generates the most revenue. But given the competitive imbalance that would result and the still overwhelming proportion of revenues derived from ticket sales and expenses doled out to salaries, it is no wonder that the NL did not adopt Ward's plan.

NL president Nick Young and Ward exchanged a series of additional letters on the matter in August and September 1887, but the league still refused to recognize and meet with the brotherhood. Young suggested that "the League would cheerfully meet a committee of its players" but would not recognize them as members of the brotherhood.[92] Furthermore, such a meeting would be possible only after the conclusion of the season. And anyway, the players' concerns could be reasonably settled by "the old and usual means," Young concluded.[93]

Ward responded with a veiled threat. "Well, unless we receive recognition there will be no contracts signed for the season of 1888," he told a *Sporting Life* reporter.[94] But "if the League steadfastly refuses to recognize your Brotherhood, and none of you sign," the reporter asked, "will another organization be formed?"[95] With a sly smile Ward replied, "I am not at liberty to say what we will do. Let me say, however, that there is plenty of money at our disposal to organize any association or league. We know of any amount of capitalists who want to invest their money in base ball."[96] In other words, the brotherhood was planning for a possible Players League (whether or not the brotherhood would call it that) as early as 1887. Such a league would be supported by a new set of capitalists but would operate according to the aims of the players. Ward further elaborated on the plans that he was "not at liberty" to discuss:

> The people now managing the business are powerful, and have plenty of money to back them up, but we believe that we will have the support of the masses in the stand we have taken. It is claimed that a new League could not be formed, because it would have no grounds [i.e., ballparks] and the other necessaries to begin with, and that it would meet the same fate as the old Union Association. Now, as to the first argument, how long would it take to get new grounds and erect new stands? Before the season was half over they would be paid for. As for the old Union Association, it would never have died had it had the Brotherhood to draw from. It lacked the proper attractions to make it a success. . . . The Brotherhood has come to stay, and if the League does not recognize it there will be another one that will. It is not the League that the public goes to see, but the players. Where could the League get men enough to run eight clubs? If they are so plentiful why does it not strengthen its weaker clubs with some of those men?[97]

Two pillars that would become integral to the Players League in 1890 rise to the surface here. One, if the players were to start a new league, they would construct new ballparks in a quick and cost-effective manner. Just how they would go about achieving such efficiency remained to be seen. But Ward's emphasis on the speed and cheapness of the project suggests that the brotherhood had considered the necessary labor involved only in terms of its cost and timeliness. Two, the players' new league would base its success on the superior product at hand: teams consisting of the vast majority of the country's best players. For it was the players themselves, not the league or its owners, who attracted fans to the game. So to put these two components together, the brotherhood's "secretive" new plan would feature reasonably high salaries for the on-field workers and the cheapest possible wages for the off-field laborers.

The National League continued to refuse to meet with the brotherhood. Nevertheless, the brotherhood sent a model of its proposed contract to the league in late October 1887. And come mid-November four members of the brotherhood—Ward, Dan Brouthers, Ned Hanlon, and John Morrill—holed themselves up in the Barrett House, a Manhattan hotel close to the Fifth Avenue Hotel, where the National League owners were about to meet. The players sent an eleventh-hour communiqué requesting recognition. After four months of obstinate refusals, the league admitted the brotherhood committee to its meeting. It made them wait two days, scheduling the players for the final item of business on the agenda, but once the meeting did take place, the National League agreed to officially recognize the brotherhood. Furthermore, the league conceded to include the terms of the reserve rule in the players' contracts. The league was not yet ready for limited reservation, as suggested by Ward.[98] Now that the reserve rule was in writing, however, Ward must have known that it would be easier to challenge one day in court. The league owners gave the brotherhood members their word that their full salaries would be written into their contracts, another concession for which the players had asked. Previously, bonuses and other special payments were kept out of contracts so that a club would not appear to be breaking the $2,000 salary limit. So by making this demand, the players were forcing the league either to acknowledge that most clubs were paying certain players more than the legal limit or to altogether revoke the salary cap. The league promised that it would proceed with the latter.

Reasonably satisfied, the brotherhood committee instructed the rest of the players to sign contracts for the 1888 season. Many of the players, including some of the brotherhood's most prominent members, sought and received significant raises. Ward earned $4,000 in 1888; Tim Keefe received a $1,000 raise; Buck Ewing would make $4,500; Hanlon's salary rose from $2,100 to $2,800; and Fred Dunlap was to earn $7,000.[99] It was as if the owners were bribing the players to stay in line and stay in the league.

Albert Spalding's "Australian Base Ball Tour"

The temporary peace, at whatever price, lasted beyond the close of the 1888 season. By October the baseball world was caught up in the excitement of Albert Spalding's proposed "Australian Base Ball Tour." The magnate made arrangements to take his Chicago club and a team of "All-American" stars gathered from the rest of the league on a barnstorming tour across the United States and over the Pacific to the Hawaiian Islands, Samoa, New Zealand, and Australia. At each stop the tourists would demonstrate the American game of baseball to throngs of excited locals. The trip, Spalding declared, would establish once and for all that baseball was America's "national game." Seeking representative Americans, Spalding invited players who were not only outstanding on the diamond but who were also "men of clean habits and attractive personality, men who would reflect credit upon the country and the game."[100] In an aside to *Sporting Life* writer Harry Palmer, Spalding also acknowledged, "In undertaking such a trip I do so more for the purpose of extending my sporting goods business to that quarter of the globe and creating a market for goods there, rather than with any idea of realizing any profit from the work of the teams I take with me."[101]

Indeed, the trip itself was a financial failure. On the way to Australia, Spalding announced that the tour would not turn around and head home, as the players had expected, but rather would continue westward, with stops in Ceylon, the Arabian Peninsula, Egypt (where, after a game, players took turns firing baseballs at the pyramids), Italy, France, England, and Ireland. Although at nearly every stop the Americans played to sell-out crowds, the expenses of such an ambitious journey far exceeded the revenue earned in ticket sales. Whether the trip was successful in terms of Spalding's ability to create new markets for his sporting goods, however, can be measured, in part, by the fact that he subsequently opened distributors in Honolulu, Auckland, Sydney, Melbourne, Adelaide, Cairo, Paris, and London.[102] And the cost of the trip, estimated, in Spalding's words, at "a minimum of thirty thousand dollars," was offset by the entrepreneur's cunning ability to convince a few other investors to share the expenses.[103] There is also the pure grandeur, whether or not Spalding's business thrived overseas, in declaring (particularly in the 1880s) ownership over a worldwide empire of retail stores (all of Spalding's factories, meanwhile, were located in the United States).[104] And likewise, with weekly dispatches sent back to the American newspapers by Ward (to the *Chicago Tribune*), Harry Palmer (*Sporting Life*), Newton MacMillan (*Chicago Inter Ocean*), and Simon Goodfriend (*New York Sun*), the tour brought attention to baseball within the United States as much as it did at any of the stops on the tour. When the S.S. *Adriatic* finally reached New York Harbor in April 1889, the players found an American public more enthusiastic about baseball, and particularly the American character of baseball, than ever before.[105] Games in 1889 were better attended than in any other season to date.

The tour also served to reinforce racist perceptions of various foreign (and domestic) "others." While in San Francisco the ballplayers received a tour of Chinatown. Reporter Harry Palmer apparently summed up many of the players' feelings when he wrote, "No religion is known in Chinatown; virtue is unknown there. The people have brought the heathenish customs and horrible practices of their barbarous country to San Francisco, and cling to them with a tenacity that shows the hopelessness of converting them to our views of life and religion and of their ever becoming desirable citizens."[106] San Francisco's Chinatown helped people like Palmer and the ballplayers construct, moralize, and naturalize a specifically Chinese race (in fact, reactions to San Francisco's Chinatown also helped shape the geographies of Vancouver's Chinese population).[107] In so doing they further constructed their own white American identity. Such constructions were not without material effect. Just days before the tour reached San Francisco, Congress reinforced the 1882 Chinese Exclusion Act, which prohibited Chinese immigration for ten years.[108]

Moreover, the tourists unflinchingly referred to Hawaiians and Samoans as "cannibals"; of the Hawaiian women, Ward commented, "The lithe forms, graceful movements, and wondrous eyes of the charming Kanaka dancers will haunt the boys for many days to come."[109] In Ceylon, MacMillan wrote, "One day in Ceylon is to the untraveled American a liberal education in Orientalism compressed into a single lesson."[110] What, exactly, did the Americans learn? Colombo, Ward noted, was "a queer sort of a place inhabited by a queer sort of people."[111] Goodfriend observed that the Ceylonian men were "weak and effeminate looking."[112] "To the Oriental," MacMillan concluded, as he explained the locals' tepid reception of baseball, "perfect repose is the ideal state. The chasing of a fly ball to him is the sheerest folly."[113]

Upon arriving in Cairo, the players decided, for a prank, to tie a rope leash around the waist of their traveling mascot, a diminutive African American man named Clarence Duval. Putting a catcher's mask on him for additional laughs, they paraded him around the train station as if he were "an angry monkey."[114] The Egyptian travelers "fell over each other in a wild effort to get out of reach of the terrible looking ape," Palmer continued.[115] But who could blame them, the reporter asked, "for could a disciple of Darwin have seen the mascot in his impromptu make-up, his heart would have bounded with delightful visions of the missing link."[116]

Cap Anson, the most outspoken racist among nineteenth-century ballplayers, variously referred in his autobiography to Duval (who was a Broadway singer, dancer, baton twirler, and actor when not performing for the Chicago club and world tourists) as "a no account nigger," "a little darkey," and "a little coon."[117] While traveling across the Indian Ocean toward Ceylon, a "man-eating" shark tailed closely behind the ship.[118] Anson suggested they throw Duval overboard as bait. Whether or not Anson was serious did not stop Duval from making, in Ward's words, "such strenuous objections that the plan was abandoned. In lieu of the pickaninny... salt pork was fastened on the hook."[119] At about the same time, Spalding realized that the ship's crew was treating Duval as if he were of equal status to the ballplayers. So he sent the mascot to the captain of the ship, who put him in charge of pulling the punka rope, which kept the ceiling fans in motion, for the rest of the trip.

Far more disturbing to Ward and the other players, however, was the news they learned in Cairo once they reached their hotel. Shortly after the players had left San Francisco en route to Hawaii, the National League instituted a salary classification scheme. The "Brush Plan" would determine players' salaries according to the athletes' graded on-field performance and off-field, "habits, earnestness, and special qualifications."[120] This plan, named after Indianapolis owner John Brush, who developed the scheme, limited salaries to a $2,500 maximum for A-grade players and a $1,500 minimum for E-grade performers, who, moreover, were required to work for their clubs as ticket takers and groundskeepers. The news, however, did not reach the tourists until February 1889, when the players had their first chance to read an American newspaper. Now, three months after the fact, with their president and other key members on the other side of the world, the brotherhood could do nothing to change the course of events. The players were livid. Ward wanted to return to New York immediately. Spalding tried to calm him by claiming that he was just as befuddled as were the players. He said he knew nothing of the plan and that he was angry at Brush, a man of whom he was already known not to think too fondly. The scheme was "not only impracticable but positively dangerous," Spalding told the tourists.[121] Ward remained on the trip but became increasingly testy.[122]

It appeared, in the spring of 1889, when the players signed their contracts, that Spalding may have been telling the truth. The Brush scheme, though on the books, was scarcely followed. Ward signed a one-year contract with New York for $4,250, and virtually none of the other players who had been making more than $2,500 had his salary cut.[123] But Spalding admitted later that season that the tour was in fact organized, in part, to make sure that Ward was nowhere near the 1888 National League meeting.[124] Burk makes sense of the raises despite the Brush Plan as a scheme focused primarily on the younger, prospective stars, who were not yet making $2,500 but would soon demand the league's highest salaries.[125] The league would grandfather in the veterans' salaries but keep the next generation of players' within an affordable maximum level.

In any case Ward and his friends were not flattered. In addition to the Brush Plan, the league's retraction of its promise to draw up an equitable and transparent contract incensed the players. After the players returned to America, the brotherhood held a meeting in late April at the majestic Fifth Avenue Hotel in New York. Ward, Dan Brouthers, Charles Radbourn, Billy Nash, and Charlie Ganzel were in attendance.[126] "When the players got together," Ward explained, "their indignation was extreme, and it was determined to insist upon a fulfillment of the original understanding."[127] Someone suggested a strike. Ward leaked to the *New York Clipper* that "demands [would] be made upon the magnates during the championship season, when, if necessary, a strike could be made effective."[128] But, the brotherhood president later noted, "wiser councils prevailed."[129] Instead, they would "ask the National League for a hearing, state the case squarely, and see if the National League was willing to make any concessions."[130] The league responded in its usual fashion, saying that it would not be able to meet with the brotherhood until November, when "every one knew . . . the players were separated for the winter," Ward wrote.[131]

In the meantime other events brought the brotherhood's anger to a fever pitch. Jack Rowe and Deacon White were nearing the end of their successful careers, spent primarily in their hometown of Buffalo and, during the second half of the 1880s, in Detroit. They had saved enough money by the start of the 1889 season to buy the Buffalo franchise, then in the International Association. But just before they made the sale, their Detroit owner, Fred Stearns, sold the pair to Pittsburgh. Rowe and White refused to relocate, choosing instead to get started in Buffalo. "No man can sell my carcass, unless I get at least half," White cracked.[132] Stearns insisted that they move to Pittsburgh or "get off the earth."[133] Rowe and White met with Ward, after which, surprisingly to outsiders, the two left for Pittsburgh.

Spalding agreed to meet with Ward on the twenty-fourth of June, but in no official capacity. The shortstop expressed the brotherhood's grievances, but Spalding declared that there was nothing serious enough to demand league action until after the season's end. "Ward says," according to the *New York Clipper,* "that while the Brotherhood threatens nothing yet, it would be an extremely unwise move for the National League to try the effect of delays."[134]

A week later brotherhood secretary Tim Keefe remarked, "Spalding and a few of the moneyed people may regret their step. I won't say what the Brotherhood will do but we will move."[135] Adding more cryptic drama to the picture, Keefe added, "There is one thing certain, they won't classify as many men this fall as they think."[136]

Several players proposed a strike on the always-lucrative July 4 holiday. Ward somehow, and for some reason unbeknown to the rest of the baseball world, convinced the players to call off the strike.

On July 14—Bastille Day—representatives from each chapter of the brotherhood met at the Fifth Avenue Hotel to "begin organizing on a new basis."[137]

The growing popularity and profits of baseball, coupled with the draconian measures the National League issued in order to make those gains, gave the league's players more reason to believe that, one, they were largely responsible for that success, and two, that they could and should fight to take a greater share for themselves. The Brotherhood of Professional Base Ball Players, led by John Ward, emerged as the central protagonist of this struggle. But like other forms of labor politics, this was a workers' movement that was deeply interwoven with gender, racial, and national politics as well.

Although imbued with these identity politics, the brotherhood's central objective was to transfer the power over player mobility and compensation from club owners back to the players themselves. It was a struggle antagonistic first to particular policies of the National League's owners and, by the summer of 1889, to the whole structure of ownership in professional baseball. Accordingly, in order to reach their objectives, the players decided on July 14 that they would need to create new policies, new social relations, and new infrastructures of the sport.

4

PREPARING FOR THE PLAYERS LEAGUE

Gathered at the July 14 meeting in the elegant halls of the Fifth Avenue Hotel were representatives from each brotherhood chapter. They decided that they would start planning for a new league. The idea was not new. After Ward first leaked a scheme to form a new league in 1887 (see chapter 3), the idea came up again during Spalding's World Tour.[1] John Ward, Jim Fogarty, Ned Hanlon, and Fred Pfeffer started planning for the "Players National League of Professional Base-Ball Clubs" sometime after they received word of the Brush Plan. While stolen away in private conversation on the decks of their various steamships, they envisioned a league in which the players would share ownership of clubs with financial backers and the clubs would divide the revenues and expenses among themselves. There would be no reserve rule and no buying or selling of players. Their contracts would be for multiple years and would clearly spell out the terms of employment, including their salaries. Expecting the vast majority of the brotherhood to follow them, the quartet was certain that the Players League's superior talent would allow them to competitively dominate the National League. After adjourning that Sunday afternoon, the players secretly went to work on organizing the Players League.

The brotherhood met again at the Fifth Avenue Hotel on November 4, 1889. After three hours of routine business, the players fell silent as Ward rose to the podium. He looked around the room at his fellow teammates and competitors, with all their eyes anxiously on him. A buzz of anticipation quickly filled the room. They knew what he was there to say but were nonetheless caught up in the excitement of the moment. "Brothers," Ward began,

> Last June a committee was appointed by the organization to wait upon President A. G. Spalding of the Chicago Club, and lay before him, at a representation of a committee appointed by the League for consideration of any differences that might arise between the two bodies. . . . It was clearly and comprehensively stated that the Brotherhood could not afford to wait until fall and we said, "If you do not meet us, we are going to get our rights in another way." From that time, as you all know, our organization has been going on and the new regime is now consummated.[2]

Ward stepped down to rapturous applause. His address was the symbolic culmination of four months of backroom planning, whispered meetings in clubhouses and on the base paths, frantic searches for contributors and supporters, and rampant rumors in the press.

A motion was then made to draft a "card" to the public that would announce the creation of their "new regime." Ward appointed Jim O'Rourke, Fred Pfeffer, Ned Hanlon, Arthur Irwin, and Ed Andrews to compose the statement. A motion was then made to add Ward to the card committee. At 7:30 in the evening, the group distributed the card to the crowd of newspapermen and other "baseball enthusiasts" who had been milling around amid clouds of cigar smoke for hours in the hotel lobby.[3] "There was a time when the League stood for integrity and fair dealing," the card read,

> to-day it stands for dollars and cents. Once it looked to the elevation of the game and an honest exhibition of the sport; to-day its eyes are upon the turnstile. Men have come into the business from no other motive than to exploit it for every dollar in sight. Measures originally intended for the good of the game have been perverted into instruments for wrong. The "reserve" rule and the provisions

of the "National Agreement" gave the managers unlimited power, and they have not hesitated to use this in the most arbitrary and mercenary way. Players have been bought, sold and exchanged as though they were sheep instead of American citizens. "Reservation" became with them another name for property right in the player. By a combination among themselves stronger than the strongest "Trust," they were able to enforce the most arbitrary measures, and the player had either to submit or get out of the profession in which he had spent years in attaining proficiency. Even the disbandment and retirement of a club did not free its players from the octopus clutch, for they were then peddled around to the highest bidder. That the player sometimes profited by the sale has nothing to do with the case, but only proves the injustice of his previous restraint. . . .

We believe that it is possible to conduct our National game upon lines which will not infringe upon individual and natural rights. We ask to be judged solely by our own work, and, believing that the game can be played more fairly and its business conducted more intelligently under a plan which excludes everything arbitrary and un-American, we look forward with confidence to the support of the public and the future of the National game.[4]

The card was the first of several moves that the Players League made to rally public support behind it. It would distinguish itself from the National League on the basis of its fairer, more "American," ways of conducting business, not to mention its far superior collection of players.

But the reality was that in most ways, the Players League would sell virtually the same product that the National League had been selling for the past fourteen years. The faces of baseball, the things representatives of the new league said, and the ways they moved would, with some exceptions, go unchanged. And the geographic arrangements of the new league would mirror those of the old. As such the Players League would face the same economic contradictions that beset the

National League. The players, therefore, would also need to construct similar resolutions to these contradictions. In so doing the Players League would directly attack the market power of the National League. But the heart of the new association would also rest on the compromise, if not outright negation, of the National League's most powerful resolution: controlling the mobility, and ultimately the cost, of players. The Players League, therefore, reintroduced the potentially debilitating contradiction by which the players served as the source of the industry's greatest cost and revenue. Without the reserve rule the new league would have to find another way to resolve it.

None of these components of the league fell into place automatically. The precise rules, regulations, arrangements, and governing structure of the league were the subject of rumor, debate, and struggle before they were promulgated. The majority of players eagerly moved to the Players League out of both loyalty to the brotherhood and disdain for the National League. There were, however, some holdouts and some deserters, whom the new league scrambled to sign. The National League's aggressive efforts to acquire playing talent made this process all the more competitive and frantic. The purchase or renting of "grounds" for the ballparks, the preparation of fields, and the construction of grandstands likewise did not happen overnight or without struggle. Ancillary markets for products that traded on the game, too, took a certain amount of time and planning. And before the players could get started with any of this work, they needed to procure a significant amount of money.

This chapter examines the players' struggles to establish the intricacies and infrastructure of their new league. In particular it details the ways in which the Players League raised money, developed its tenets and governance, signed players, and secured grounds on which to build ballparks.

Financing the Players League

While their exceptional skills empowered the players to begin thinking about breaking free from the National League in the first place, there was still a need for at least an initial outlay of money to pay for those players and the ballparks in which they would play.

Once the decision to form the Players League was made at the July 14 meeting, "each representative," Ward recalled, "was instructed to look up the feasibility of securing capital in his own city, and report at any early date."[5] Players were encouraged to invest in their own club, but thanks to the relatively dismal salaries that the National League clubs had been paying them the past several years, there was simply not enough money among them to finance eight new clubs and ballparks. Outside investors, the league decided, would have to be sought. Finding financial backers who would be interested in a business scheme where the workers would receive the bulk share of the revenue would be difficult.

Each team was to eventually raise $20,000 in $100 shares of stock. The brotherhood decided that its new league would establish clubs in six of the National League's eight cities—Boston, New York, Philadelphia, Pittsburgh, Cleveland, and Chicago—and two new cities—Buffalo and Brooklyn—in place of the financially bearish Washington and Indianapolis. Buffalo was chosen in order to give Rowe and White an opportunity to return to their hometown. It had also enjoyed a National League club between 1879 and 1885 and an International Association team ever since. Rowe and White were certain that there was enough interest among investors and fans to again support a major league club. Brooklyn had been home to an American Association club since 1884. The "city of churches" was ripe with baseball excitement in 1889, as its Brooklyn "Grays" were on their way to their first AA pennant. Plus the city's proximity to New York gave the players a much deeper pool of potential investors.

At the November 4, 1889, meeting, when the brotherhood's representatives announced the results of their search for interested capitalists, "a decided glow of contentment settled upon the players."[6] "Men were found willing to advance the necessary money to start a new league and upon terms most liberal to the players," wrote Ward.[7] But just who were these men? And why did they invest in the Players

League? The simple answer is that they were capitalists—investors, financiers, backers—who expected to earn a profit. While this is generally true, the picture is more complicated when the particular individuals' investment choices are examined. In short investment is not a disembodied force. It cannot be separated from the people who set it into motion. Finance, in this sense, breathes, eats, walks, talks, feels, and makes decisions—some advantageous, some disastrous. It has histories, geographies, identities, life, and death.

According to the brotherhood, whose descriptions of the men *Sporting Life* paraphrased, the backers were, "without question, representative men of their various communities; men whose connection with anything stamps it to a certainty with eminent respectability; of good judgment, wealthy, and to a man deeply interested in the welfare of the new organization. It was also stated that these men had been made acquainted with all the ups and downs of base ball, of its business chances and of its management."[8] There is some truth to this statement. The men who invested in the Players League were generally locally based, well known, wealthy, and interested in baseball. The importance of geographic proximity between backers and clubs should not be underestimated. Finding investors in the local community was easier than finding them elsewhere, as the players were reasonably well known among, if not already familiar with, several prominent local citizens. Given the barriers of travel, it was also a matter of practicality to assemble and thenceforth meet with a group of investors in the same city. And it made far more sense for someone to buy stock in a club from his own city than from one located elsewhere. Many of the Players League investors owned businesses—such as hotels, trolley lines, or newspapers—or land, which would directly benefit from the presence of a major league baseball team. For the politicians in on the plan, the patronage of a popular baseball team could enhance their public standing among the thousands of baseball fans across the city. In some cases the city officials used their backing of the Players League, an association that resonated with unionized tradesmen, to strengthen their ties to organized labor.

Ward went so far as to suggest that "many of them were even willing to put in the capital without any return whatever, but of love for the sport and a desire to see it placed on a plane above that upon which it was being operated."[9] While certain backers may not have cared whether they received a return on their investment, the fact was that the constitution of the league—which the investors helped draft— guaranteed them a significant portion of the profits. But Ward's statement, nonetheless, reflects the need among players and backers alike to at least dress the financial capital up in philanthropy.

The story of the Players League suggests that, in general, the kinds of people able to, and interested in, financing a segment of this culture or entertainment industry are men (and much later down the road, women) who have already earned a lot of money elsewhere, in a business that could be further enhanced by linking it—geographically or discursively—to a particular form of cultural production. And the wiser of the cultural capitalists are those who also realize that their other business activity can and should continually support their interest in cultural production. Moreover, the best among them also know a thing or two about, in this case, the baseball business. That is not to say that all of the Players League's backers fit this description. But it does mean that their success and failure largely rested on their ability to figure these things out.

Several dozen men agreed to buy stock in Players League clubs. The work to secure these people was not easy, nor was it finished by the November 4 meeting.

Albert Johnson, a Cleveland-based trolley-car mogul and baseball fanatic, was the first capitalist in on the plan. When Ned Hanlon's Pittsburgh club visited Cleveland during the first week of June 1889, Hanlon broached the idea with Johnson. "Ed [sic] Hanlon called on me and told how the League had broken faith with them so often," Johnson told a reporter.[10] The following evening Johnson spoke with another Cleveland player, Larry Twitchell, and "after a long talk, [he] agreed to lend all the assistance within [his] power to help them accomplish their aim."[11] For the rest of the summer, brotherhood members met with Johnson each time they visited Cleveland, "until every League player had heard our views and had a chance to express himself and suggest whatever he thought would be for the best interests of such an organization," said Johnson.[12] The meetings, which took place in Cleveland's Hollenden Hotel, were guarded by police officers paid off by Johnson.[13]

According to *Sporting Life* Johnson was "a large, fine-looking blonde man, with a slight mustache," taken to wearing a diamond brooch "as big as a pen."[14] In Cleveland he was "very popular about the town" and was regularly seen at Cleveland's home games.[15] A friend to many ballplayers, Johnson once owned stock in the Cleveland NL team. But at the point when he and the "other stockholders lost money [and] the club went to pieces," Johnson quickly sold his shares.[16] Although only in their early thirties, Johnson and his older brother, Tom, had already built an expansive empire of trolley-car lines. By 1889 they owned the Brooklyn and South Side lines in Cleveland and additional lines in Brooklyn, Indianapolis, and Louisville. They also owned a steel-rail mill near Johnstown and several trolley-related patents.[17] Heavily influenced by the teachings of his friend and mentor Henry George, Tom Johnson ran for Congress in 1888. He lost a close race, running as a Democrat in the heavily Republican Twenty-First District of Ohio. But he won the seat in 1892. In 1901 he was elected mayor of Cleveland. Serving until 1909 Tom Johnson was one of the most progressive mayors in the city's history.[18] Throughout his political career, of which Albert Johnson stood on the sidelines, Tom Johnson championed the causes of ordinary people, advocating a single-tax plan that shifted the burden toward wealthy property owners and the reformation of municipal institutions such as prisons, hospitals, schools, and parks. At one point he hired a socialist political scientist to help bring all of Cleveland's city services—including the trolley-car lines—under public ownership. The Players League seemed to fall in line with the politics of the elder Johnson, but he was not interested. In fact Albert Johnson recalled that his brother had "urged [him] to get out" of the scheme, fearing tens of thousands of dollars in losses.[19] But, Albert explained, "I had seen the cars on the opposition street road loaded down with people going to the games, and it occurred to me that here was a chance to make a good investment, as I could get grounds on the street car line owned by my brother and myself. Visions of millions of dollars of profits loomed up in front of my eyes."[20] These comments, however, were not made until November 1890, after the Players League's first season. Johnson was speaking to a group of backers at an all-night, wine-infused meeting, at which the fate of the league was to be decided. It was always clear that the Johnsons' businesses would benefit from the league, but in the fall of 1889 and the spring of 1890, Johnson couched his support as, first and foremost, a philanthropic endeavor. In November 1889 Johnson explained that he was going to help "liberate [the players] from the tyrannical rule of the League."[21] To this comment a *Sporting Life* columnist then sarcastically wrote, "He of all others should be the ball players' Moses to release them from their $2000 to $5000 bondage."[22] It is well within the realm of possibility, however, that Johnson's contributions and those of the other backers were motivated by both philanthropic and self-interested impulses. After all, the players were driven by these same forces. And such business ventures were not new to Johnson. In 1888 he put up the money for Dr. E. E. Beeman to mass-produce pepsin, which Beeman had discovered as a cure for indigestion. The pair made a fortune by selling pepsin-based chewing gum.[23] But in professional baseball there was a finer line between philanthropy and profit making, between casting the PL as an endeavor to right the NL's wrongs, in which some profit was necessary to keep it afloat, and casting it as a sheer moneymaking opportunity. The image of the game, as discussed in chapter 1, helped form part of the game's value. And while baseball was clearly by this time a legitimate business, it still needed to present itself as something more.

Topping off Cleveland's club with Johnson were Chris Gover, a "vessel owner and businessman"; Henry Purdy, a "wealthy gentleman of the West Side"; J. J. Coleman; E. H. Hopper; Edward French; and L. A. Russell, the club's attorney.[24] John "Cub" Stricker, who had worked with Johnson from the start, secretly monitoring the city's National League turnstile so that they could estimate their potential market, and Fred Pfeffer were the only players to take ownership of the Cleveland club.[25]

Johnson sought funding for other clubs as well, traveling to Brooklyn, New York, St. Louis, and Philadelphia, where he had business contacts.[26] In late September and October, following the *Chicago Tribune*'s leak of the brotherhood's plans, rumors of possible investors started appearing in the newspapers.[27] Johnson's name was mentioned repeatedly, but the Cleveland tycoon adamantly denied any knowledge of the scheme. His denials, however, were soon overwhelmed by the multitude of "anonymous correspondents" who named Johnson as one of the leading figures of the new plan. By the third week in October, Johnson had admitted to his involvement.[28]

Also named in the rumors was New York NL owner John Day. Throughout the remainder of the season, Day would neither confirm nor deny reports that he was in on the scheme. His 1887 spat with Ward notwithstanding, Day was considered a friend to the players, someone who mingled and sympathized with the men on the field more so than did other owners. The notion that Day would back the New York Brotherhood club (the "Players League" had not yet been named) received further credence when the Giants reincorporated themselves in the first week of October 1889. The team, which had hitherto been incorporated as the "Metropolitan Exhibition Company," changed its name to the "New York Base Ball Club." The move ensured that no other baseball team in New York (particularly, the rumored brotherhood club) could call itself the "New Yorks" or the "New York Base Ball Club."[29] But Day, who was the principal stockholder of the team, was not listed on the new incorporation papers as one of the club's directors. His excuse for not signing the papers—that he was in Chicago at the time—ended up lending more grist to the rumor mill. While in Chicago, Day was invited to meet with Spalding, Boston owner William Conant, and Cleveland owner George Howe to discuss strategies for dealing with the possibility of a renegade brotherhood league. But

Day neither attended the meeting nor gave a reason for not doing so. Unlike just about every other man invested in the National League, Day did not publicly scoff at the idea of players running their own association of baseball clubs.

Meanwhile, Day's New York club was running neck and neck with Boston toward the National League pennant. The race went down to the final game of the season, with New York finally pulling ahead after defeating Pittsburgh on the road. With the league pennant (and Dauvray Cup) secured, they headed back to New York ready to celebrate. Hung over the side of their Erie Railroad carriage, as they rolled into Jersey City, was a banner reading, "We are the People!" the slogan that manager Jim Mutrie would induce Giants fans to yell out during home games. "Who are the people?" he would ask. "We are the people!" the crowd and players would respond. The phrase, whether invoked in the Declaration of Independence or at an 1880s labor rally, has been used to subjectively establish any group as a solidified and empowered public, one that legitimately represents the common masses. Here, however, the mostly bourgeois New York crowd seems to have participated in the cry out of an imagined solidarity with the players. Their claim to be "the people" seems to have less to do with the broader public than with an empowered sense of supremacy (in the world of baseball, at least). After all, the cheer was associated with winning games and championships, similar, but ultimately only parallel, to workers' and activists' association of the phrase with winning a strike or a political battle. The players' participation in the cheer at this point, however, given their impending break from the National League, may have meant something more.

In any event, soon after they returned, Day declared his unending allegiance to the National League. Asked about a story in the press regarding his possible support of the brotherhood, Day responded: "That story is a lie! It is made out of whole white cloth and the writer of it knows it. I told him that I had had no communication with Mr. Ward, Mr. Coogan, nor with any one else looking towards a compromise with the Brotherhood. I further told him that I would not desert the League or the New York Base Ball Club until I had first applied to the Legislature for permission to change my name to Benedict Arnold. The whole story is a lie."[30] The truth of the matter may have been that Day's flirtations with the brotherhood were simply an act of humoring his players so that they would not become disgruntled and lose the 1889 pennant.

Sporting Life attributed New York's triumph over Boston exactly to this factor. With Day seemingly on their side, "the Giants had nothing to worry them, and they devoted themselves to business and got there. [Boston owner] Conant made no end of talk in public and in private. He threatened his manager and his players. Result, the soup. See?"[31] In this light one might reconsider Mike Kelly's drunken tirade on the final game of the season (see chapter 2). Perhaps he was just an alcoholic, out of control and out of his mind. But perhaps also his failure to remain sober enough to play was the result of his expired loyalty to Boston's management. Why continue working for a lame-duck employer who never treated you that well in the first place? The rest of Boston's club did seem to be playing their hardest, but Kelly at least, in a sort of strike of inebriation, may have taken advantage of his relative control over the labor process to bend the fortune of his employers. There is also a good chance that he had been drinking with Albert Johnson (among others) the previous evening, as the trolley-line owner (who was no teetotaler himself) would have been very interested in fully securing Kelly's services for the Players League. In any case Day's bluff reflects the relative weakness of baseball's investors in relation to the players. With the prospect of a mobilized workforce, Day had to express his loyalty to his employees in order for them to work at their most productive capacities. And winning the pennant, in this case, was more than symbolic. The National League champion played the American Association winner in a best of eleven "World Series." In what could have been dubbed the "Brooklyn Bridge Series," New York outlasted Brooklyn six games to three in a well-attended, but darkness- and weather-impaired, string of contests.[32]

Whether the brotherhood was actually courting Day is unclear. But it was certainly going after other prominent New Yorkers. Chief among those who ended up signing on with the Players League were Senator and Postmaster Cornelius Van Cott; Republican League Club of New York president Col. Edwin McAlpin; Excise Board president Alexander Meakin; stockbrokers E. B. Talcott and E. B. Robinson; Judges Howland and Bacon; and James Coogan. Coogan managed the land at and around 155th Street and Eighth Avenue on which the NL Giants had just built their new "Polo Grounds" (also known as Manhattan Field) as well as other tracts belonging to the Lynch Estate in uptown and downtown Manhattan. Also the co-owner of a furniture business, Coogan twice ran (unsuccessfully) for mayor. He served as Manhattan Borough president from 1899 to 1901. The mayor of New York in 1889, Hugh Grant, was rumored to own stock in the team, but as the National League began threatening legal action against the players, he denounced the scheme: "I do not care to buy a lawsuit," he quipped, thereby ending rumors of his involvement.[33] McAlpin, who was described by the *Chicago Tribune* as "strong in social and political circles [in New York], young, rich, and popular," took a lead role among New York's stockholders.[34] With only the evidence in newspapers as a guide, it is impossible at this point to know exactly how much stock each investor owned and whether there were additional stockholders. It does seem, however, from the ways in which they represented themselves that McAlpin, Van Cott, Talcott, and Coogan owned a majority (or at least a plurality) of the New York club's stock. More players on New York's PL club owned stock in their team than in any other. In fact every single player, according to Ward, held shares.[35] Four of these men—Buck Ewing, Roger Connor, Tim Keefe, and Jim O'Rourke—would later be inducted (all posthumously) into the National Baseball Hall of Fame, a reflection of the extraordinary talent the club possessed.[36]

The money invested in Boston's Players League club is more readily apparent. The National Baseball Hall of Fame Library has archived the correspondences and financial records of Frederick Long, Boston's treasurer (and PL stockholder). Included in this collection are the preseason and midseason lists of Boston PL stockholders. Owning the most shares were Arthur "Hi Hi" Dixwell (thirty-five shares) and Julian B. Hart (twenty-eight). Long bought ten shares. These three stockholders, in addition to a handful of other minor owners of the PL club, had previously owned shares in the Boston National League club. Why did they move their investment from the old to the new club? It is quite likely that they believed the Players League team would fare better than its crosstown rival. By the time many of the backers had signed on, the club had secured commitments from most of Boston's players. Quite simply, the PL franchise looked like a better investment. But there is also a backstory to their participation in the new league. In 1888 Boston's "Triumvirate" of majority owners (J. B. Billings, William Conant, and Arthur H. Soden) stopped issuing season passes to all minority stockholders, as they had been doing for the past twelve years. The "Triumvirs" had not only owned most of the club's stock, but they also held an exclusive grip over club affairs. Charles Porter (who now owned two shares of Boston Players League stock) and Hart (whose brother, Jim Hart, served as financial manager of the Chicago NL franchise throughout the 1880s and into the 1890s) organized a petition that year to reinstate the season passes perk. But the Triumvirate refused, arguing that "the unwise custom of giving complimentary season tickets to stockholders" had brought "serious financial loss" to the club.[37] When the seventeen minority stockholders asked for a financial report, the Triumvirs decided to take a vote. But each owner's vote, they declared, would be weighted according to the number of shares he owned; the result, not surprisingly, fell in favor of not disclosing the report, which would have revealed that the team had more than $130,000 in assets.[38] In this context the Players League backers' choice to jump leagues seems as much rooted in revenge and enmity as in rational economic decision making.

Moreover, Dixwell, at least, had befriended many of the players. He traveled with the team and was quite generous with his money. When pleased with certain players' performances, he often gave them boxes of cigars or other gifts.[39] After the 1889 season Dixwell was so impressed with the New York club that he gave each of its players a diamond scarf pin, despite the fact that they had just beat his beloved "Beaneaters."[40] This sort of behavior, divorced from the expectations and antagonisms that would have accompanied a more powerful owner, must have impressed the players. Given Dixwell's allegiance to the players, bitterness toward the owners, and pockets loaded with money, the brotherhood, in all likelihood, viewed him as an ideal backer.

Long's position in relation to the National League and the Players League was a bit more complicated. He was the treasurer of the Boston NAPBBP club from 1871 to 1875 and of the NL club from 1876 to 1888. As such he was the only minority stockholder intimately familiar with the club's financial well-being. Perhaps afraid of the risk this posed, the Triumvirs did not revoke Long's season ticket pass. In fact they gave him a lifetime ticket pass, a move unprecedented in the team's history. But at the same time they forced him out of the treasurer position, replacing him in 1889 with Billings. Long had not been excluded from team affairs to the extent that the other minority owners had, but he could very well have been bitter over his abrupt dismissal from the treasury. Moreover, as someone thoroughly attuned to the financial side of baseball, Long most likely believed that the Players League would be a success.

Twenty-two other men, including six players, owned at least one share of Boston stock. All but two of the nonplayer stockholders (George Wright and John Morrill) had formerly owned Boston NL stock.[41] Among the players were Arthur Irwin (twelve shares), Frank Foss (ten), Hardy Richardson (ten), Dan Brouthers (ten), William Nash (five), and Mike Kelly (five).[42] In short Boston found no trouble raising the $20,000 in stock.

Even those who held relatively few shares were more than capable of increasing the number of shares if need be. John Haynes, for example, was the president of the Oliver Ditson Company, one of the country's largest music publishers and instrument manufacturers.[43] *Sporting Life* claimed that he was a multimillionaire and was still disgruntled over being "frozen out" by the Triumvirs.[44] Haynes bought nine shares of stock on December 13, 1889, and, at the request of Hart, bought an additional ten shares late in the 1890 season.[45] Charles Corey was a "gentleman of leisure" and friend of Haynes.[46] He bought one share in December and four additional shares in August 1890.[47] The presence of wealthy men such as Haynes and Corey on the Boston stockholders' list provided some insurance against financial insecurity; there was always the possibility of increasing the team's capital stock.

Pittsburgh had more difficulty finding money to support a new team. Hanlon and Johnson did come up with W. W. Kerr. Kerr was the manager of Exposition Park, a piece of land across the river in Allegheny, where the Post Percheron Horse Association held races and Charles Arbuckle put on circuses. There was still unused space at Exposition Park, and both Kerr and the brotherhood must have been attracted to the idea of putting a ballpark there, which would garner steady rent and was just a walk across the bridge from downtown Pittsburgh. Kerr then convinced Pittsburgh's mayor, William McCallin, to join, but he did so only under certain conditions. Just what those conditions were was never revealed, but it is possible that they had something to do with the league's relationship with organized labor. Shortly before McCallin committed to the Players League, Ward met with some of the city's labor leaders. William Martin, secretary of the Amalgamated Association of Iron and Steel Workers and vice president of the American Federation of Labor (AFL), and Secretary Dillon, of the National Flint Glass Workers' Association sat down with Ward and assured him of their support.[48] Perhaps it was just a coincidence, but there is reason to believe that McCallin, who depended on the working-class vote, egged on Ward. Following McCallin was M. B. Lemmon, a local judge and member of the Elks. Lemmon had reportedly invested $5,000 in the club, but *Sporting Life* called this figure "a sweller."[49] Lemmon must have had something invested in the team, though, as his name (along with Kerr and McCallin) appeared on the club's incorporation papers.[50] George Meyers, an agent with the Brunswick Baike Billiard Company, was also said to be a backer, as were attorneys W. P. Potter, Col. W. A. Stone, and John Beemer. Ned Hanlon and Fred

Carroll appear to be the only Pittsburgh players to buy stock in the team.[51] Pitcher John Tener (who later was elected to the U.S. House of Representatives and also governor of Pennsylvania) became the secretary of the club, but there is no evidence that he invested any of his money in the team.[52]

By November Pittsburgh had still not raised its requisite $20,000 in stock. Johnson and Hanlon scoured the city for additional money but came up short. They pursued James Chambers, a millionaire involved with a glass company, but he was not interested. C. L. Magee, a politician and owner of a Pittsburgh trolley line, expressed interest but only if the team would locate its ballpark adjacent to his line. Kerr, who depended on the club's grounds on Exposition Park, objected, and Magee withdrew his support. By mid-November, *Sporting Life* commented, "If Pittsburg had to raise money for a World's Fair, that important event would be held [in] about 2092. No doubt Ned Hanlon and Al Johnson believe this to-day. Not knowing this town's coldness to schemes of public education and ventures not clearly sure things, they have been hustling to sell an article known as base ball in this money tight burg for nearly a week, and the result is about a horse and horse with that of the man who tried to sell cold boiled ham in the neighborhood of Tunnel street, the Jewish quarters."[53]

Pittsburgh's moneyed men were not buying into the scheme. In fact several commentators and baseball men suggested that the problem was skepticism concerning not just the Players League but also professional baseball more generally.[54] Although no reliable data exist, Pittsburgh's nineteenth-century NL club is scarcely mentioned as a moneymaker. It may have been just a ruse, but the team's president, Jim Nimick, claimed that the club rarely made a profit.[55]

Hanlon stated at a November 5 meeting of players and backers that he had had a hard time securing backers in Pittsburgh. But "no sooner had he made known this fact," *Sporting Life* reported, "than a half dozen New York capitalists jumped to their feet and told him not to be discouraged on that score, that if the capital was not forthcoming in Pittsburg, it would be in New York, and that Pittsburg would not go without a club for the need of it."[56] Ward then traveled to Pittsburgh with Johnson and Hanlon to search for willing contributors. Headquartered at the Hotel Anderson, the trio raised its $20,000 in capital stock by the end of November. Hanlon estimated that only about $3,500 of the stock was bought by "outsiders."[57] One relatively local man, E. C. Convers of McKeesport, Pennsylvania, bought a majority of the club's stock. Convers, the superintendent of the National Tube Works of McKeesport, a position that garnered him an annual salary of $25,000, said after offering the money, "I virtually dropped $13,000 in the present venture through love of the sport but am determined to fight the old players and will drop five times that amount in the endeavor."[58] Once again that strange combination of baseball fanaticism, antagonism toward the National League, and excess wealth came to the rescue of the Players League.

Across the state in Philadelphia, outfielders George Wood and Jim Fogarty and pitcher Charlie Buffinton found a number of men interested in the league. Wood's and Fogarty's affiliation with the Union Republican Club probably led them to Magistrate William Aheren and former common councilman Lew Young, both prominent members of the club who signed on to the Players League.[59] Adam Forepaugh was a locally renowned circus promoter, who owned the vacant land on which the club would eventually build its ballpark. Forepaugh's involvement with the team was most likely predicated on the club's guarantee that it would use his grounds, as was the case with Kerr in Pittsburgh. It is telling that Forepaugh denied rumors that he was backing the club until after the team signed the lease for his land. Benjamin Hilt was the treasurer of the Philadelphia National League club in 1889, but after the close of the season it was revealed that he had invested money in the Players League. Philadelphia's NL owner John Rogers accused Hilt of sharing the club's financial data with its stockholders in order to convince them to shift their investment to the Players League club.[60] Unfortunately, the names of Philadelphia's NL minority stockowners are nowhere to be found in the historical record, but given Rogers's accusation and Hilt's failure to deny it, there is a good chance that at least some of the Philadelphia PL backers had been involved in the National League. More importantly, that any investor here (as in Boston) would shift his money from one league to another so easily suggests either that he had a sudden idealistic streak that favored players' rights or that he felt the new league would yield higher returns on his investment, or perhaps some combination of both. Hilt, moreover, was the owner of Philadelphia's Hotel Hilton on Filbert Street, near Eleventh.[61] Hoteliers had long capitalized on the proximity of professional baseball parks and on exclusive agreements with visiting clubs. This possibility could have played a part in Hilt's decision to buy stock in the club. The archives do not indicate at which hotel visiting Players League teams stayed in Philadelphia, but given Hilt's role with the club, it is a safe bet that the Hilton received the PL's business.[62]

Several other Philadelphia businessmen bought Players League stock. These investors included Henry Love, a manufacturer of knit goods amid the city's booming textile industry; William Whitall, a cotton manufacturer; J. Earl Wagner and George Wagner, dealers in Chicago beef; Frank Elliot, an attorney; John Vanderslice, an attorney for the B&O railroad and former city official; Harry L. Taggart, the owner of *Taggart's Sunday Times*; and William McGunnigle, a Chestnut Street saloon owner.[63] McGunnigle, whose name surfaced on the pages of *Sporting Life* in November 1889, was most likely the anonymous "well-known saloon-keeper on a prominent thoroughfare," whom the *Philadelphia Inquirer* interviewed in early October.[64] Said the man in question, "I do not hold any stock at present because it has not been delivered, but I have subscribed for some of it. It will be a go, and the American Association will have to go with the [National] League. In the words of the New Yorkers, 'We are the people.'"[65] McGunnigle's invocation (assuming that it was, indeed, McGunnigle) of "we are the people" takes on an added meaning to that of Mutrie, and even to that of the Giants' players and fans, mentioned earlier in this chapter. For McGunnigle the "we" ties, principally, players to backers (particularly as the new league had yet to play a game) in their struggle against the

National League. We, the integrated force of performers and patrons, McGunnigle seems to suggest, are the legitimate public that will prevail over the old league. In this sense "we are the people," insofar as it invokes the labor struggle waged by players against their owners, comes closer to the more common usage found in late nineteenth-century working-class politics. But by slipping himself into the "we," McGunnigle makes it signify a fight between capital on the one side and capital and labor on the other. To the extent that it is viewed that way, the problem, then, is seen not as one created by capitalism's general antagonism toward labor but rather as one between particular capitalists and particular workers. The solution, as McGunnigle and the rest of the Players League apparently saw it, was a reformation of the relationship between capital and labor in this particular instance, not a full-scale revolution in the political-economic system in which all such relationships developed. Moreover, "the people" in McGunnigle's statement still do not stretch beyond or beneath the baseball world. In other words, McGunnigle, at least, had not connected (beyond a parallel association) the Players League to other workers' struggles.

Other politicians and city officials involved in the Philadelphia club included James Allen, a former common councilman, and Edwin E. Wells, an active member of the Republican Party.[66] Harry Disston, whose family owned Henry Disston and Sons, one of the country's most prosperous steel companies, was the only "gentleman" mentioned as a Philadelphia stockholder.[67] Wood, Fogarty, and Buffinton were listed as player-stockholders, with Wood taking the greatest number of shares.[68] Second baseman Al Myers also bought stock in the Players League club but sold it before the season started, when he jumped to the National League.[69]

Henry Love played a lead role among the nonplayers. Throughout the late summer and early autumn of 1889, he hosted secret meetings of these men at his spacious brownstone at 1418 Diamond Street. In November Love was elected president of the team; Allen was secretary; Hilt served as treasurer and manager.[70] Vanderslice handled the club's legal affairs.[71]

Despite otherwise extensive and eloquent baseball coverage, the *Chicago Daily Tribune* did not offer much information on Chicago's PL backers.[72] The omission may have been intentional on both ends, as Frank Brunell, the *Tribune*'s chief baseball writer, was intimately involved with the league.[73] It was Brunell who originally broke the details of the league in September and later was elected as the Players League's secretary-treasurer.[74] It is possible that Brunell was a backer himself, given his early and steadfast association with the league and his residence in Chicago (Brunell was also a close friend of Ward).[75] But it is more likely that he did not invest money in the new league. When the PL's players and contributors met in November and December 1889, they agreed to elect an "outsider" as secretary-treasurer. Although Brunell's knowledge of and association with the league hardly placed him outside the Players League's activities, a lack of financial stakes (notwithstanding his $3,200 salary for serving as secretary-treasurer) in the endeavor may have put him in sufficient "outsider" territory. Still, Brunell served as a loyal gatekeeper for news on the Players League. And whatever the reason, he provided virtually no information on Chicago's backers, outside stating a few of their names.

Publications from other cities and additional research on the names that were provided add some light to the picture. Fred Pfeffer, Chicago's "crack" (as was said, in admiration) second baseman, led the effort to find Chicago capitalists. The *Tribune* and the *Philadelphia Inquirer* reported that Pfeffer gathered a few of his friends from the Chicago Board of Trade to support the new team (the *Tribune* refers to these men as "the brokers from section A").[76] Exactly who these brokers were is never specified, but at least one or two of the names that were otherwise mentioned as contributing to the Players League—F. Orton, Lot Smith, F. Auten, and James Murdough—were probably affiliated with the Board of Trade.[77] No matter what their names were, though, Board of Trade members were investors through and through. The stakes may not have been as high, but if the tenets and governance of the Players League, which they played a key role in constructing, are any indication, the backers were as concerned with the return on their investment here as they were in any other endeavor. John Addison, a wealthy Chicago building contractor and architect, was one of the leading investors in the club. As discussed in further detail later, he was a significant figure in the construction of the team's ballpark. Also deeply invested in the club and the construction of its ballpark was C. A. Weidenfelder, a man *Sporting Life* described as "a typical Chicagoan of about 30."[78] Weidenfelder was president of the Metropolitan Insurance Company and the owner of "considerable real estate in the Windy City."[79] Chicago's players are said to have bought $8,000 in stock, with Charles King and Dell Darling holding the most shares, each buying $1,000.[80] Charles Comiskey, Jimmy Ryan, and Hugh Duffy each bought $500 in stock, and Fred Pfeffer owned an undisclosed amount of stock in the team.[81]

When the club incorporated itself (as the Chicago White Stockings) in November 1889, the investors decided to increase the capital stock from the league-mandated $20,000 to a total of $25,000. Orton was said to have put up the additional $5,000. The increase was never explained, but it probably was in preparation for the bidding war over players in which Spalding was promising to spare no expense. Chicago also would have the most expensive travel arrangements of any club in the league, as its shortest road trip (to Cleveland) was still 350 miles by train.

Sporting Life described Brooklyn's money capitalists as "among the wealthiest and most influential in the City of Churches."[82] Most of these men came to the Players League through Johnson or Ward. Some were from New York. The first person in on the plan was Wendell Goodwin. Goodwin was involved with Johnson in the Kings County Elevated Railway Company.[83] It was no accident, then, that Brooklyn located its ballpark on Goodwin and Johnson's rail line in what is now considered the neighborhood of East New York. George Chauncey, who worked as a Brooklyn realtor with the D&M Chauncey firm, also bought Brooklyn stock. It is not clear whether Chauncey brokered the deal over the club's land, as he was no more eager to speak to the press as Brunell was to write about the PL's backers. (As the Brooklyn correspondent to *Sporting Life* wrote, Chauncey "is so careful not to cross the leaders of the Brotherhood discretion in talking about the affairs of the organization, that anything he might know is still a dark, dark secret.")[84] Edward Linton was another "wealthy" and "influential" Brooklyn financier. A banker in Brownsville, Linton was also active in the development of the New Lots neighborhood, where he owned property and was involved with the water works and gas industries.[85] Another Brooklyn property owner, Austin Corbin, also bought stock in the city's Players League franchise.[86] Brooklyn real-estate developers John Wallace and Henry F. Robinson bought shares in the club as well. George H. Wirth, another investor and the secretary of the club, was involved in the railway business.[87]

The connection between the Players League and Brooklyn property owners may have been just coincidental, but there was also some logic in realtors' interest in professional baseball. As ballparks were generally built on vacant property on the fringes of developed areas, they stood as small vanguards to urban expansion. The ballparks brought people and ancillary businesses to new parts of the city. While at times ballparks were seen as impediments to further expansion (the original Polo Grounds, near the northeast corner of Central Park, for example, was forced to move when the city decided to build 111th Street through the outfield), they were also, for many of the same reasons, good investments for property owners.[88] The land, which was usually rented by the clubs, could be bought for relatively low prices and, once the surrounding areas developed, sold for a considerable profit. In Brooklyn, a city that was rapidly expanding in the late nineteenth century yet always in the shadow of New York (and by 1898, within its very borders), baseball and real estate (not to mention mass transit) made a perfect combination.

In addition to the realtors, banker, and trolley-line executive, Brooklyn's Players League team was owned by Ward and outfielder Ed Andrews, the only players on the young team to hold stock. It is not clear how many shares Andrews bought, but Ward owned ten shares, the same number as Linton, Chauncey, Goodwin, Robinson, Wallace, and Wirth.[89] Ward's move from Manhattan to Brooklyn was not in his initial plans. As late as the Players League's November meetings, Ward was scheduled to play for New York. His presence in Brooklyn may have been arranged as an inducement to potential investors. Without Ward the club's prospects for a winning season, given its plans to consist primarily of Washington's 1889 players (who finished the season in last place, with forty-one wins and eighty-three losses), were dismal to say the least. Ward's agreement to play, manage, and invest in Brooklyn might have been necessary to ensure that the other backers would sign on.

Jack Rowe and Deacon White played a similar role in Buffalo. Indianapolis, which finished in next-to-last place in 1889, was also lacking in star power. The team's move to Buffalo, as mentioned earlier, would never have happened if not for the interest and leadership of longtime Buffalo residents Rowe and White. And once returned to the city, Rowe and White could both improve the team's chances for success (and thus desirability among investors) and help to find men interested in the team in the first place. The pair (whose professional and personal inseparability is worthy of further research) were the first to invest in the Buffalo franchise, White putting in $1,500 worth of stock and Rowe, $1,000.[90] Cornelius "Connie" Mack, a mediocre catcher who later became one of baseball's most celebrated managers, put $500, his entire life savings, into twenty shares of stock.[91] Moses Shire, an attorney and real-estate developer, invested $6,000 into the club.[92] Charles R. Fitzgerald, the high secretary of the High Court of New York, put in $5,000.[93] And Frank T. Gilbert, a former sheriff, paid $6,000 for Buffalo Players League stock.[94] George Myers, who played with Rowe and White in Buffalo in 1884 and 1885 but retired after the 1889 season, was also rumored to have bought shares in the club.[95]

Tenets and Governance of the Players League

The day after their November 4 meeting (on Guy Fawkes's Day), about thirty or forty players met with most of the principal backers at Nick Engel's saloon at Twenty-Seventh Street and Broadway in New York.[96]

Engel was a friend to many players and often traveled with the Giants to their away games. According to the *Philadelphia Inquirer*, Engel's saloon was "one of the biggest beer shops in New York" and served as "a great resort for actors, literary men and ball tossers."[97] The players met upstairs in a locked room from 2:00 to 6:00 p.m. An official statement from the group reported that they "did nothing," but anonymous informants said that they discussed possible proceedings for the following day's official meeting of backers and players.[98]

The following day's official meeting included two delegates from each club (one player and one backer), who hammered out much of the league's governing policies. Representing the clubs were McAlpin and Ward (New York), Corey and Brouthers (Boston), Love and Buffinton (Philadelphia), Wallace and Andrews (Brooklyn), Hanlon (Pittsburgh; Kerr was unable to attend), Johnson and Stricker (Cleveland), Shire and Rowe (Buffalo), and Addison and Pfeffer (Chicago).[99] The brotherhood's executive committee, together with Johnson, had already started this work earlier that summer. Johnson's clandestine summer meetings with the players between July and October included the signing of an agreement, which bound players to later sign a contract with a Players League club once the league had organized itself. The agreement spelled out many of the regulations and governing structures that went to a vote at the November 6 meeting.

At issue during the afternoon session was the original plan to pool all revenues and expenses. Stockholders from clubs in larger markets did not want to be responsible for the well-being of the smaller-market teams in Buffalo, Cleveland, and Pittsburgh. Johnson protested but to no avail. It was agreed by a majority vote to instead share gate receipts on a fifty-fifty basis between home and away clubs. The National League had, for the most part, been splitting the proceeds from ticket sales on a seventy-thirty basis, except on state and national holidays, when the receipts were evenly divided between home and away clubs.[100] This change would provide some improvement for the smaller clubs but would still put them at greater risk than the teams in the more populous cities.

That said, the delegates did decide to pool the profits among all the teams and distribute them according to the following plan: the first $20,000 in profits would go to a prize fund, with the first-place team receiving $7,000; second-place, $4,000; third, $3,000; fourth, $2,000; fifth, $1,500; sixth, $1,200; seventh, $700; and eighth, $500.[101] Each team would distribute this money exclusively to the players. The unprecedented plan would offer a strong incentive for every team to remain competitive throughout the season. The next $80,000 in league profits would be divided among the stockholders according to the number of shares they owned. All the players (regardless of whether they owned stock) would equally share among themselves the next $80,000. Any remaining profit would go to the players and stockholders, split evenly between the two groups and distributed to the stockholders according to the number of shares they held. The plan gave a decided advantage to the players who owned stock, as they were, of course, more likely to reap profits (not to mention earn higher salaries) than the lesser players.

A committee on contracts (consisting of Love, Arthur Irwin, McAlpin, Shire, Ward, and Bacon) composed a standard Players League contract, which would grant all players the same salaries that they had received in 1889 unless the Brush Plan had reduced their 1888 salaries in 1889.[102] The contracts would be for three years, after which the players would become free to sign with any other team. Players could not be transferred during the season from one club to another, and never could they be bought or sold (a player could, however, request to be transferred during the off-season).

Each club was to be governed by an eight-man board of directors, consisting of four players (elected by their teammates) and four non-playing backers (as elected by the capitalists). A central board of directors, consisting of two delegates (one player and one backer) from each club, would serve as "a tribunal for the consideration of all questions respecting the general welfare and the final decision of all questions appealed from the decisions of the local boards of directors."[103]

A follow-up meeting on December 16 and 17 further solidified the

PL's governing rules and regulations. It was then, again at the Fifth Avenue Hotel, that the new organization ratified its constitution and playing rules and officially established itself as a business. The delay occurred primarily because the lawyers present at the November 6 meeting agreed that the Players League could not legally incorporate itself until the individual clubs first did so. Once Brooklyn finally incorporated itself literally minutes before the December 16 gathering began at 2:00 p.m., the league was set to go. "The Players National League of Base Ball Clubs" was promulgated, according to its constitution, as an organization intended, "to encourage, foster, and elevate the game of base ball; to enforce proper rules for the exhibition and conduct of the game; to protect the mutual interest of professional base ball players and base ball clubs; and to establish the base ball championship of the world."[104] The passage is almost identical to the National League's purpose, as stated in its 1876 constitution. Similar to the Players League, the National League was meant to "encourage, foster, and elevate the game of baseball," "enforce and enact proper rules for the exhibition and conduct of the game," "protect and promote the mutual interest of professional base ball players and base ball clubs," and "to establish and regulate the baseball championship of the United States."[105] The barely indistinguishable language here, as well as the similar name (plus "Players"), was no accident. The Players League was simultaneously seeking to model itself (in most ways) after the National League and to usurp the older organization's singular grip over that model. It is telling that the PL, like the NL, called itself a league of *clubs*, rather than a league of players. This difference, a historical shift from the National Association of Professional Base Ball *Players*, established the team and the organized league of teams as the central components of professional baseball. What this meant was that there were constitutional and contractual limits to the freedom and power now granted to the players. Most of the players would enjoy more mobility and governance than they had ever had in their careers, but not to the extent that it would mitigate the power of their clubs to operate as profitable businesses. Hence, the three-year contracts, the prohibition against intrayear player transfers, and the sharing of governance and profits between players and investors, not to mention the strict regulations on the players' behavior on and off the field, would serve as a barrier to the players' autonomy and a protection for investors. But the eradication of the National League's most hated policies—the reserve rule and the buying and selling of players—was still tremendously significant in terms of empowering and enriching players.

In response to players' concerns about the original plans, the constitution also included a clause that guaranteed the payment of their salaries, regardless of gate receipts or otherwise gloomy economic conditions. Each club contributed $5,000 to a league insurance fund, which would be used exclusively to pay salaries if a club could not do so through gate receipts alone. Before the delegates included this clause in the constitution, clubs were required to use the gate receipts to pay players' salaries on the first and fifteenth of every month (between April 1 and November 1), but only after all other expenses were met.[106] The fund would not only ensure the players of their paychecks in the future but would also induce wavering brotherhood men to sign in the present.[107]

The rumor mill churned away during the cold days of December with stories of a possible amalgamation of American Association clubs by the Players League. Following the formation of the Players League in early November, the National League accepted former AA powerhouses Brooklyn and Cincinnati into its ranks. The moves, everyone seemed to agree, spelled disaster for the association, as these two cities were its strongest. Scrambling to stay alive, some AA clubs, including Philadelphia and particularly Chris Von der Ahe's St. Louis Browns, pleaded with the PL for admittance. But on the second day of the December meeting, the PL gave no such welcome. It was decided that an eight-club league was a better arrangement than a ten-club organization, as the latter would dilute the talent to an unsustainable degree. In November someone suggested that the two AA clubs could take the place of Buffalo and Brooklyn, as it appeared that these teams lacked sufficient funding. But by mid-December the clubs showed a remarkably solid financial footing. Therefore, the PL Board of Directors sanctioned the eight-club league as initially planned.

A committee on playing rules, consisting of Hilt, Hart, Ewing, Ward, and Pfeffer, instituted several changes to the National League's rules, four of which were quite significant. First, the Players League would feature two umpires during every game. Previously, one umpire would race across the diamond, trying, impossibly, to keep his eyes on all parts of the game. That players would often distract him while one of their teammates, say, skipped second base altogether, made the one-umpire system a troubling feature of the National League. The umpire was not uncommonly attacked by players and fans alike and would therefore often change his ruling on a disputed call rather than risk personal injury. Throughout the 1889 season baseball's critics, players, and mangers issued a chorus of calls for the two-umpire system. The second man would improve judgments on close plays, which he could be better positioned to see, and thus provide the game with more order and decorum. The Players League's adoption of the two-umpire system was therefore not a new idea (two umpires were also used in some World Series games), but it gave the organization an added layer of respectability. Despite the push for such a system and its adoption by the PL, the National League stuck with one umpire in 1890.

Second, the playing-rules committee ruled to move the front of the pitchers' box back to fifty-one feet from the center of "home base" rather than from forty-nine and a half feet, as in the National League. The change gave hitters a valuable additional split second to see the ball, thus tilting the balance between pitching and hitting back toward the batter and making the game more attractive for fans. Third, with similar intentions, the committee prohibited the use of one's cap to catch a ball in the air, which hitherto had been permitted. Players were using, at best, rudimentary gloves that covered half their fingers, similar to modern biking gloves. Given the sting, catches in the air with one's nearly bare hands were a rarity. Taking a players' hat away from his legitimate defensive arsenal gave yet another advantage to the offensive game. Fourth, the committee decided to use a tighter ball, which flew longer and faster upon making contact with a bat. Control over the specifications of the balls were firmly in the league's hands, as it was Tim Keefe's new sporting-goods company (Keefe & Becannon), which would hold the exclusive license to manufacture the official Players League baseball.[108]

Other policies put in place by the new league reproduced some that were long instituted by the National League. Most significantly, no games would take place on Sundays; the sale of alcohol within ballparks was strictly forbidden; tickets would cost fifty cents; and "professional gamblers" were barred from admission (to which *Sporting Life* sarcastically responded, "*unprofessional* gamblers are not barred").[109] The intent behind these policies, just as in the National League, was to enhance the respectability of the ballpark among the middle and upper classes. Fifty-cent admissions, moreover, were necessary in most places to cover the high costs of salaries. And so long as they could consistently fill grandstands with five to ten thousand people while charging fifty cents, the policy made good economic sense. But the difference between fifty and twenty-five cents also meant the de facto exclusion of many working-class fans. That this was a more or less stated goal of the National League prompted some commentators (and many more contemporary historians) to posit that the Players League shared the same intentions. The prohibition of alcohol, too, has led many to believe that working-class fans were therefore not interested in the PL and that league directors wanted it that way.[110] But as will later be seen, the situation was more complicated than that. And there were other, perhaps more important, ways—besides merely catering to its fans in one manner or another—in which the Players League engaged in relations with working-class people.

Signing Players

Part of the reason the PL adjourned in November without incorporating until mid-December was, as stated earlier, because its lawyers realized that each club needed to incorporate itself first. But another stum-

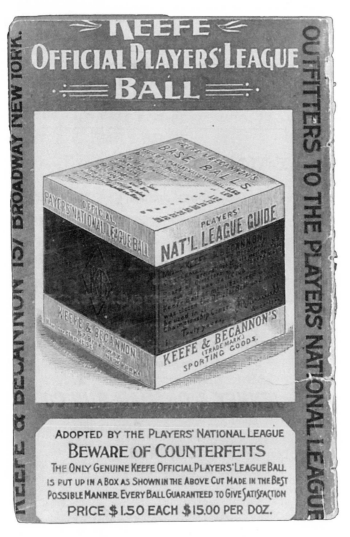

Fig. 5. Keefe Official Players League Ball. Used with
permission from Legendary Auctions, Inc.

bling block was the trepidation felt by stockholders. Before they were
really going to put their money down (initially, most investors only
subscribed for the stock), the backers wanted a guarantee that they
were going to get what they were paying for—most importantly, teams
that featured the best baseball players in the country.

Beginning the second week of November, several designated agents, some of whom were players, others nonplaying backers, set off on a mad dash to points across the United States in order to sign every brotherhood member (which included all but three of the National League's players in 1889). Meanwhile, the National League was determined to either sign these same players or legally prevent them from joining the new organization. To the extent that the NL could convince some players to stick with the old league, the Players League sought players primarily from the American Association to take their places. Young players from various minor leagues, in addition to some American Association "ball tossers," filled the several dozen remaining spots on the National League's rosters.

Before the dawn of the Players League, the reserve rule had more or less frozen the labor market in place, as it largely prevented clubs from having to travel great lengths to find new players or to sign old ones. New or temporary replacement players came by word of mouth or by a single sighting during a National League team's exhibition games against nonleague clubs. Tryouts on the clubs' grounds took place every now and then. As both cause and effect of these practices, most players still hailed from the urban Northeast.[111]

But the emergence of the Players League forced agents to travel to new corners and crevices of the country and revisit old ones to sign both rookies and veterans. From Massachusetts to Minnesota, to California, to Indiana, to Ohio, to Pennsylvania, to West Virginia, and so on, the men traversed the land in pursuit of an ever-scarcer supply of baseball players. The shortage of exceptional performers, a standard scenario in the broader entertainment industry but one now exacerbated by both the mobility of players and the addition of eight new teams, pitted the two leagues in fierce competition with each other over available labor (clubs within each league more or less agreed not to compete for particular players). This competition pushed club owners to expand the geographic edges of the labor market in search of extraordinarily skilled players. To the extent that new diamonds in the rough were either not found or not considered very valuable, the existing batch of players earned higher salaries. Ironically, it was the players' power to largely control the price of their own labor, for which reason the Players League had invented itself, that served as one of the new league's biggest stumbling blocks in signing players. In other words, now empowered by the Players League to retain a greater proportion of the value they created, some of the players asked for more than the league was willing and able to pay. Moreover, the friction of real time and material space played an active role in the competition between the two leagues for players. The men who could better overcome these barriers—in other words, the agents who could reach a player sooner—were often more successful at signing the ballplayers. More than just a "great race," however, the competition for labor also involved players' preexisting sense of loyalty or lack thereof to their "brothers," the effective use of deception and persuasion, the rule of law, and the power of money.

Every National League player except Cap Anson, Bill Hutchinson, and Tom Burns (all of Chicago) had already signed an agreement to "play base ball for the season of 1890 under the direction and control of [the Players League] . . . and to sign, when requested . . . a regulation form of players' contract to be hereafter adopted by . . . the Players National League of Base Ball Clubs."[112] This agreement, secretly signed during the previous summer and built in essence by the four years of apparent solidarity accrued since the brotherhood's founding, gave the Players League an early advantage over the National League. But once the agreement was leaked to the press, the National League employed a team of lawyers to refute its legality. Column after column of NL-sponsored arguments regarding the illegitimacy of the brotherhood's agreements filled the sporting press. Whether the oath was, in fact, legally binding was never tested in court, but the threat of its invalidity scared a number of players enough to prevent them from signing contracts with their teams.

The NL backed its attack on the legality of the brotherhood agreement with an invocation of its own reserve clause, which, it claimed, would prevent any player from signing with the new league. On October 21, 1889, each National League player received a letter composed by Philadelphia owner Col. John Rogers. "Dear Sir," the letters began,

> You are hereby notified that in accordance with the eighteenth paragraph of your contract with the____Ball Club, dated the____day of____, 1889, you have been reserved for the season of 1890 (together with thirteen other players now under contract with said club), at the same salary mentioned in the twentieth paragraph of your said contract, and that said club will require your services as a ball player for said season of 1890.[113]

Evidently some of the players did not take the letters too seriously. An unidentified Philadelphia player tore his letter to shreds and tossed the pieces into the air while making "contemptuous remarks."[114] Ward called the letter "a big bluff."[115] The reserve rule could stop a player from moving from one team to another within the National League, Ward argued, but it could "no more prevent a player from playing with another organization than [it could] prevent him from earning a livelihood by keeping a hotel or driving a dray."[116]

Nevertheless, some players chose to stay with the National League. Indianapolis third baseman Jerry Denny was the first brotherhood member to desert the movement and remain with the National League. "I have fully decided to remain in Indianapolis," Denny told the *Chicago Tribune*, "and no offer the brotherhood can make me will change my purpose. I am looking out for myself, and shall not leave a place where I have been well treated and am sure of my money and take up with a visionary scheme with no bottom."[117] So according to Denny, his defection had less to do with a higher salary figure offered by the National League than it did with the instability of the Players League (he ended up playing for NL New York in 1890 when the Indianapolis NL team folded). But this was after he tried to sign with the Players League for $1,500 more than he had been paid in 1889. It is not known how much Denny made with the NL in 1890, but it's probable that he earned more than what the brotherhood was willing to offer.

Denny's defection on November 8 was a big loss to the Players League, particularly to the team in Brooklyn, for which he was scheduled to play. The native New Yorker hit eighteen home runs in 1889, a figure topped only by Philadelphia's Sam Thompson, who hit twenty. Denny was also an excellent fielder, a skill that received far more attention then than it does today. His departure from the Players League left a gaping hole on the left side of Brooklyn's infield. At least they still had Jack Glasscock at shortstop. Or so they thought.

Glasscock had led the league in hits in 1889 with 205, stole 57 bases, and batted .352. He had played in the National League since 1879 (except in 1884, when he jumped midseason to the Union Association), captained the Indianapolis club since 1887, and was a fan favorite. Glasscock was also an outspoken member of the brotherhood, frequently complaining about National League management and urging the players to keep fighting against their bosses. Earlier that year Glasscock's push for a July 4 strike was voted down by the rest of the brotherhood.

Ward arrived at Glasscock's home in Wheeling, West Virginia, on November 18 with a contract in hand. There had been rumors in the press that Glasscock was going to sign with the National League. Glasscock had denied them, but Ward was wasting no time now to sign the Indianapolis shortstop. Ward arrived, however, to an empty home. John Brush had reached Wheeling the previous day and signed Glasscock for an undisclosed salary. The pair immediately traveled back to Indiana, where they were met by Denny and two additional Indianapolis deserters, pitchers Henry Boyle and Amos Rusie. To add insult to injury, Glasscock agreed to serve as a "missionary" for the National League; he would travel the country, trying to convince as many players as he could to play for the old organization in 1890.

Although most of the players who were signing contracts at the time were still going with the Players League, the majority had yet to sign with anyone. The PL needed to make a splash as big as that generated by Glasscock in order to pull everyone else in line. With this in mind Ward, who was now traveling out west to sign other players, sent Al

Johnson to New York to secure Mike Kelly. At one o'clock in the morning on November 25, Kelly signed for $5,000. "I signed the first paper the boys brought to me," Kelly explained, "because I wanted to show my utter contempt for that deserter, Jack Glasscock."[118] Echoing other players who had recently commented on the diminutive size of Glasscock's head, Kelly continued, "There is a good ball player, but he wears a No. 4 hat. He has a head like a pigeon."[119]

Hours later Kelly boarded a train for California. Several Boston players were already on their way to San Francisco, where they were scheduled to play against local teams. Kelly had been instructed by Johnson to try to sign every last one of them. On his way Kelly stopped over in Chicago, where he acted as a policeman in a local performance of the play *Brass Monkey*. Taking advantage of the opportunity to address a theater full of people, Kelly embellished the role, incorporating a scene in which he dramatically signed a Players League contract. The audience responded with lavish applause.

Meanwhile, Ed Andrews was busy on his own adventures trying to sign players for Brooklyn's Players League team. According to Andrews's dramatic retelling of his travels, second baseman Lou Bierbauer, of the Philadelphia AA club, was out hunting when Andrews reached his Erie home.[120] His brother escorted Andrews through the woods, across a muddy swamp, and into a clearing where Bierbauer, shotgun in hand, was standing. "He was glad to see me," Andrews said, and the two chatted for a short while in the cold, autumn-colored forest.[121] But on their way back to Bierbauer's house, Andrews recalled, "the tide had risen and the swamp was covered with water to the depth of about two feet."[122] After a bit of discussion, Bierbauer, who was wearing gumboots, decided to wade through the swamp with Andrews on his back.[123] When they returned to the house, Bierbauer signed the contract "without any coaxing."[124]

Andrews was not as fortunate the following week in Cleveland. When Andy Sommers didn't answer Andrews's tug on his doorbell one afternoon, Andrews took it upon himself to climb the fence into the catcher's backyard.[125] Lo and behold, Sommers was there, stripped down to his underwear and about to hop into the washtub. When Andrews handed him a contract to sign, Sommers hesitated, saying that he hadn't decided where he would play in 1890. Just then Sommers's German-born father burst through the back door and barked to Andrews, "It vas [*sic*] all your own misdakes in vaiding so long to send Andy's gondract. Andy would not haf signed wit Glassgock yisderday ef you had go here furat."[126]

While Kelly was on his way to California, Arthur Dixwell and John Morrill launched their own attempt to sign Boston's players. The backers had traveled along with the team to the West Coast and were in a good position to get players on the Players League's side.

In the first week, according to Morrill's December 8 letter to Frederick Long, they signed several players, including Charlie Radbourn, Hardy Richardson, Tom Brown, Dick Johnston, and Billy Nash.[127] "Mr. Dixwell worked on the men every moment," Morrill wrote, "and I am sure no one could have done better. I did all I could to induce the boys to sign. It was not so easy as some people think to have all the boys sign as these men."[128] Morrill's tone here is more defensive than it might seem. While the two backers had signed several players, they were having a difficult time signing the others. Boston's star pitcher, John Clarkson, was holding out, as was catcher Charlie Ganzel. The inability to sign these players, particularly Clarkson, was testing the patience of Hart and Long back in Boston.

Complicating matters was Kelly's arrival on the scene. "It made me very mad," Dixwell wrote to Long, of his discovery that Kelly was trying to sign players. "I was not willing after that to talk to a single player as I was afraid that Kelly might have more authority than I was given and that if I signed a player for his old salary that Kelly might curse out and say that he, Kelly, would have given him [a] higher salary if he had waited."[129] Dixwell's letter points toward the hazy line that the Players League had drawn between and within player and investor control. It was the first, but definitely not the last, instance of disagreement between the players and their financial backers. The incident also speaks to the fundamental dilemma embodied by players who were interested in larger salaries and who now at least should have also been concerned with the financial well-being of the club in which they invested. These tensions, between players and backers, on the one hand, and between the individual and collective interests of the players, on the other hand, would remain throughout the Players League's short history.

When first approached, Clarkson told Kelly that he wanted a $10,000 salary.[130] The pitcher had had a stellar year in 1889, leading the league in wins, games pitched, shutouts, innings pitched, strikeouts, and earned run average, so his wish for a hefty salary can be understood. But Clarkson's request was several thousand dollars more than any player had ever before received. And he was still not as popular among the fans, or arguably as valuable, as was Kelly.

Informed of Clarkson's demand, Long wrote to Dixwell, "Sign Clarkson [for] six thousand."[131] Kelly added to this offer $500 out of his own pocket if the pitcher would sign. But Clarkson refused, signing instead for $7,500 with Boston's National League club.

The *New York Clipper* suggested that Boston's futile attempt to sign Clarkson, among other endeavors, was informed by espionage: "Early in the fight a National League agent on a player foray, dropped a bundle of half a dozen telegrams in a St. Louis hotel. A boy who sympathized with the Brotherhood found and promptly mailed them to Ward. Clarkson's treason was first uncovered by means of a similar accident, and another one of the same kind enabled the Brotherhood men in San Francisco to know that Clarkson was in communication with a man in Williamsburg [Kansas]."[132] Nothing else in the archives confirms this accusation but it does reflect, at the very least, the suspicion that clubs were going to extraordinary lengths in their attempts to sign players.

Charlie Ganzel was about to embark on a short hunting trip when the Boston backers wanted to sign him. Hoping to catch him before he left, Dixwell raced to Ganzel's mother-in-law's house in Oakland, where Ganzel and his wife were staying, but learned that the catcher had already left. Dixwell and a friend then set off for a town about forty miles outside San Francisco, near which Ganzel was said to be hunting. "When we reached [indecipherable]," Dixwell wrote in a letter to Long, "we found the worst place I think I ever stopped at and were told that the men were at least eight miles away and likely several miles further off."[133] Frustrated, Dixwell returned to the comforts of his room at the Hotel Baldwin in San Francisco. Not to be defeated, though, he went back to Oakland each of the next two mornings, hoping that Ganzel had returned. On the second day, just after 8:45 in the morning, Dixwell found his man, but it was to no avail. Ganzel had already signed with the National League.

Despite these few setbacks, the Players League was in good shape. By December 11 at least ninety-seven players had signed with the Players League, eighty of whom had played in the National League the previous year. Twenty-one former brotherhood members deserted the new movement and signed with the National League, Denny, Glasscock, and Clarkson, the only prominent players among them.[134] It was no matter to the National League, its spokesmen claimed, for they were finding, in the minor leagues, talented young players who would soon replace the PL's men as the game's top stars. "I tell you," Spalding said to a reporter, "the youngsters play livelier ball than the old Leaguers."[135] "Are we worried?" he later asked. "Pshaw! Certainly not!"[136] Boston started these efforts by signing nearly the entire Omaha team of the Western Association to replace the players who left for the Players League. Ted Sullivan traveled throughout the Midwest in search of ballplayers for several National League teams. For Pittsburgh he signed Saginaw pitcher Frederick "Crazy" Schmidt, Quincy infielder Sam Laroque, and McKeesport pitcher Henry Jones. He found Quincy catcher Malachi Kittridge for Chicago and Evansville first baseman Louis Whistler for Washington. Philadelphia's new manager, Abe Cushman, signed a handful of players from the Western Association. Other players came from American Association teams, which both the PL and the NL raided after Brooklyn and Cincinnati joined the National

League. Even among these clubs the Players League got the better end of the stick, signing the biggest AA star, Charles Comiskey, to play for and manage the Chicago team, as well as several other players. Nearly all of the PL's players came from either the NL or the AA, with most coming from the National League.

All this progress, however, was threatened by the legal action that the National League was preparing to take. "I shall serve every player with an injunction restraining him from playing ball with this new organization," said New York owner John Day, although he actually sought injunctions only for Ward and Keefe.[137] Not able to sign enough marquee players to legitimately call themselves a major league, the National League owners reverted back to their old ways of restraining players from moving from one club to another: they would seek to legally apply the reserve rule.

John Rogers sought an injunction against Philadelphia shortstop William Hallinan, pitcher Charlie Buffinton, and PL shareholder Henry Love. Rogers contended that the reserve rule, as articulated in paragraph 18 of the 1889 contracts, legally prevented the players from playing elsewhere in 1890. Love, therefore, was unlawfully hiring them to play for his club. Rogers argued that the loss of these players "will break up your orator's team of skillful players, and will injure, if not destroy, its drawing power in public exhibition and cause great losses of money, the amount of which it is impossible to estimate or assess."[138] In other words, the minor league players that Philadelphia and the rest of the National League were signing could not effectively replace the men lost to the Players League. Perhaps the game's stars were interchangeable over time, but they were in limited numbers over space.

Some legal precedent stood on the National League's side. In *Lumley v. Wagner*, an 1852 English case sporadically cited by American judges in the nineteenth and early twentieth centuries, the court ruled that a theater owner could prevent a singer who was contracted to perform only at his theater from performing at any other theater during the time of the contract.[139] Key to this decision, legal scholar George

Clark argued, was "that [the defendant] was a person of extraordinary qualifications."[140]

A more recent legal decision, however, ruled differently. The decision in *Ford v. Jermon* (1865) prevented a theater owner from forcing an actress to perform only for his Philadelphia theater and no other. "Is it not obvious that a contract for personal services thus enforced would be but a mitigated form of slavery?" Judge John Hare wrote.[141]

But the NL's legal action may have had as much to do with intimidating players into signing with their old clubs as it did with actually legally enjoining them from playing for their new ones. In other words, perhaps they knew the law was not on their side, but if they could convince enough players in advance that it was, any legal losses could become moot. Along these lines the league hired a team of lawyers to write threatening opinions in the press. Typical of these pieces, New York attorney George Duysters concluded, "The player who joins the [Players League] now . . . assumes two very serious risks. First, that he may be unable to play at all if the court should decide that an injunction would lie; secondly, that after the season begins, and he should become dissatisfied with his position in the Brotherhood, he may not find the League magnates so anxious to take him back after they have made all their other preparations for the season of 1890."[142] Duysters was covering all his bases. The players were damned if the ruling came out against them, and they were damned if the Players League went on. The safe course of action, he suggested, was to stick with the National League.

As described in the introduction, Judge Morgan O'Brien's ruling in John Ward's case set the stage for the Players League to proceed. "I do not fully concur in the claims made by the plaintiff that the probability of finally succeeding is of the strongest and most certain kind," read O'Brien at the conclusion of the hearing.[143] And the meaning of the word "reserve" was not sufficiently explained in the contract. Nor does the reserve rule "provide the terms and conditions of the contract to be made for 1890," announced O'Brien.[144] And even if it had been articulated, the rule allowed clubs only to reserve Ward's "services ... to the exclusion of any other member of the league of base-ball clubs."[145] It did not allow the New York owners to reserve Ward from playing in another league. Furthermore, the contract's lack "of fairness and of mutuality, which [were] fatal to its enforcement in equity," rendered it unenforceable by the court.[146]

Despite the threat of appeal and additional lawsuits, the players were jubilant upon hearing Judge O'Brien's decision. The National League's final strategy to restrain them from playing with the Players League had failed. With the ruling, and subsequent victories in Ewing's and the Philadelphia cases, the new league was effectively open for business. The players who had delayed signing PL contracts until after Ward's case largely signed on in the following weeks and months.

Securing Grounds

The production of Players League baseball needed to take place on particular grounds and in suitable ballparks. But this element of the Players League's landscape could not be located just anywhere on any open urban space. Suitable land may not have been as hard to find as appropriately skilled players' bodies, but it also did not come very eas-ily. The Players League's grounds, as mentioned earlier, were often selected based on their proximity to a backer's trolley line or real-estate holdings. But there are more general principles guiding the location of late nineteenth-century ballparks, which the PL's decisions and sub-sequent press statements reflect. Other advantages and complications arose in particular circumstances. The three most important qualities in baseball grounds were proximity to the city center, the size of the plot, and the preexisting levelness.

Quite simply, the closer, or more accessible, ballparks were to the central business district, the easier it was for fans to attend games. But the closer a location was to the city center, the higher its cost and the less likely it was to be open, undeveloped space. So teams were forced to locate on, at best, the periphery of downtown areas. Trolley lines somewhat alleviated this contradiction, as they could form an artery directly from the city center to the ballpark. Where locations within walking distance of the central business district were not available, therefore, the proximity to existing or potential trolley lines was key.

The importance of a spacious ballpark may come as a surprise to contemporary baseball enthusiasts. Nineteenth-century baseball fans did not value home runs and power hitting as much as they did speed, defense, and consistent hitting. Where possible, therefore, clubs built ballparks on grounds large enough to prevent most balls from traveling over the outfield fences. One site that Cleveland was considering, for example, was criticized in the press for its short distances between home plate and the outfield fences. "The loss of balls will be tremendous," *Sporting Life* wrote.[147]

It was just as difficult in some cities to find open and accessible space as it was to find smooth and level land. Crews of laborers graded and leveled grounds using relatively simple equipment (spades, it appears, were the most common tools) when the land was not already flat to begin with. The desired result, if the language repeatedly used to describe attractive grounds is any indication, was to make the field "as level as a billiard table." Level grounds were not just an aesthetic consideration. As anyone who has played baseball on a field riddled with bumps and holes can understand, smooth grounds lend to better fielding. Injuries are less likely to occur, too, on a diamond that prevents fewer terrestrial obstacles.

These and other factors came into play in the selection of each Players League ballpark site.

Philadelphia allegedly sought to lease the grounds on which the AA Athletics' park, at Jefferson Avenue and West Twenty-Seventh Streets in the northwest part of the city, was already located.[148] According to *Sporting Life* a man from Cincinnati who was associated with the brotherhood offered to pay a higher rent to the city government, which owned the land, than the Athletics were already paying.[149] Another report had "a black-mustached man, who gave a name that evidently was fictitious" and who "said he was acting in the interest of a syndicate," attempted to lease grounds in Gloucester.[150] But the Players League ended up at Broad and Dauphin Streets, on land owned by

Adam Forepaugh and adjacent to land that now serves as the campus of Temple University. This spot was advantageous not only because it belonged to one of the PL's backers, but also because it was adjacent to six different streetcar lines and two blocks from the Reading Railroad's Huntingdon Street Station. The club signed a multiyear lease of $5,000 per year. *Sporting Life* described the Players League's new Philadelphia park in November 1889 as "a beautiful piece of ground about 600 feet square, level as a billiard table and well located."[151] The NL Phillies, housed nearby at Huntingdon and Broad, enjoyed the same locational advantages but played on what was considered one of the worst infields in baseball.[152] Evidently, however, the PL still considered the Athletics' "Jefferson Avenue Grounds" a better location, as it waited until December to sign the lease at "Forepaugh's Park" in hopes that the AA club would fold and thereby make its land available.[153]

New York was one of the first clubs to sign a lease for grounds when James Coogan brokered a deal between Ward and Sarah Lynch of the Lynch Estate. The club agreed to rent the land for the next ten years. The grounds were bound by Eighth Avenue on the southeast, Harlem River Drive on the northwest, 159th Street to the northeast, and the Polo Grounds (along what would be 157th Street) to the southwest.[154] The lease on the Polo Grounds, which the NL New York club also rented from Lynch (via Coogan), was to expire after the 1891 season, when the Players League would have the option of moving there if so desired. There are conflicting reports on the grounds' rental costs. The *New York Times* claimed that the club paid $10,000 per year, while *Sporting Life* had the cost at $4,000.[155] The former figure was most likely an error, as this amount, although the property was in New York, is exceptionally greater than any other club's rent. Moreover, both accounts note a $2,000 fee charged by Coogan, which an additional story reported was equivalent to six months' rent.[156] In any event the grounds were slightly larger and not as hilly as the neighboring Polo Grounds.[157] The Sixth and Ninth Avenue elevated trains and the Eighth Avenue horse-car line directly served both fields, and with the construction of the PL's ballpark, the railway installed a new stop at 159th Street.[158] It was a fifty-minute commute from "the remotest part of the city," but given the expansive growth of the city in the 1880s, there were not many other options.[159] And with the NL club just next door, the relative disadvantages of location were rendered moot.

The location of Brooklyn's Players League grounds was a mystery to the baseball world for quite some time. On November 3, 1889, Ward, Al Johnson, Buck Ewing, Jay Faatz, and Ned Hanlon went to Brooklyn to search for grounds. They announced in the following days that they had found a suitable location, but they would not reveal where it was. The truth of the matter is probably that they were still searching. Few suitable options, according to a *Sporting Life* writer, were available in Brooklyn.[160] It is at this point that the club's realtors may have come in to help. According to Ward a syndicate of real-estate men, whom neither he nor the press identified, bought a ten-acre plot of land in the Twenty-Sixth Ward of Brooklyn. The land stood next to the intersection of the Kings County and Manhattan Beach elevated trains and was bordered by Vesta Street to the northeast, Sutter Avenue to the southeast, Rowell Street to the southwest, and the Eastern Parkway on the northwest.[161] The Manhattan Beach Railroad planned to build an enclosed pedestrian walkway from its station at Snediker Avenue directly into the ballpark's grandstand.[162] Much of the wood for the grandstand itself, as well as for the fences, was purchased by the club from a company in Brighton Beach, Brooklyn, which had built a grandstand there for fireworks displays.[163] The realtors leased the land to the PL club for an undisclosed rate. Although one of the backers boasted that the grounds were "just twenty-one minutes' ride from the Brooklyn Bridge," they were nonetheless on the very outer fringes of Brooklyn (even by today's standards), near Jamaica Bay.[164] Ward noted, "The ground is as flat as a billiard table and not a spadeful of dirt will be needed for grading."[165]

John Morrill began searching for grounds in Boston all the way back in September 1889. By mid-October he had found two potential sites, one near the NL park on Huntingdon and Columbus Avenues and the other by the Boston Harbor between Congress Street and the New

York and New England Railroad Terminal.[166] When a handful of backers plus Ward visited the sites, they nearly unanimously chose the grounds on Congress Street. The location was but a fifteen-minute walk from Post Office Square, the *Chicago Daily Tribune* reported, and much of the city's central business district was even closer.[167] "It will be extremely convenient for clerks and business men," *Sporting Life* claimed, "to stay at their desks up to the last minute and then go down in time to see the game."[168] For those spectators further away, the New York and New England railroads would drop passengers on platforms directly connected to the park, and the Lynn and Revere Railroad would also make stops at the grounds. The only drawback to the location, some stockholders complained, was that ladies, who were largely excluded from the downtown area, were less likely to reach the grounds. Not to fear, Dixwell responded, because "where one lady was lost six men would be added."[169] Thus the added respectability lent by the presence of women, though deemed important, was not seen as valuable as an increase in white-collar ticket sales. In addition to being more accessible, the "Congress Street Grounds" were larger than Boston's otherwise beautiful South End Grounds.[170] "There can be a home run made easily on a hit inside the fence," *Sporting Life* wrote, in reference to the spacious outfield, whose exterior barriers were to stand nearly one hundred feet further from home plate than those on the other side of town.[171]

Cleveland's grounds were, as anyone would have suspected, on one of Johnson's electric streetcar lines. The location he found was situated at Wilson Avenue (later named East Fifty-Fifth Street) and the termination of a road called Diamond Park. It was adjacent to the Nickel Plate Railway and Brooklyn streetcar terminals. Michael Woolrich and a man referred to as Dr. Barr leased the grounds to the club for two years at $2,000 per year.[172] Johnson announced that he and his brother would run special Brooklyn streetcars every fifteen minutes directly from Superior Street, downtown, to the ballpark without stopping. The ride, Johnson claimed, would take seventeen minutes and would thus make the grounds nearer to the city center than Cleveland's "League park, which was between Payne and Euclid Avenues to the north and south and East 35th and East 39th Streets to the east and west."[173] The PL's grounds were longer than those of its rival, at 975 feet, but much narrower, coming in at 430 feet.[174] The field was reported "level" in October 1889, but in December the club hired a crew to grade the grounds.[175]

Jack Rowe and Deacon White were readily familiar with Buffalo's Olympic Park, at the corner of Richmond Avenue and Summer Street, as they had played there with the city's NL club in 1884 and 1885. The park was subsequently used by the International Association club, for which Rowe and White had planned to play in 1889. The city's adoption of a Players League club led to the temporary disbanding of the IA team, which left Olympic Park vacant. The pair therefore sought to use the park for the 1890 season. The costs of constructing a new ballpark ran in the tens of thousands of dollars, which, particularly for a small-market club like Buffalo, was no minor expense. But as Johnson recalled, "It was decided that Buffalo must erect a new grand stand, so as to be in with the rest of the procession."[176] In the end the decision to expend more money in this regard may have backfired, but it did accord with some economic logic. The call to construct a new ballpark in Buffalo points again toward the value of attractive architecture and suitable amenities, which Olympic Park probably did not have. Nonetheless, the club's new park, located at the corner of Masten Street and East Ferry Street, came to be known as Olympic Park as well, though historians refer to it as "Olympic Park II."[177]

The only potential problem with Pittsburgh's Exposition Park (which was actually located in what was then the city of Allegheny) was that the nearby Allegheny River tended to flood into it. The lower end of the grounds, which was home to a horse track and previously to the Pittsburgh Alleghenys of the American Association, frequently flooded, while the upper end did not. Exactly why the Post Percheron Horse Association and the Alleghenys chose that end is not clear, although it could have had something to do with changing landownership after the grandstands were constructed. Fortunately for the Players League,

W. W. Kerr leased the upper end of the park to his club. There the grounds were bound by the river to the south, School Street to the east, South Avenue on the north, and Grant Street on the west—approximately the same spot where the Pittsburgh Pirates' Three Rivers Stadium would be located eighty years later.[178] According to *Sporting Life* Fred Pfeffer was thrilled to learn in November that the PL grounds were fifteen to twenty minutes closer to Pittsburgh's central business district than was the NL park, also in Allegheny, at Pennsylvania and Allegheny Avenues.[179] The PL club signed a five-year lease for the grounds.[180] Other than an ash heap on the south side of the space, the grounds were already reasonably level.

Chicago ran into more problems searching for grounds than did any other club. Perhaps it was the backers' audacity that got them into so much trouble. Just as the 1889 season concluded, backers from the Chicago club attempted to lease the land occupied by the NL team right from underneath Spalding's feet. Spalding was apparently planning to build a new ballpark in a different location anyway, so he had let his lease on West Side Grounds, at Congress and Loomis Streets, expire at the end of the 1889 season. Fred Pfeffer had an insider's view of the situation, as Spalding still trusted him as faithful to the National League. So as soon as the lease expired, agents for the PL club (probably Pfeffer, a backer or two, and perhaps Ward) secured a three-year lease at $7,500 per year (Spalding had been paying $4,000).[181] When Spalding visited his new grounds, which had been selected by an underling, he was disgusted to find them in horrible, perhaps irreparable, shape. He hurried back to the landowner of his previous site only to find that the brotherhood men had beaten him to it. Spalding was furious but resolute. Only after giving the landlord $10,000 did Spalding retain his lease (now at the new rent figure).

The PL contingent had to look elsewhere. In November it seemed that they had found the perfect location. An empty piece of land right on the lakefront between Ontario and Ohio Streets could not have been more convenient. It was a ten-minute walk to the Palmer House Hotel and five minutes from the Clark Street Bridge. The space was roomy, attractive, and flat. The club signed a lease in December from the Ogden Estate for $2,500 a year.[182] There was but one obstacle. The neighborhood's posh residents did not want them there. "The small boy is jubilant," the *Tribune* wrote after the ballpark's location was announced, "his older sister sniffs as she thinks of the noise, and the stern parent says it will depreciate property 50 per cent."[183] Whether true or not, the neighbors argued that a ballpark would attract saloons, rambunctious fans tearing down the tree-lined streets, and excessive horse carriage traffic. Speaking for the Ogden Estate, E. H. Fishburn countered that without the park, the vacant land was overgrown, ugly, and attracted "disreputable characters."[184] The ballpark would be an improvement, he said. Arguing along these same lines, the Chicago City Council approved an ordinance that allowed the club to close off the end of Ohio Street, which ran perpendicular to where the outfield would lie.

Not to be defeated, the people of the neighborhood gathered "a large number of signatures" for a remonstrance against the ordinance. The mayor, who had been sitting on the fence on the matter, was now leaning toward a veto of the Ohio Street ordinance. Faced with the possibility of thorny legal problems and hostile neighbors, the PL club gave up the site. Desperate for a location, the club quickly found empty grounds at the corner of Thirty-Fifth Street and Wentworth Avenue on the southside of Chicago (just across the street from where the Chicago White Sox, twenty years later, would construct Comiskey Park, coincidentally named after the Chicago Players League's player-captain). The team had moved from one of the wealthiest areas of the city to one of the most militantly working-class neighborhoods. Its troubles were far from over.

5

THE MEN WHO DO THE WORK

The Players League had secured sufficient investment, players, and grounds by the spring of 1890. But there was still more work to do. Some of the grounds needed leveling; the construction of grandstands was essential if the games were ever going to take place; and the production of uniforms and equipment was necessary for the players to actually play the games. Moreover, after the season would begin in May, the ballparks would still need music, security, maintenance, and refreshments. Most of the work involved in furnishing these goods and services fell into the hands not of the players but of ordinary working people. Common laborers leveled and prepared the fields; carpenters and bricklayers put together the grandstands and outfield fences; painters colored them in bright hues; musical bands played patriotic tunes as they marched into the ballparks before the start of the game; young boys peddled scorecards, fruit, and tobacco to the fans; policemen tried to keep the patrons (and players) under control. The political and economic aspirations of these workers necessarily intersected with those of the players. But they did not always coincide so harmoniously.

Without the reserve rule to contain players' salaries, the Players League had to find another way to limit its costs. Some people associated with the PL took measures to reduce the costs of the ballparks and equipment. In particular contractors hired by the Players League in at least Chicago and Boston underpaid and overworked the carpenters who were constructing ballparks in those cities. Despite the support of organized labor, the league did not consistently attempt to hire unionized workers or to stop the abuses in Chicago and Boston.

This chapter examines the political and economic struggles of the Players League's off-the-field workers. It focuses most of its attention on the carpenters, particularly those in Boston and Chicago, whose work stoppages directly collided with the Players League's interests. Furthermore, this chapter reinforces the general need to look beyond the surface of the baseball industry, beyond the performances and heroics, past the labor relations between players and their bosses, and toward the people who produce the industry's built environment and ancillary commodities.

It is the relations between these workers and the Players League—mediated by the contractors and manufactures—that reveal the limits to any notion that the new league was somehow radical in its orientation. That the PL outsourced the work involved in constructing its ballparks to contractors does not make the league any less materially connected and responsible for these workers' exploitation.

Ballpark Construction

The Players League employed more workers to construct and operate its ballparks than it did baseball players to play in them. Given the predominance of wood in ballpark construction (most parks include some brick in their facade; some clubs did not use it at all), and the evidence provided in newspapers and secondary accounts that point to the limited number of in-season employees, it is safe to conclude that the majority of the workers were carpenters.

While it is impossible to know exactly how many carpenters or other workers toiled in and on the ballparks, the detailed records of Frederick Long offer a clue. Long's papers include the twenty-five-page receipt issued by W. H. Keyes & Co., the contractor in charge of constructing Boston's ballpark.[1] Keyes measures labor here only in workdays and daily rate, not in the actual number of workers. But if one assumes that a full "day" equaled a single worker (and the definition of a full-day was a source of serious contention, as discussed later), an average of

49 workers showed up each day between March 10, when construction began, and June 12, when the final touches on the outfield fence were put in place.[2] The workers constructed the ballpark in seventy working days (labor generally did not take place on Sundays, and there was a short break before the fence was completed). As many as 143 people worked for Keyes on one day, while as few as 3 did on a handful of other occasions.[3] The total cost of construction, according to Long's end-of-the-season financial report, was $41,346.88.[4] Labor constituted just over $10,000 of that figure, according to Keyes's account.[5] The carpenters earned between $2.50 and $2.70 per day.[6] The salaries of Boston's seventeen players, in contrast, cost the club $45,868.13.[7]

If one presumes an average of 49 workers to be typical, then a minimum of about 400 men, mostly carpenters, worked full-time for two to three months on the construction of Players League ballparks across the league. Given Boston's varied crew numbers from day to day and the likelihood that some people did not stay on the job throughout the duration of the project, the number is probably higher. The costs of constructing a ballpark varied from city to city; in Boston and Chicago, where carpenters' union militancy was relatively high, the labor costs must have been greater. But in any case the point is that a majority of the league's workers received a disproportionately smaller amount of its wages. No one even considered (publicly at least) including carpenters or other off-the-field workers in the Players League's profit-sharing plans.

Nevertheless, months before the hammers and saws were put into motion, Ward declared the players' solidarity with working-class men. But he also tacitly drove an economic wedge between baseball players and the workers who would build the venues in which their games were played:

We count, again, on the support of the public, because we have the sympathy of the labor organizations. The [Players League] is an experiment on our part to have the men who do the work participate in the profits of the pastime. If we are successful, it will be a demonstration that such a principle can succeed. That we receive larger salaries and that our hours of work are shorter leaves us none the less workingmen. We are hired men, skilled in a particular employment, who work not only for the profit, but the amusement as well of our employers.[8]

Ward's conception of "work" within the realm of professional baseball is limited to that performed on the ball field. Surely, he considered carpentry and bricklaying work as well, but his (and the PL's) exclusion of these off-the-field workers from also participating "in the profits of the pastime" suggests that ballparks and the men who construct them do not add value to the game. In other words, carpenters "work," but they do not "do *the* work" necessary for baseball games to take place. This subtle distinction has deeply political and economic consequences. Had Ward correctly identified ballparks as value-adding components of professional baseball, he would have had to either include the off-the-field workers in the Players League's profit-sharing schemes or abandon his argument that those who "do the work" should reap the benefits. But his exclusive conception of "the work"—his comparison of baseball playing and other forms of work as parallel but not materially connected to one another—allowed the Players League to both discursively align itself with working-class people and to share the game's profits only with its partner investors. This alignment was, in part, an attempt to attract working-class fans, on whose support Ward counted. Thus Ward's statement of solidarity and the policies behind it were meant to open the door for the league's off-the-field workers to *contribute* to the profits in the form of ticket purchases, not *share* them in the form of dividends. So in this sense, the Players League was an *intra*class struggle as much as it was an interclass one.

Nevertheless, tradesmen, and particularly carpenters, were quick to support the Players League upon its creation. Maj. Samuel Leffingwell, a nationally recognized organizer with the International Typographical Union, conveyed the support among skilled tradesmen for the Players League shortly after its inception. "A peculiar interest," he said in November, "is being manifested in the trade union element favoring this Base Ball Brotherhood movement."[9] The brotherhood was "a legitimate organization of skilled workmen," he argued, and as such, should "make application to the American Federation of Trade and Labor Unions or to the . . . Knights of Labor."[10] If so aligned with "organizations representing over 1,000,000 of skilled mechanics," Leffingwell concluded, the Players League would receive the support of "the working men."[11]

The players did not join any larger labor organization, but they nonetheless received an official endorsement from the American Federation of Trade and Labor Unions (AFL). On December 13, 1889, at its annual meeting, the AFL adopted a resolution against the buying and selling of baseball players and in favor of the Players League.[12] Individual trades and various local unions also endorsed the league. The New York clothing cutters' branch of the Knights of Labor, for example, issued a statement of support for the league that same month.[13] The United Brotherhood of Carpenters and Joiners of America (UBCJA) stated, through its official organ, the *Carpenter*, "The sympathy of organized labor is most emphatically with the Brotherhood."[14] The Players League also received endorsements from the Amalgamated Association of Iron and Steel Workers, the Central Trades Council of Western Pennsylvania, the Brotherhood of Locomotive Firemen, and the Caster's Protective Union of Boston.[15]

A delegation of powerful and prominent labor leaders, including Samuel Gompers, president of the AFL; P. J. McGuire, vice president of the AFL and general secretary of the UBCJA; W. J. Shields, vice president of UBCJA; and James Dey, business agent of the Philadelphia local, Union No. 8, of the UBCJA, attended a meeting of the Philadelphia Players League club on January 16, 1890.[16] "Messrs. Gompers, McGuire, Shields and Dey," recalled Philadelphia PL backer John Vanderslice, "called to say that the laboring men all over the country were in sympathy with the players in this fight, and to assure us that we would receive their moral and financial support."[17]

The support of organized labor did not (initially at least) go unrequited by the Players League. There was an expectation, and in some cases spoken agreements, that the league would hire only union workers in the construction and operation of its ballparks. The *Carpenter* reported that the New York, Boston, and Philadelphia clubs had agreed to hire no one but union carpenters in the construction of their ballparks.[18] The meeting minutes of Chicago's United Carpenters' Council (UCC) reveal that a similar agreement was reached in that city.[19] After speaking with UCC secretary T. G. Howard, PL secretary-treasurer Frank Brunell "promised," according to the union's minutes, "to do all in his power to have work done in accordance with [the union's] wishes."[20] That Brunell was the league's, not Chicago's, secretary-treasurer, further suggests that the PL as a whole intended to hire union workers.

Labor Struggles of the Carpenters

This turned out not to be the case, however, in Boston and Chicago.[21] In both cities contractors hired nonunion carpenters at one point or another. Carpenters' strikes related to these actions disrupted the construction of Players League ballparks. Although on different scales, the strikes in both cities were launched to reduce working hours and increase pay. As in the players' rebellion, the carpenters in Boston and Chicago sought to take control of the labor *market* in order to better take control of the price of their labor. But without extraordinary skills to fall back on, the carpenters needed to rely on other strategies. Producing and controlling the geographic scale of the labor market through concerted strikes was one such configuration. An examination of the processes by which carpenters first lost control over their labor market helps to better clarify the essential differences between the labor processes of carpentry and baseball, and thereby, the differing labor struggles that emerged in response. The case of Chicago is particularly significant, as the citywide strike there, which lasted from April 1890 to March 1891, impacted carpenters across the country.

Contestations over the spatial and numeric expansion of the American carpentry labor market trace back to the turn of the nineteenth century. In the late eighteenth and early nineteenth centuries, carpenters were expected to apply a broad set of skills to the interior and exterior construction of houses and buildings. "House carpenters" were also responsible for the design and engineering of structures, often reproducing European styles that they had learned as apprentices or from specialized periodicals. The relative scarcity of these skilled craftsmen allowed individual carpenters, and subsequently small, urban-based guilds of carpenters, to set their own prices, relatively unhindered by market forces.[22] Carpenters thus enjoyed relative monopolies over the labor market; their ability to determine the price of their labor was relatively strong.

But the industrialization of carpentry, which began in the 1830s and 1840s and was in full steam by the late 1880s, increased the ready supply of carpenters by systematically de-skilling their labor process. The first significant innovation to the construction process was the development of the balloon-frame house in the 1830s. Augustine Deodat Taylor, a Chicago carpenter, started building houses out of several two by fours instead of the traditional massive posts. Enabled by new technology that made it easier to cut and shape logs, the balloon-frame design demanded less wood and fewer hours of labor.[23]

As industry began to grow across the American economy in the years before the Civil War, companies started demanding larger buildings with more intricate designs. The task of design was separated from that of execution, as architects and structural engineers performed the former job and carpenters stuck with the latter. Larger work crews necessitated the distinction of a foreman from other journeymen.[24] And although foremen still enjoyed autonomous power in certain cases, the rising costs of construction were out of their reach.[25] Thus the guilds collapsed, and contractors, financiers, and landowners rose to power.[26]

In the years after the Civil War, new woodworking machines and the geographic dispersal of construction into specialized factories rendered many long-established skills of carpenters useless, and thus a good number of carpenters found themselves out of work.[27] "The mechanization of much of the work that the old artisan-carpenter had done on the jobsite or in his employer's shop," argue Richard Schneirov and Thomas J. Suhrbur, "increasingly turned the late nineteenth-century carpenter into a mere installer of factory-made woodwork and enabled the piecework system to invade the trade."[28] Piecework, which involved the delegation of specific tasks to individual workers, replaced careful craftsmanship with hurried mass production. New building materials, such as stone and iron, and the increasing hesitation to construct with fire-prone wood (particularly in Chicago), further alienated carpenters from the larger production process and decreased the relative demand for their labor.[29]

Despite the increasing prevalence of factory-made piecework, most of the carpentry industry's production was still conducted on site, at the same location where it would be consumed. Thus the degradation of carpentry's labor processes did not allow building capital to move the sites of production wherever it pleased, as capital did in most other industries. Instead contractors encouraged and facilitated the mobility of carpenters on an ever-broadening labor market. The expansion of national railways between 1850 and 1873 assisted in this endeavor, as it allowed carpenters from across North America to work in virtually any city's building industry.[30]

That Chicago in particular was the regional hub of this rail network, and that its growth surpassed that of any other city in the American West at the time, made migration to this city easier and all the more attractive for carpenters from other parts of the United States, Canada, and Europe. Chicago soon became the "dumping-off place for traveling carpenters who were willing to work for anything," recalled Peter McGuire, the general secretary during the 1880s and 1890s of the UBCJA, the national organization founded to regulate the migration of carpenters between cities.[31]

Without the need for skill or the time-space barriers of travel, a much larger pool of men became available to work as carpenters. According to Frank Duffy in his history of the UBCJA, "The once honored craft of carpentry lost its exalted position, its prestige and its standing not only among the other skilled trades but with the public as well."[32]

The growth of large building companies, which both implemented these changes and were born from them, drained even more power from individual carpenters. In the mid-1870s contractors formed urban-based builders' associations and a National Association of Builders to internally regulate the industry. The largest handful of Chicago's contractors formed the Carpenters' and Builders' Association (CBA) "for the purpose," according to the preamble of its constitution, "of uniformity in action in regard to matters involving [their] interest."[33] By 1889 five Chicago contractors employed 75 percent of the city's carpenters.[34] Such "unscrupulous and irresponsible contractors," complained Duffy, "swarmed into the building industry and introduced all sorts of newfangled ideas and questionable practices. Quality did not count. Quantity was what they wanted. A big day's work was demanded at a very low wage. Competition was keen. Cheapness had become the prevalent rule to the detriment alike of contractors and journeymen, to the injury of the public and the degradation of the trade."[35]

The contractors whom Duffy bemoaned were often former carpenters themselves. But now as employers they answered to the dictates of competition, a force that could be harnessed to work against the interests of their employees. With the supply of carpenters exceeding demand, contractors were able to insist on low wages and long hours. It was now the contractors, cooperating at the urban and national scales, not the carpenters, whose monopoly power could set the price of labor.

Efforts to organize carpenters to counter these forces took place in a variety of forms and at various locations after the Civil War. During the two decades of serious labor activity before the 1890 strike, Chicago's carpenters seesawed between integrated solidarity and divided partisanship. Ethnic, political, and geographic differences meddled with the need to present a united front against increasingly powerful bosses. Periodic influxes of outside carpenters made it more difficult to achieve solidarity. Until the 1890 work stoppages, Chicago's union carpenters had launched only a small handful of marginally successful strikes and bargaining campaigns. Work stoppages in 1872, 1882, and 1886 brought Chicago's carpenters closer to an eight-hour day and an acceptable wage, but their strikes had yet to pressure the city's contractors into recognizing their unions. The creation of the UCC in 1887, which included carpenters from the brotherhood, Amalgamated Society, and (sometimes) the Knights of Labor, sought to change these circumstances. Under this umbrella the carpenters struck in 1887, 1888, and 1889. And while these struggles did not result in outright victories, they did serve to significantly increase membership and teach the UCC some valuable strike tactics.

By December 1889 carpenters held a prominent position within the American Federation of Labor. At the same annual meeting in which the Players League received an official endorsement, the American Federation of Labor asked the UBCJA to lead a renewed effort for eight-hour working days. Carpenters from cities across the United States and Canada were to strike on May 1, 1890, for shorter working days and, in most cases, wage increases. Once these strikes proved successful, the AFL would designate another trade (the miners) to walk out in support of eight hours. Chicago's union carpenters, under the umbrella of the UCC, struck first, walking out on April 7, 1890. The city's carpenters were forced to strike a month earlier than those in the rest of the country because the unusually mild spring enabled contractors to begin construction sooner than usual. Also Chicago's carpenters were widely regarded as the most organized and therefore as having the greatest potential for success among all the unions of the trade.

On March 24, 1890, before any of these larger strikes began, however, the carpenters working on Boston's Congress Street Grounds walked off the job. While the UBCJA and the AFL did not sanction the strike, it was organized amid this same climate of carpenter agitation for shorter hours and better pay. Boston's union carpenters, under the leadership of Local 33, had already achieved a standard nine-hour working day, at $2.50 per day, and were planning to press for eight hours come May 1. But the carpenters employed on Congress Street Grounds were earning $2.70 for a ten-hour day.[36] Also Boston's contractor, Keyes, hired both union and nonunion men. At some point during March, the secretary of Local 33, J. G. Clinkard, complained to John Ward. Ward referred him to Julian Hart, Boston's principal stockholder. Clinkard met with Hart "a number of times" to discuss the situation, but according to the carpenters, Hart "declined to intervene."[37] "The only alternative left for the union," Clinkard decided, "was to call the men off the job."[38] Seventy-one of the eighty carpenters at work that day struck. Later that evening members of Local 33 met at Dexter Hall in the Wells Memorial Building. After the meeting started, Keyes arrived and asked to meet with a committee from the union. The two parties held "a pleasant conference" during which the contractor completely acquiesced to the union's demands.[39] The carpenters would work nine-hour days at $2.50 per day and Keyes would hire only union carpenters. The settlement "was received with great satisfaction by the union" and set the course for a much more positive relationship between the carpenters and the Players League. When Local 33 threatened to launch strikes on May 1 against each employer who did not adopt an eight-hour working day, Keyes promptly granted his carpenters the shorter day.[40] On May 8, a few weeks after the season started, an estimated five hundred carpenters marched from the Wells Memorial Building to Congress Street Grounds in support of the new team. (Unfortunately, however, the game was rained out.)[41]

Boston's strike enabled the carpenters to control the labor market at the worksite itself. Upon exercising their power to strike, the carpenters at Congress Street Grounds were able to force their employers to pay a specified wage and hire a particular group of people. The success of this labor strategy had mixed ramifications for the Players League. On the one hand, the carpenters' strike increased labor costs. But on the other hand, because they were able to amicably settle, the carpenters paid the league back in a sense by buying its tickets and publicly supporting the league. Still, it is possible that the carpenters would have turned out in even larger numbers for baseball games had the Boston club been more receptive to the union in the first place. Either way the strike itself sheds light on the contradictory relationship between the industry's on-field and off-field workers.

The conflict between the Players League and its carpenters was readily apparent in Chicago. Immediately after Ward's injunction case was settled in January, the Chicago club set to work on its southside ballpark. Leveling the grounds did not present too many difficulties, and by March work on the grandstand had begun. But despite Brunell's initial claim that the club would use only union men, its contractor, Frank Reynolds, hired nonunion carpenters from the beginning. "I went to Brunell and made a kick, and a hard one," said UCC secretary Howard. "He promised to make it all right. But he didn't."[42] Toward the end of March, according to the UCC's minutes, Chicago PL owner C. A. Weidenfelder suggested that they "should advertise for union men and he would see to it they were put to work."[43] But nonunion carpenters continued to work on the ballpark. Meanwhile, the citywide strike was just about to begin.

The CBA refused even to meet with the UCC to discuss its demands for an eight-hour day and a minimum forty-cents-per-hour wage. But the UCC had organized most of the city's carpenters and was ready for a protracted labor struggle. "So thoroughly did it do its work," UCC founder and historian James Brennock observed, "that on April 7, 1890, the sound of the hammer and swish of the saw was hushed throughout the city, and the greatest strike in the history of the craft was inaugurated."[44]

When the strike began, the greatest threat to Chicago's UCC was the presence of nonunion carpenters. The carpenters' unprecedented solidarity, coupled with promised "moral" and financial support from the AFL, the UBCJA, and nearly every trade union in Chicago and across the country, offered a measure of protection against internal disintegration. But if the contractors could put nonunionized men to work, if they could expand the boundaries of the labor market beyond Chicago and thus beyond the UCC, they could circumvent the strike and render it and the union irrelevant. Two conditions outside the contractors' control put even greater pressure on the labor market to expand across Chicago's borders. First, Chicago was experiencing a boom in construction. The World's Fair was coming in 1893, and the city was preparing for it with several new skyscrapers, houses, apartment buildings, department stores, and, starting in 1891, structures constructed specifically for the fair. Before there was even any talk of a strike, the city's boosters announced that they would not have enough building tradesmen to fill all the necessary jobs. Already journeymen had started coming to Chicago to find work. Second, Chicago's carpenters, for all their grievances, earned higher wages than those in most other towns and cities. The widespread vacancies that would be created with a general strike among Chicago's carpenters could exacerbate the contractors' need, and the outside journeymen's desire, to begin construction.

Compounding the problem for the UCC was not just that Chicago was an attractive place to which carpenters would travel on their own for work, but that the CBA, after the strike began, advertised for outside carpenters, and in many cases, escorted them into the city. CBA president, William Goldie commented: "If we decide not to recognize the union we must advertise for men. I am informed that carpenters in Albany, Buffalo, Syracuse, and Detroit are only waiting for a call to come here."[45] Such "calls," whether issued by the CBA or another city's builders' association, directed the migratory traffic of carpenters but were often made under false pretenses (of readily available employment or higher than normal wages, for example) in order to attract a surplus of carpenters to a particular place where union militancy was high.

Well aware of these threats, the UCC attempted to secure the city from nonunion and outside carpenters. This was not only a means to win the strike but an end of the work stoppage as well. By forcing the CBA to hire only carpenters from the Chicago unions, the UCC could institutionalize a geographically bound monopoly over the labor market. The union exercised a two-pronged strategy to reach these ends. On the one hand, the UCC attempted to prevent carpenters from entering Chicago. On the other, its members picketed those carpenters who did manage to get into the city and those nonunion men already in Chicago who tried to work during the strike.

The carpenters' thick security system served to halt nearly all construction in the city. Most of the remaining nonunion carpenters joined one of the UCC's locals. Contractors began calculating their losses, as it seemed that many jobs would not be completed by the end of the summer, even if work did resume.

Yet on one patch of land on the southside of Chicago, "the sound of the hammer and the swish of the saw" could be readily heard. Chicago's Players League club desperately wanted to finish construction of its ballpark before the season opened in May. On just the second day of the strike, it sent a crew of nonunion carpenters to the site. But soon after the crew arrived, an organizing committee approached the men and convinced them to stop working and join the union. Less than a week later, a new, smaller group of men went to work on the ballpark, some constructing the grandstand and others sodding the field. Probably misinformed by their contractor that the union approved of their presence, the carpenters actually "raised a flurry at the headquarters of Union No. 28 by asking for their $5 a week which they said had been promised them."[46] The local, of course, refused to pay them, and after a long argument, the carpenters joined the union.

Players League secretary Frank Brunell pleaded with the union to allow construction to continue. He promised to hire a new contractor, use only union carpenters, and pay them the requested wage. Not surprisingly, since the strike was citywide, the UCC refused his demands. Brunell insisted, then, that the club would finish construction with or without union carpenters.[47]

On April 18 the club arranged for a group of forty carpenters to reach the city by rail from the northwestern entrance to Chicago, but they were stopped by picketers and unable to enter the city.[48] A crew of twenty-five carpenters did manage to find the ballpark on April 21 and set to work on the upper tier of the grandstand. Soon after they began work, however, hundreds of UCC carpenters marched to the ballpark in protest. Surrounding the strikebreakers, the union carpenters threatened bodily harm if they did not leave the worksite at once. They left, but not before Reynolds, the contractor, had called for police protection. As soon as the police showed up, however, the bricklayers, who had been working all along under a favorable agreement their union had already reached with contractors, walked off the job as well. As part of their arbitration agreement, the bricklayers would work through carpenters' strikes but not when police protection was called for strikebreakers.

In the end the Players League managed to finish construction in bits and pieces before the season began. The carpenters ended up winning (albeit nearly one year later) recognition of their union, an eight-hour working day, and a pay raise. The Players League's failure to abide by the union's demands may have been driven by local circumstances. After all, one of Chicago's chief backers was John Addison, a powerful contractor and architect within the city's building industry. While Addison's voice is noticeably absent from the club's negotiations with the UCC, it is well within the realm of possibility that he was calling some of the shots from behind the scenes. Addison also took a lead role in finding a location for the ballpark and in designing it. The team's new captain, Charles Comiskey, may have also had an opinion on the matter, as he had recently bought several properties in the city, on which he was planning to build houses.[49]

But like the situation in Boston, Chicago's treatment of its carpenters points to larger issues. Although there would have been benefits to serving the UCC's needs (namely, its members may have been more supportive of the team once the season started), the costs of, one, paying carpenters at the union rate and, two, not finishing the ballpark in time for the season to start were greater. With the National League breathing down its neck, ready to go on the other side of town, and salary costs spiraling nearly out of control, the Chicago PL club faced considerable pressure to construct its ballpark as efficiently as possible. In other words, without the ability or desire to contain the salaries of the players, it had a greater need to contain the wages of the men who built the ballparks in which the players would play.

While Boston and Chicago appear to be the only cities where the Players League ran into difficulties with its workers, it does not mean that these pressures were felt any less by the other clubs.

Other Labor Struggles of the Players League

Another way the Players League saved money was through its ball supplier. Five manufacturers competed for the opportunity to be the league's exclusive purveyor of baseballs, including two companies owned by Players League stockholders.[50] Nothing is known about the actual people who produced the league's official, Keefe & Becannon ball (they also made bats, gloves, and uniforms). But if the state of industrial manufacturing more generally is any clue, it is safe to presume that the Players League saved money by relying on the skill degradation and exploitation of the ball manufacturer's labor. Moreover, the exclusive licensing of products that were associated with professional baseball was, and is now more than ever, a surefire way to create revenue for both the manufacturer and the league.

Individual clubs sold contracts for the exclusive right to sell products within the ballpark or items that somehow related to the game. When the Players League met in Cleveland in March 1890, "the meeting room was filled toward the close of the session with agents of printing companies, who wanted to sell their wares," according to the *New York Clipper*.[51] Boston sold the right to sell scorecards in Congress Street Grounds to A. Bronson Cooper for $40 per game.[52] "In consideration of this exclusive right," Cooper also agreed to "assign . . . to the Boston Base Ball Club his contracts for advertising on the score cards."[53] John Patterson wrote to Boston treasurer Frederick Long on December 2, 1889 (two days before the league was formally announced), asking for the privilege of selling "Brotherhood League Base Ball Tickets at [his] store #10 School St., for the season of '90."[54] It is not evident whether the club granted Patterson the right, but it is easy to understand why he would apply for such a task. In his case the sale of baseball tickets would facilitate the sale of cigars. Asher Hyneman and Charles Bryant paid $650 for the right to sell "cigars, cigarettes, tobacco, fruit and refreshments" within Boston's Congress Street Grounds.[55]

The labor that went into the production of these ancillary products, and any sort of labor struggles therein, is beyond the scope of this research and the contents of the available archives. But it would not be too difficult to garner a generalized picture of the social conditions beneath these vendors' contracts. That exploitative social relations governed the production of Keefe's equipment, Hyneman and Bryant's concessions, Cooper's scorecards, and Patterson's cigars is a reasonable conclusion, based on what is already known about nineteenth-century garment manufacturing, cigar making, printing, and fruit harvesting. Through the sale of these exclusive contracts, the Players League stood to receive a portion of the profits produced by hundreds of additional workers.

Had this analysis of the Players League's labor struggles stopped after examining only those between the players and their erstwhile owners, it would have hidden a significant portion of the league's workforce. But by examining the economic incentives, social relations, and workers' struggles that compose and intersect the production of Players League baseball, one can see other social relations, other production processes, and other workers' struggles.

Indeed, in order to better understand how the baseball industry works economically and how so many workers work and struggle with it, it is analytically and politically necessary to study the multiple, intersecting, and sometimes antagonistic social and economic relations of an organization like the Players League, not just those apparent on the commodity's surface.

6

THE 1890 PLAYERS LEAGUE

Opening Day

Boston's Congress Street Grounds was packed beyond capacity on the afternoon of April 19, the opening day of the Players League's 1890 season. Every chair on both decks of the grandstand was occupied; the bleaching boards down the right and left field lines were full; horse-drawn carriages crowded the outer edges of center field, where the fence had yet to be completed. American flags and red, white, and blue bunting adorned the ballpark. The men in the audience wore dark suits and top hats; the women wore light-colored, full-length dresses. Young boys and grown men climbed to the tops of telegraph poles overlooking the field. Some took refuge on the roof of the adjacent firehouse, but they were soon doused in water by the engineer's hose. Another group of men sat on top of a few nearby train cars despite the fact that the switch engine moved them back and forth, in and out of the depot, throughout the day. From the upper rows of the grandstand, spectators could see Boston Harbor. The sun was bright, the sky was clear, and the air was brisk. It was a great day for baseball.

Just before three o'clock, Reeves's American Band marched into the grounds from left field. Following the Providence-based band and its lively tunes written specifically for the occasion were John Ward and his Brooklyn teammates and Mike "King" Kelly and his Boston club.[1] The Brooklyns were dressed in their visiting grays with blue belts and stockings; Boston wore white suits with red belts and stockings. Three

Fig. 6. Boston's Congress Street Grounds. Courtesy of Boston Public Library.

"tally-hos" of friends and luminaries brought up the rear. The cheering of the crowd nearly drowned out the rhythm and melody of the band. When the players and their entourage reached second base, they posed for a photograph. Then the procession continued toward the grandstand, and the band broke into an already popular number written for the home team's captain, titled, "Slide, Kelly, Slide!" As the band played the accompaniment, the crowd sung the chorus, "Slide, Kelly slide! Your running's a disgrace! Slide, Kelly, slide! Stay there, hold your base! If someone doesn't steal you, And your batting doesn't fail you, They'll take you to Australia! Slide, Kelly, slide!"[2]

Even the umpires were caught up in the excitement of the day. When former National League umpiring veteran John Gaffney and rookie Ross Barnes walked onto the field, clad in their perfectly pressed blue suits, the crowd broke into applause.[3] At 3:38 Gaffney called play, and the season was under way. Hardy Richardson led off for Boston (the home team, in most cases, still batted first in 1890). After working the count to three balls and one strike, Richardson sent a scorching line drive toward the left side of the diamond. It was sure to be a hit if not for the quick hands and well-timed leap of the shortstop, John Ward, who caught the ball right out of the air. Despite the setback for their beloved Bostons, the home crowd showered Ward with "liberal applause."[4] Harry Stovey was the next batter. He drove the second pitch from Brooklyn "twirler" George Van Haltren, over the left-field fence for a home run. In the top of the third inning with Stovey now on second base and the score still 1–0, Kelly hit the ball well over the center fielder's head and into the crowd of carriages, sending one overweight man running for safety. Stovey scored easily, and Kelly reached third, standing. Meanwhile, Boston pitcher Matt Kilroy held the Brooklyn batters to no hits through the first five innings.

The score remained 2–0 in favor of Boston until the ninth, when the home team added another run in the top half of the inning on a sacrifice bunt by Joe Quinn. "It was a pretty piece of work on Quinn's part and the proper way to win games," wrote the *Boston Daily Globe*.[5] The run seemed all the more important after Brooklyn put two runners on base in the bottom half of the ninth inning. There were two outs when the veteran outfielder Emmit Seery stepped to the plate. Fatigued from a full day of work, Kilroy hung a curveball, which Seery hammered into left field. Hardy Richardson raced back to the fence to catch it, but the ball landed just above his outstretched left arm. Luckily for Boston, however, the carpenters had built the fence "about six inches too high," and the ball bounced back into play.[6] Two runs scored, but Seery was held to a double. The next batter hit a sharp groundball to Billy Nash at third base. Nash scooped up the grounder and fired the ball to first, where Dan Brouthers "hung on to it like a burr to a dress coat."[7] And with that Boston was the winner, 3–2.

After the fans rushed the field, reveling in the opening-day win, the backers and the players celebrated a victory of another sort. Between 8,000 and 10,000 people passed through the turnstiles of Congress Street Grounds that afternoon.[8] On the same day only 3,800 people saw the NL's Boston and Brooklyn clubs compete at the nearby South End Grounds.[9] "After the gate money had been counted," the *Globe* wrote, "the Only Kelly publicly declared that the Congress street experiment in self-government is not a failure while the Napoleonic Ward announced unhesitatingly that the people reigned and the brotherhood still lived."[10]

Boston was not alone among the Players League clubs in enjoying opening-day success: 8,500 people attended the home opener of Pittsburgh's Players League team against Chicago, in which the visitors won by a score of 10-2, while only 950 saw the National League Pittsburgh club beat Cleveland 3-2.[11] A total of 11,606 people bought tickets for the Players League's first four games at Pittsburgh's Exposition Park; only 1,697 paid to see the National League in the city's Recreation Park.[12]

The dismal showing in the Pittsburgh NL park was due in part to an AFL boycott. The AFL had ordered all union men to boycott the Pittsburgh NL park, not out of an allegiance to the Players League (though it did support them), but specifically because the older club had hired the Great Western Band, a musical group that had fallen out of favor with the AFL and joined the Knights of Labor.[13] The city's Musical Protective Union refused to recognize the Great Western Band as a union band and called on all the unions of the city to boycott the National League.[14] The boycott may have accounted for the relatively miniscule crowd at the NL's Recreation Park, but the abundance of people at Exposition Park cannot be separated from the widespread contention that the Players League provided a better product. Indeed, months before the Great Western Band had even left the AFL, a *Pittsburgh Commercial Gazette* poll found that, "out of 2,257 signatures on the base-ball question in this city, only 421 [were] in favor of the old [National] League club," a reflection, most likely, of the city's deep connection with organized labor.[15] Either way, despite the Opening Day loss, the *Pittsburg Press* praised the spectacular play of the city's Players League club: "Old man Galvin's slick throw out of clever Duffy at first; Hanlon's long run and remarkable catch in right center; Kuehne's and Beckley's slugging; together with the meritorious work of the other old and new players individually, show conclusively that our

Players League boys will not only put up good ball during the coming season, but will crowd the ambitious pennant winners."[16]

Both New York ballparks—Brotherhood Park and the Polo Grounds—flew pennants on opening day claiming that their club had won the championship the previous year.[17] But the legitimacy of the Players League's pennant was stronger than that of the National League, as only three players on the 1889 New York club remained on the 1890 NL club, while eleven men who won the championship in 1889 played for the PL team in 1890. Accordingly, more than twelve thousand people filled the stands on Opening Day at Brotherhood Park in New York, where the visiting Philadelphia club beat its hosts in a game that featured "brilliant fielding, stupid errors, heavy batting and darling base running."[18] Only 3,524 fans (2,004 of them with free tickets) saw the National League Philadelphia club shutout New York, 4-0, literally a stone's throw away.[19]

The following week Philadelphia hosted 17,119 people at its beautifully decorated Forepaugh Park in the home opener against Boston. The contest on the field, however, would go in favor of the team from New England, 9-6, as "the home players were either visibly affected by the cordiality of their reception, or from the superior strength of their opponents, as a certain degree of nervousness marred their work."[20]

After three consecutive rainouts Brooklyn hosted an estimated 6,240 fans at Eastern Park, where the "Twenty-third Regiment Band played many choice selections" and Judge Henry Howland made the opening address.[21] "The day was perfect," the New York Clipper declared, "and many of the ladies present were attired in bright spring costumes, lending an additional charm to the already attractive picture. The mammoth grand stand was tastefully decorated with flags and banners of all nations."[22] And the home team beat the visitors from across the East River by a score of 10-5.

Only in Chicago did the National League's Opening Day attendance rival that of the Players League, but even there it still did not surpass it. The National League contest, on April 29, between Cap Anson's

Fig. 7. Opening day fans at the New York ballparks. *Frank Leslie's Illustrated Newspaper*, May 3, 1890, courtesy of John Thorn.

Fig. 8. Opening day fans and concession hawks. *Frank Leslie's Illustrated Newspaper*, May 3, 1890, courtesy of John Thorn.

Chicago nine and Pittsburgh's hapless squad of men, attracted 2,365 spectators.[23] This number, however, should be read in light of the fact that the Chicago PL club was in Buffalo that day. And while a relatively meager number of fans, 2,625, showed up for the Players League's opener a week later, only 125 people passed through the turnstiles of the NL Chicago's West Side Grounds on that same day in conditions the *Chicago Daily Tribune* called "good weather for pneumonia, but bad for outdoor sport."[24] Nonetheless, Chicago's PL opener was the most poorly attended Opening Day match-up in the entire league. Even

Buffalo, where "cold and raw" weather also dampened the festivities, drew more fans—3,200—than did Chicago.[25] Friends and allies of Chicago's striking carpenters, who later that same day reached a partial settlement with some of the city's contractors, had perhaps not yet forgiven the Players League for breaking their strike just a month earlier.

At the end of the first week of play, Boston led the Players League with five wins and two losses, while the league as a whole led the National League in attendance by the estimated score of fifty thousand to thirty thousand.[26] And nearly half of the NL's total came from Cincinnati, where the Players League did not have a team.[27] The *New York Clipper* declared, "The attendance at the [Players League's] opening games far exceeded anything that even the most sanguine admirers of the organization dared to expect, which goes to show that the players are popular with the public and that they can look for a liberal share of patronage if they behave themselves, and at all times play the best game of ball they are capable of doing."[28]

Charles D. Blake, a popular songwriter from Boston, took advantage of the early success by publishing a new song, "Hurrah for the Brotherhood Boys":

Hurrah for the gallant lads who boldly struck for right!
The dauntless souls, like knights of old, who fought and wont the fight!
Mammon's greed, Oppression's power, they boldly now defy.
So cheer them to the echo lads, and fling your hats on high!

chorus:

Cheer them to the echo lads make a ringing noise,
Hurrah, hurrah, hurrah, hurrah for the gallant brotherhood boys.[29]

The Battle over Fans

While the various teams battled it out on the field, the real competition seemed to be over which league would lead in attendance. The league with the better attendance, it seemed, would prevail. The other would have to fold. While aggregate attendance may have marginally increased from 1889 to 1890, it became clear very quickly that there were still only enough baseball fans in each city to sustain one major league team. As National League president Nicholas Young predicted shortly after the season began, "Divided attendance means diminished gate receipts, and somebody must go to the wall."[30] Spalding agreed: "The two opposing leagues are waging a war of extermination. It cannot last. One of the two must give way.[31] The 1890 season, in other words, would end with the fall of either the Players League or the National League. The American Association, meanwhile, was on its last legs in either scenario.

The 1890 season suggests that there simply were not enough players of sufficient quality to sustain two major leagues. The location of Players League teams in National League cities, of course, exacerbated the problem. The 1890 season included seven cities with both a National League and a Players League franchise (Boston, New York, Brooklyn, Philadelphia, Pittsburgh, Cleveland, and Chicago). Brooklyn and Philadelphia also held American Association teams. Buffalo, for the Players League, and Cincinnati, for the National League, stood on their own. By choosing these cities, the PL directly challenged the "territorial rights" that the National League had institutionalized in 1876 as a means to create and protect its monopolies over the markets for baseball clubs. But the PL chose these cities as much out of necessity as from a sense of predatory competition. Like the National League the Players League needed to play in cities large enough to provide sufficient markets for its baseball games. But by destroying the NL's territorial rights, the PL also abdicated any such privileges for itself. Without an artificial monopoly imposed over the consumer market for professional baseball, the Players League had to compete with the National League for a limited number of paying customers and therefore an even more limited margin of profit. The reasoning for both leagues, it seemed, was that only through direct competition in these key cities could one or the other emerge as the sole purveyor of major league baseball. Competition, in other words, was a prerequisite for monopoly power.

The competition was made even more intense (and intentional) by the leagues' nearly identical schedules. The Players League put the finishing touches on its 140-game schedule in early March.[32] Then, as John Ward recalled, "A skeleton was given out so that the National League could avoid conflicting dates if it wished."[33] But instead the NL "went out of its way to conflict as often as possible."[34] Each of the seven shared cities featured both NL and PL games on the same days at virtually the same times. The New York PL club, for example, played only eight home games when the NL club was not playing at home as well. While Ward claimed that the Players League was not "inspired by a spirit of extermination," asserting, "We believe this country [is] big enough for all of us," he and the rest of the board of directors still did not change their schedule.[35] In fact only Albert Johnson wished to avoid conflicting schedules. "My associates disagreed with me," Johnson recalled of the preseason Players League meeting, "and we did not change our schedule."[36]

"As players and men," Ward explained, "we could only accept the issue and I believe that of all the stupid mistakes the magnates have made this conflict of dates will prove for them the most costly."[37] Whether or not the conflicting dates were part of its original plan (the chance that the schedules would have ended up identical had the PL *not* published its in advance seems extremely slim), the retention of its original schedule indicates the new league's willingness to engage in direct competition with its rival. And the identical schedules, as Ward's comments make clear, became a competition not just over the baseball industry but also over a sense of manliness. Despite his initial reluctance, Johnson agreed: "The National League people forced the fight, and now, rather than turn tail and run, they should take their medicine like men."[38] Tim Keefe was even more adamant about his position on the matter. "I feel so strongly about the success of our cause," he said, "that I would be eager to change the schedule right on to their dates if they make a single change. Why, bless you, we are not the weak side. We are the winners, we are the people."[39]

Nevertheless, the conflicting schedules did coincide with decreased ticket sales for each league relative to the National League's 1889 numbers. A month into the season, the Players League's Pittsburgh club, plagued by low attendance, petitioned the league to reschedule its games so that they would not conflict with the National League club of that city. But in a meeting on May 31 in New York, six of the eight clubs voted to keep the schedule as is.[40]

Given the nearly identical schedules, baseball fans in the PL and NL cities had to choose between one league or the other, or none at all. Several factors affected these choices, including the reputation of the players, the accommodations and accessibility of the ballparks, the weather, the perceived quality of play, and the extent to which the games mattered in the pennant race.

The biggest factor in drawing fans to the Players League's ballparks rather than those of the National League was the reputation of the players themselves. An overwhelming majority of the 1889 National League players played in the Players League in 1890. A fan of the 1889 National League pennant-winning New York Giants, for example, had no reason to watch the 1890 NL Giants, as most of the championship-winning team was now in the Players League. In fact, 80 of the 126 players who played at least ten games in the Players League in 1890 had played in the National League in 1889 (29 had been in the AA, and 17 came from minor or amateur leagues).[41] The 1890 National League included only 36 players who had played in the NL in 1889; 66 came from the minor or amateur leagues, and 34 were in the AA. Several more amateurs and minor leaguers appeared in just one or a handful of game for the National League, as the NL clubs tried and usually failed to find quality players to replace those who were not as good or as popular as their Players League counterparts. The National League was not without its superstars—11 of its players would later make the Hall of Fame (17 PL men would be inducted)—but at this point, the new league simply had more recognizable players than its rivals.

The ballparks in which these men played were also a factor in attracting fans. Once completed, the Players League's ballparks were, by all accounts, beautiful pieces of architecture and, in most cases, were regarded as more attractive and accommodating than the National League's venues.

The Brooklyn Players League's Eastern Park was designed by the celebrated Brooklyn architect Walter Montague Coots.[42] Measuring 432 feet in length, the horseshoe-shaped grandstand was "of Swiss design, with the front eaves so arranged as not to interfere with a perfect view of the diamond and field."[43] The park featured "a handsome ladies' parlor and toilet room" at the back of the grandstand behind home plate, fifty private boxes, and three cupolas atop the grandstand, the center one housing the directors' and reporters' boxes.[44] Costing nearly $45,000 to build, the grandstand seated 5,330 people in elegant folding chairs.[45] Similar to other ballparks of the era, several thousand additional spectators could watch the game from bleacher boards beyond the outfield fence and down the outfield foul lines. The *New York Clipper* editorialized in May 1890, while the finishing touches were being added, "The grand stand at the Brooklyn grounds of the Players League, when completed, will be the handsomest pavilion ever erected on any baseball grounds, and in point of comfortable arrangements, architectural beauty there is none that can approach it."[46]

Upon comparing New York's Brotherhood Park to the adjacent ballpark that housed the National League club, the *New York Clipper* declared, "From present appearances it is evident that the Players League Club [has] the most attractive grounds."[47] Furthermore, the *Clipper* later wrote, "It is a large, convenient and handsome structure. It will seat a great many people." And similar to Eastern Park, New York's Brotherhood Park featured a comfortable and accommodating press box, a feature certainly aimed at pleasing the ever-important sports media: "The choice part . . . is the section reserved for the newspaper men, which is the best arrangement yet offered a reportorial staff at any of the ball grounds in this country."[48] While the National League's New York park was referred to in 1890 as the Polo Grounds,

Fig. 9. Brooklyn's Eastern Park. Courtesy of John Thorn.

Fig. 10. New York's Brotherhood Park (later renamed the Polo Grounds)
in the background and Polo Grounds (also known as Manhattan
Field in the foreground). Courtesy of John Thorn.

it was Brotherhood Park that would later take on that name in its fourth and most famous iteration. It was on this same field, within the horseshoe-shaped, double-decked grandstand in the shadow of Coogan's Bluff, where Willie Mays would decades later play most of his Major League games.[49]

"Nothing but commendation and admiration could be heard" about Pittsburgh's Exposition Park when it opened on April 19, according to the *Pittsburg Press*.[50] Of the press box, which sat atop the grandstand, "even the erstwhile reporter of kicking proclivities failed to find any fault with his quarters, which are of a substantial and comfortable nature. Light, ventilation and location are all that could be desired."[51] Costing nearly $30,000 to build, the grandstand seated ten thousand spectators.[52]

John Addison, the president of the Chicago Players League club and the architect who designed the team's Brotherhood Park (also known as "South Side Grounds" and "White Stocking Park"), insisted that the new league's parks were more accommodating than those of the National League: "The National League has made no provision for the accommodation of the public, and has persisted in planting them on hard boards, in the sun. The Players League has sought to give to the public covered stands, with comfortable opera chairs, in place of the old bleachers."[53] While the PL ballparks were not the only ones with covered grandstands, nor were they without sun-drenched bleachers themselves, the *Chicago Daily Tribune* nonetheless reported, "The local brotherhood club can truly boast of one of the handsomest and most commodious parks in the United States."[54] Indeed, within the light green, covered grandstands, Chicago's Brotherhood Park featured a "ladies retiring room," in which, "there [was] a lady attendant and everything [would] be done for the comfort of the fair sex."[55] Private boxes behind home plate in the upper deck of the grandstand comfortably seated 100 people, while an additional 2,300 could sit in opera chairs.[56] Pavilions on the first- and third-base sides of the diamond held up to 5,000 fans, and an additional 5,000 seats were available, if necessary, on temporary, tiered benches.[57] Access to the park from downtown Chicago was considered "excellent," as "the State street cable road [ran] within a block of the park, the schedule time from Madison street being twenty five minutes."[58] Upon arriving at the corner of Thirty-Fifth Street and Wentworth Avenue, fans could enter the ballpark through four turnstiles, all on Thirty-Fifth Street, and then walk through "broad and commodious" passageways to their seats within grandstand or pavilions.[59]

Regardless of covered grandstands and lovely sightlines, miserable weather kept many fans away from both National League and Players League ballparks during the first two months of the season. Several games were postponed because of rain, and many others were beset by cold and wet conditions. Only 1,408 people showed up for a May 7 Players League game against Pittsburgh in Chicago, for example, as "the weather was raw and cold and made it very disagreeable for the spectators, as well as the players."[60] Two days later in Cincinnati, a National League game against Pittsburgh "was twice stopped on account of rain and the closing innings were played in mud ankle deep."[61] A May 15 Players League contest hosted by Brooklyn, against Chicago, drew only 400 people, as "rain had been falling for some hours previously."[62]

The most spectacular weather-related incident took place in Cleveland during a June 5 Players League match-up against Buffalo. Heavy rain forced the players from the field during the third inning. The rain gave way to hail, and a "wind storm of cyclonic dimensions began."[63] Then lightning struck the grandstand, sending electricity down to Buffalo's rookie catcher, Jocko Halligan, who had been leaning against a post. Halligan fell to the earth, knocked out. The accompanying clap of thunder and falling debris from the grandstand alarmed the crowd: "Women screamed, and some fainted, men yelled, and general pandemonium reigned."[64] Halligan was seriously hurt, confined to his bed for several weeks, and "his left arm [was] badly swollen."[65]

The weather negatively affected the finances of both clubs, as traveling expenses still accrued when games were postponed, and attendance was down when games were played in the cold or damp conditions. Nonetheless, Players League secretary Frank Brunell claimed during the first week of June that the league was in good shape: "Our clubs in Buffalo, Cleveland and Pittsburg, despite bad weather, are ahead of their expenses up to date. All their players have been paid up to June 1. Brooklyn has lost some money, but its players received their salaries May 31 in my presence."[66]

These claims may have been true, and the PL may have fared better than the NL during the rain-soaked months, but the bad weather undoubtedly decreased both leagues' attendance and revenue.

When the rain finally did stop and summer temperatures arrived, in mid- to late June, the quality of play improved and attendance increased, particularly in the Players League. For the most part the players lived up to their reputation, putting together dazzling performances and nail-biting action. The June 21 Saturday-afternoon game against Brooklyn at Chicago's Brotherhood Park, for example, featured "the greatest battle between pitchers ever seen in this city," according to the *Brooklyn Daily Eagle*.[67] Silver "Cannonball Charley" King pitched a no-hitter for Chicago but nonetheless lost the game 1–0. This was the first time in baseball history that a team had won a game without getting a hit. Gus Weyhing, who "was in grand form," gave up four hits and was credited with the win.[68] The only run was set up by a two-base error by the Chicago shortstop, Dell Darling, on a groundball by George Van Haltren. The runner advanced to third on a bunt by Paul Cook. In what looked like the game's first hit, Lou Bierbauer drilled a ball to right field, but "little [Hugh] Duffy by a marvelous stop and magnificent throw retired him at first."[69] The run scored. Although not getting any hits, the Brooklyn team "played a grand all round game, running bases well and showing lots of ginger."[70] The *New York Clipper* described the no-hitter-loss as "one of the most remarkable games in the annals of baseball," and the *Chicago Daily Tribune* predicted that the sizable crowd of 4,021 fans "augured well for the future, as it showed that the people [had] commenced to take an old-time interest in the game."[71] Two days later King pitched eight innings in the second game of a doubleheader against Brooklyn and gave up just two runs. He would go on to win thirty games, strike out 185 batters, and post a 2.69 earned run average, the lowest in the league. He also led the league in shutouts, games started, and, although it was not calculated at the time, opponent's batting average.[72] King's teammate Mark Baldwin also pitched well in 1890, winning a league-leading thirty-three games while giving up just 3.35 earned runs per nine innings pitched, fourth best in the league. Tim Keefe went 17 and 11 with a 3.38 ERA, but he broke the top of his forefinger in late August, thus making him unavailable for New York during the pennant race.[73] Just five feet seven and 140 pounds, lefthander Bill Daley won eighteen games and lost just seven for his Boston club.[74]

The Players League also featured some fine defensive play. King's excellent pitching throughout the 1890 season, for example, was supported by the outstanding fielding of first baseman Charles Comiskey. "The phenomenal first base playing of Comiskey in the Chicago-Boston game June 26, at Chicago," wrote Tim Murnan of the *Boston Globe,* "was the best the writer had the pleasure of witnessing."[75]

In Pittsburgh Players League centerfielder Ned Hanlon "made one of the grandest running catches seen in this city this season—a high fly from Richardson's bat, taken in deep left centre field" in a 4-2 loss against New York at Exposition Park on June 28.[76]

Two days later in the same ballpark, Boston turned a triple play. With runners on first and second and no outs, Ned Hanlon popped a fly ball to shallow right, which looked as though it would fall safely. Both runners started running, but Quinn, "after a hard run, captured the ball and threw to Kelly, who covered second, and he threw to Brouthers" at first for the third out.[77]

Boston's defense provided spectacular plays even while the weather was still cold and wet. During a June 4 contest at Brotherhood Park in New York, Boston leftfielder Hardy Richardson "made several brilliant running catches. The first catch was with the left hand while in full chase after a long hit by [Roger] Connor, the second one was from [Jim] O'Rourke's bat. Either hit was good for a home run."[78] It was not just Richardson who was capable of making "brilliant" catches. "The

Boston Club of the Players League, may have the best outfielders in the profession," one newspaper posited.[79]

Great defense was often accompanied by the risk of, or in spite of, physical injuries. Pittsburgh's second baseman, William "Yank" Robinson, for example, was hit in the head by a pitch early in his June 11 game against Chicago. He stayed in the game, and despite the probable concussion, his subsequent "fielding was exceptionally brilliant."[80] Later in the game he took a ground ball in the face, which "injured him severely" but did not prevent him from finishing the game.[81]

These defensive spectacles, along with the good pitching of King, Baldwin, Keefe, and Daley, are even more remarkable when one considers the relatively high number of runs scored by the Players League in 1890. Early on in the season, sportswriters and pitchers alike speculated that Keefe & Buchanan's official Players League ball was "livelier" than Spalding's National League ball, thus resulting in enhanced offensive performances for the new league.[82]

Players League secretary Frank Brunell countered, "The reason for the larger scores in our championship games is not that our playing ball is livelier, but on account of the hard hitting being done by the batsmen of our teams."[83] But, Brunell added, "the extra eighteen inches in the pitching distance has made it necessary for [pitchers] to almost learn over again the effect of their curve balls, and our larger grounds have increased the value of long hits as factors in runs."[84] Whatever the cause the Players League did score more runs in 1890 than the National League. By the end of the season, the PL averaged 6.88 runs per game, while the NL scored only 5.58 runs per game (the National League had averaged 5.84 runs per game the previous season).[85] The Players League batted .274, with a .351 on-base percentage and a .358 slugging average.[86] The National League's 1890 numbers, in contrast, were .254, .329, and .342.[87] And while it may never be known whether Keefe & Buchanan had purposely "enlivened" the ball, the distance between the pitcher's box and home plate was, according to Brunell, "increased to reduce the number of small score games, in answer to a public demand."[88] These measures fall in line with baseball's long history of altering the game in favor of hitting when the need for popularity outweighed the need to reduce player salaries.

Much of this offense came in the form of base hits and singles stretched into doubles and triples. Twenty-eight players hit ten or more triples, for instance. Jake Beckley, Pittsburgh's twenty-two-year-old first baseman, slugged twenty-two triples to lead the league. Home runs were still relatively rare (and most were of the inside-the-park variety rather than over the relatively distant fences); only five Players League batters hit ten or more home runs, with New York's hefty first baseman, Roger Connor, leading the league at fourteen. Boston's veteran third baseman, Hardy Richardson, hit home runs in five consecutive games in early July. He would go on to hit thirteen, a career high for him, and a number that probably would have been higher had he not contracted a temporarily debilitating case of malaria shortly after his streak.[89]

Whether the Players League's star-studded rosters and elevated quality of play would bring more fans into its ballparks than those of the National League was put to the ultimate test on Independence Day. After opening day the biggest opportunity for fan support was the annual Independence Day doubleheaders. The Players League again led the day. According to the *New York Clipper*, 45,700 fans attended the Players League's double-admission doubleheaders, while only 32,244 people saw the National League's games.[90] Like most attendance figures in 1890, these numbers most likely were inflated, but neither league disputed the proportions.

Unlike on opening day, when it barely outdrew its National League counterpart, Chicago's PL team led both leagues in attendance on the Fourth of July: 8,700 people attended the Players League's morning game against New York, and 14,823 raucous fans watched the afternoon contest.[91] The grandstands were completely full, and several thousand fans lined the field, trampling over "the gaudy flower beds near the catcher's position" to get a better view of the action.[92] The fans jeered and threw firecrackers at police officers who tried to keep spectators away from the field. Later in the game someone set off a firecracker behind Chicago infielder Dell Darling while he was trying to make a play at first. Others blew horns "in a vigorous and unseemly fashion" throughout the contest.[93] And despite the chaos, the games were good—closely contested and well played. Chicago won the first leg, 3–1, behind the excellent pitching of Silver King, and the second, 4–2, after scoring the go-ahead runs in the top of the eleventh inning. With the sweep and an additional win over New York the following day, Chicago was just a half game behind Boston in the win-loss columns.

Cincinnati was leading the National League following the midseason holiday, with Brooklyn, Philadelphia, and Boston not too far behind. Pittsburgh's National League club, however, had won only sixteen games by July 7 and lost forty-six, for an abysmal .238 winning percentage. Cleveland had won just nineteen games. At the end of the month, the club's manager, Gus Schmelz, resigned.[94] Both clubs were suffering at the box office.

Pittsburgh's troubles began shortly after the season started. An April 23 game drew only 162 people, and "even this small crowd was disgusted by the burlesque game the Pittsburg and Cleveland clubs played," wrote the *Boston Daily Globe*. [95] "The ball was wet and hard to handle, and the men played as though they cared nothing about the game."[96] Pittsburgh won by a score of 20–12 in a game described by the *Pittsburg Press* as "largely of the nature of a farce" and by the *New York Clipper* as "long drawn and tiresome."[97] The club that would later be called the Pirates hit five opposing batters in the game, a team record that, as of September 2015, still stands.[98] Shortly after the game the club's owner threatened to move the team to Indianapolis, where the Players League did not have a club.[99]

Two weeks later the Jenny estate, which owned the land on which the club played, sued the team for $3,000 in past-due rent from the previous six months. The estate threatened to buy the club if the payment was not made within thirty days. Upon finally paying the rent, Pittsburgh's president, William Nimick, claimed, "In the worry of the past few months, the matter has been neglected. I had the check in my possession, but forgot to sign it."[100] Nimick apparently forgot to sign his rent checks again, as the Jenny Estate sought $1,400 in unpaid rent on July 4. The club paid its rent on July 7.[101]

Nevertheless, the club was losing and not drawing any fans to its games. The *Boston Herald* declared, "The utter collapse of Pittsburg as a valuable member of the National League was fully proven June 26, when only a few over a hundred persons assembled to witness the second game of the series between the Pittsburgs and Bostons."[102]

As the team's regular cast of characters was not getting the job done, Pittsburgh's management began signing amateurs and minor leaguers to step in for a game or more. A June 19 doubleheader against Cleveland featured two rookie pitchers. In the first game a local amateur, Billy Gumbert, started for Pittsburgh. "He did excellent work," wrote the *New York Clipper*, "holding the visitors down to three scattering hits" and getting the win, 9–2.[103] The *Pittsburg Press* reported, "Gumbert, a local player who won much fame with the East End Athletics, did yeoman service for the 'Allies' in the first game, and will probably be signed."[104] The Pittsburgh National League club indeed went on to sign Gumbert, who pitched nine more games in 1890 and posted a 5.22 ERA and a 4–6 win-loss record.[105] But his baseball career had already reached its apex, as Gumbert would go on to pitch only eight additional professional baseball games after the 1890 season, his final outing, in 1893 with Louisville, ending before he could get three men out in the first inning.[106] Good enough for the National League in 1890, Gumbert was not up to par for major league pitching in any other season.

In the second game of the same doubleheader, Pittsburgh put a five-foot-eight, eighteen-year-old named George Ziegler on the mound for the home team. Ziegler, a Jewish pitcher from Chicago, had already played semiprofessional baseball with Sacramento and Wheeling in 1889 and again with the same clubs during the spring of 1890.[107] Paid fifty dollars for the game, Ziegler "suffered considerably at the hands of the visitors" in his major league debut, giving up seven runs in five innings.[108] Ziegler would never pitch in the major leagues again. But he would continue to play baseball, pitching for Olean in the New York Pennsylvania League in 1891; Mansfield in the Ohio-Michigan League in 1893; Staunton/Newport News-Hampton, Lynchburg, and then back to Staunton/Newport News-Hampton, all of the Virginia League in 1894; St. Joseph (Missouri) of the Western Association in 1895; and finally Austin of the Texas Association in 1896.[109] Ziegler's career of crisscrossing the country in search of employment with any ball club that would pay him was typical of many nineteenth- and early twentieth-century marginal baseball players. But George Ziegler, who may have been quickly forgotten by his Pittsburgh teammates and has been barely noticed by baseball historians, should be seen as pathbreaking. His five innings in Pittsburgh in 1890 marked the first ever appearance by a Jewish pitcher in the history of Major League Baseball.[110]

On the one hand, Ziegler's appearance, which was one among many trials given by National League clubs to minor and amateur league players in 1890 (Pittsburgh alone used nineteen players for eight games or less), appeared to signal a certain desperation to find suitable talent.[111] Having lost most of their men to the Players League, the National League teams struggled to fill their rosters with major-league-caliber players. On the other hand, these sorts of moves may have reflected a salary dump, whereby clubs would replace salaried players with cheaper temporary signings. Indeed, Cincinnati released veteran catcher Clarence Baldwin and outfielder Hugh Nicol in late July "in order to cut down expenses," according to the *New York Clipper*.[112] When Pittsburgh's managing director, J. Palmer O'Neill, resigned in late July (he would remain affiliated with the club), he seemed to indicate that he was hired precisely in order to reduce salaries: "I resigned because my work is really finished. . . . Now the fight is virtually over, and, as I have brought the team from a big losing venture to a place where it is self supporting I feel perfectly satisfied and turn it over to [club president] Nimick in good shape."[113] The *Clipper* further explained, "O'Neill took the team on May 14, when a month's salaries were due, and the team was playing very poor ball. The salary list was then about $4,000. Since then the salary list has been reduced to about half what it was, and the club is nearly paying its own way."[114] Indeed, the club released veteran second baseman, Fred Dunlap the day after O'Neill took over.[115] Rookie infielder Henry Youngman was the next to go, receiving his release papers on June 2.[116] Later that summer Pittsburgh traded star outfielder (and ordained Presbyterian minister) Billy Sunday for two rookies and some cash on August 22.[117] The club may have reduced its expenses by hiring cheap, relatively unskilled labor, but these players could barely win a game. Between July 4 and October 3, when the season ended, Pittsburgh lost 72 games and won only 7. It finished the season with 23 wins and 113 losses, the second worst record in Major League Baseball history.[118] Fans had virtually stopped coming to Pittsburgh's Recreation Park by the end of July, forcing the team to move many of its remaining home games to its opponents' cities or to neutral locations, including Wheeling, West Virginia, and Canton, Ohio.[119] It would take more than George Ziegler and Billy Gumbert to bring fans back to Pittsburgh's National League games.

Not all of the National League's midseason signings were busts. Denton Young, a farmhand from outside Gilmore, Ohio, had been lighting up the Inter-State League in 1890, striking out 201 batters while walking only 33 for an otherwise hapless Canton, Ohio, club. Nicknamed "Cyclone" (later shortened to "Cy") for his blazing fastballs, Young pitched a no-hitter on July 24 in McKeesport, striking out 18 and walking none. "Cash" Miller, a scout for Cleveland's struggling National League club, who had already had his eye on the twenty-three-year-old right-hander, shortly thereafter bought the young pitcher's contract from Canton for $300. As long as his services were needed, Young would be paid $75 per month for the next two months, a prorated salary of $450 per year, an abysmally low figure even for the penny-pinching National League.[120] On August 6, 1890, Cy Young made his major league debut during the first game of a doubleheader against Cap Anson's Chicago club. Having read about "the Cyclone" in the papers, about two thousand excited fans turned up at League Park on a warm Wednesday morning in Cleveland.[121] In spite of the hype for Young, Anson commented before the game that Young was "just another big farmer."[122] Young would relish for the rest of his life the vindication he felt after beating Chicago that day by a score of 8–1.[123] Anson went 0 for 4, as Young gave up just three hits and no earned runs.[124] After the game Anson reportedly offered Cleveland's owner $1,000 for Young's contract, a proposal that was quickly declined.[125] A year later, when Cy Young was a very good but still not yet elite pitcher, Anson declared, "If I had Young I'd win the championship in a walk."[126]

The Players League's failure to sign Young appeared to be the result of the league's ideological stance against buying and selling players. After all, it was John Ward's excoriation against the "sort of speculation in live stock, by which [baseball players] are bought, sold, and transferred like so many sheep" that gave rise to the Brotherhood of Professional Base Ball Players and the Players League in the first place.[127] About a month after Young's debut, PL Chicago manager, Charles Comiskey, was accused of attempting to sign two American Association players before their 1890 contracts expired. In line with Ward's comments made a few years earlier, Comiskey called the rumor "an infamous falsehood" and asserted, "I would never sign a man who has broken his contract."[128] Buying Young's contract from Canton, as Cleveland's National League club had done, would have placed the Players League in a state of hypocrisy, though it is doubtful that Young minded the sale. But insofar as a Players League club could have at least signed Young before the season started, his absence from the Players League may also just have been the luck of the draw. There were scores of young amateur and semiprofessional baseball players who were regarded by one scout or another to be the fastest, strongest, or heaviest-swinging they had ever seen. The vast majority of these players never excelled in the major leagues. There was, and still is, simply no guarantee that a highly touted prospect will meet expectations. In fact they rarely do. The National League (and after 1901, the American League) merely lucked out that this young man ended up becoming one of the greatest pitchers ever to pick up a baseball.

The Players League was generally drawing more fans to its games than was the National League. But some of the PL teams were, in fact, struggling by mid-July. Chief among them were Philadelphia and Buffalo. Neither club was able to pay its bills, including at times the players' salaries, and both were marred by internal disputes. Resembling many of the National League clubs, Buffalo was signing various amateurs and minor leaguers to take the field for its last place club. John Buckley, a twenty-year-old pitcher from Marlborough, Massachusetts, who had been playing for Joliet of the barely professional Illinois-Iowa league, signed with Buffalo on July 15 to pitch against Boston. He gave up seven earned runs in a 12–9 victory. He would pitch in three more games with Buffalo that year but then never pitched in the majors again. The next day Dan Cotter, a pitcher without any professional experience at all, was sent to the pitchers' box for Buffalo. He gave up nineteen runs, six walks, and twenty hits in nine innings of work, as the team lost to Boston, 19–0. Cotter played for the Lewiston, Maine, team of the New England League in 1892 but otherwise never saw professional action again.

In response to the situation, the Players League's Board of Directors held a meeting on July 17 in Philadelphia. The first order of business was to grant $2,500 to each of the league's clubs for "campaign purposes."[129] An "emergency committee," composed of Buffalo director Moses Shire, Cleveland backer Albert Johnson, and league secretary Frank Brunell, was formed to address the Buffalo situation. The committee concluded that the team should acquire a new infielder, outfielder, and two pitchers.[130] Later that month, by means that may have violated the league's policy regarding the buying and selling of players, Buffalo acquired pitcher Bert Cunningham from Philadelphia and right fielder and first baseman Larry Twitchell from Cleveland. First baseman Jay Faatz was appointed captain. And C. R. Fitzgerald, "the unpopular business manager, [was] retired, and the players [were] happy."[131]

But "the principal reason why this special meeting was called," one of the directors said, "was to settle the trouble in the Philadelphia club."[132] Despite having several top-quality players, Philadelphia was losing money. According to an anonymous PL director, "The stockholders were fighting each other, and this has had a bad effect upon the team as well as upon the attendance. The men behind the club evidently did not trust each other, and, by not being able to agree upon anything, bills were left unpaid, though there was plenty of money in the treasury to meet all outstanding debts."[133] To settle the disputes J. E. and G. W. Wagner bought 148 of the club's 200 shares.[134] The Wagner brothers, according to the same anonymous director, "will, in the future, run [the club] on business principles. [They] will promptly pay any outstanding bills, and the club is now in a healthy financial condition. There will be no more cliques and factions among stockholders. The players now know who controls the club. Their salaries will be paid promptly, and, knowing who is boss, they will no longer be annoyed by conflicting orders."[135] Although the Philadelphia shakeup did, indeed, improve the club's financial situation, the move to operate under "business principles," where players would know "who is boss," was, along with Buffalo's endeavors, the first crack in the Players League's ideological facade.

Nevertheless, shortly after the club was reorganized, Philadelphia's "playing was in a striking contrast with that of the past month or so, and at no period of the season ha[d] they put so much 'ginger' in their work. In the field, they were especially active in going for any ball within reach. At the bat they sacrificed as never did before, and on the bases they were as lively as kittens."[136]

As the summer moved on, a race for the Players League pennant was beginning to take shape. By the July 4 doubleheaders, Brooklyn had won thirty-two games and lost thirty. But the team proceeded to win eleven in a row between July 9 and July 21, going 18 and 10 for the month. Boston, winning thirteen of their twenty-two games in July, was still leading the league but now only by three games. Chicago cooled off some during the month, winning fourteen and losing fourteen, dropping them to third place. While Philadelphia, despite its improved play, found itself mired in fourth.

Brooklyn continued to win in August. Team captain John Ward led the charge, putting together several flawless games in the field and productive appearances at the plate. He was backed by five-foot-eight, 140-pound second baseman Lou Bierbauer, who was on his way to finishing the season with a .306 batting average, .350 on base percentage, and .431 slugging average, all career bests.[137] His defense, too, was routinely praised in the newspapers: "Remarkable stops were made by Ward [and] Bierbauer," wrote the *New York Clipper*, of an August 7 performance against Philadelphia.[138] The durable Gus Weyhing continued to pitch well, nearing the top of the leader boards in wins, strikeouts, and innings pitched.

Brooklyn swept Philadelphia in a three-game series at Eastern Park before boarding the train to Boston for a three-game series against the league leaders. Brooklyn won the first game, on August 9, by a score of 6–2, putting it just a game and a half out of first place. Ward went three for five with two runs and made six assists and no errors. In the following game, played after Sunday's off day, Ward scored his team's only run and was one of two Brooklyn batters to get a hit. But down 5–1 Ward may have been pressing too hard, for after he made a base hit in the eighth, "he was then put out in trying to steal second."[139] Boston won 7–1 behind the nearly flawless pitching of Bill Daley; timely hitting by Quinn, Brouthers, and Richardson; and the aggressive base running of Mike Kelly. During the rubber match the following day, Charles Radbourn "pitched superbly" for Boston, giving up seven hits, a walk, and four runs, none of which were earned.[140] "Weyhing's pitching" similarly "proved puzzling to the home team, and for seven innings they made only one safe hit off him."[141] Boston put together a two-out rally in the eighth, with consecutive singles by Brown, Stovey, and Kelly, the third of which drove Brown home. Dan Brouthers, the brawny, future Hall of Famer first baseman, then sent a long drive to center, "which looked good for three bases" and certainly capable of tying the game, "but Andrews made a phenomenal catch," and the threat was over.[142] Shut down in the ninth, Boston lost 4–1. Brooklyn was, again, a game and a half out of first place.

For the rest of August, both teams continued to win, Boston taking twelve of the next seventeen games, Brooklyn eleven of fifteen. But Chicago and New York began to surge as well. Comiskey's men won eight out of ten games between August 9 and 18, putting Chicago in second place, two and a half games behind Boston and a half game ahead of Brooklyn.[143] New York ignited its own hot streak, taking eighteen of twenty-one games between August 12 and September 4.[144] By then Chicago had already started to swoon, having lost eleven of twelve games between August 19 and the 29.[145] On September 4, with a month left to play, Boston remained in first place, but now New York was in second, three and a half games behind; Brooklyn was in third, four games out of first place; and Chicago had already fallen out of contention, at eleven and a half games back from Boston, tied with Philadelphia for fourth place.[146] Pittsburgh, Cleveland, and Buffalo, meanwhile, had effectively been eliminated from the pennant race by the Fourth of July.

It looked as though an exciting September was in store for the Players League. But Boston proved too good for its competition. Led by the hot bats of Harry Stovey and Dan Brouthers, the pitching of Bill Daley and Charlie Radbourn, and the captainship of Mike Kelly, Boston won eight of its next ten games, clinching the pennant with a week and a half to go on September 24. Brooklyn put up a valiant effort, winning six of eleven during that stretch, while New York dropped eight and won just three. Boston was the champion of the Players League.

The next week, an even bigger victory took place. At 8:00 p.m. on October 4, just a few hours after the final out of the 1890 season was recorded, a group of Players League officials purchased the National League's Cincinnati franchise. Albert Johnson, Edward Talcott, John Ward, and Frank Brunell pooled together $40,000 for the club. Rumored in the press for weeks beforehand, the deal was nevertheless a bombshell for the NL. The club would replace Buffalo, which had finished the season at the bottom of the league in wins, attendance, and revenue. Cincinnati was an important baseball city, one with a rabidly loyal fan base, a strong set of players, and a long history. It was the home of baseball's first all-professional team, the Cincinnati Red Stockings, in 1869 and played host to a National League club from 1876 to 1880. With perennially high attendance the only reason that Cincinnati had stayed out of the National League from 1881 to 1889 was its refusal to abide by the NL's no-alcohol policy. Soon after its dismissal from the NL in 1880, Cincinnati's club owners took the lead in creating the American Association. The team did not have a bad year in 1890, finishing the season in fourth place with seventy-seven wins and fifty-five losses. Its attendance, estimated by the *Boston Globe* at 131,080, was third highest in the league, behind only Philadelphia and Boston.[147] So in one fell swoop, the Players League replaced one of its weakest teams with one of the National League's strongest. Ward, who took a leave of absence from his team that day to finalize the deal, said, "It will not only bring into our league one of the best ball teams in the country and a strong drawing card abroad, but it will give us an ideal circuit. . . . Under such circumstances I do not see how we can fail to do well."[148]

These circumstances included not just the upgrade from Buffalo to Cincinnati but also clear evidence that the Players League had defeated the National League in the battle for fans. While precise figures for 1890 are unreliable, as both sides seemed to inflate their reported attendances on a regular basis, the Players League nonetheless outdrew the National League. All reports, even the comments of National League magnates, confirm this fact. The only mysteries are the actual numbers. *Sporting Life* printed figures that were "computed by the eminent statistician, Clarence Dow, of the Boston *Globe* [sic]."[149] Dow had the total PL attendance at 980,887 and the NL at 813,678. "As the lying was equally generous on both sides," *Sporting Life* stated, "it is fair to presume that they represent something like the correct ratio."[150] But it was suggested that "you might want to knock off thirty per cent" to come closer to the actual numbers.[151]

There was more than one reason to celebrate, therefore, when Boston was officially awarded its Players League pennant on October 11. The Boston club was to play a five-inning exhibition contest against New York, most of whose players had captured the NL flag in 1889. Led by the Reeves' Band, two tally-hos paraded the players from their hotels, through the "principal streets" of the city, to Congress Street Grounds.[152] Along the way "there was much applause and cheering, and the sidewalks were lined with people, while every window was filled with observers."[153] Once the tally-hos reached the grounds to the applause of eight thousand adoring fans, the players marched toward the infield. The cheering increased as they approached the grandstand and continued for several more minutes. Eventually the players removed their caps and made room for Col. Charles Taylor, a writer for the *Boston Globe*, who walked onto the field with the pennant in his hands. "I congratulate you upon your success," Taylor told the players. "It has been a credit to the great national sport which you represent, to your League, to yourselves as individuals, and as a club, and to the city of Boston, which you have so ably and so successfully represented."[154] Before Taylor could formally hand the pennant over to the team, Mike Kelly, always the showman, snatched it from his hands and sprinted out toward the center-field flagpole. Both teams followed in an excited heap of laughter and jubilation. When they reached the pole, Kelly attached the pennant to the rope and raised it high into the air. Waving gently in the breeze, the white flag with red lettering read, "Boston Champion Players League, 1891."[155]

7

THE FALL OF THE 1890 PLAYERS LEAGUE

After Kelly raised their pennant into the sky above Congress Street Grounds during that October 11 celebration, and after the footrace around the bases between Tom Brown and Harry Stovey (they each made it in fourteen and a half seconds), Al Johnson called the teams and a couple of reporters together for a meeting in the Boston clubhouse.[1] It seemed fitting that the man who had played an instrumental role in starting the Players League nearly a year and a half ago was going to personally offer his congratulations for a successful season. Was he also going to give the champions new suits and the men from New York boxes of cigars? Was he there to present Boston with their cash prize for finishing in first place? These questions must have passed through some of the players' minds as they walked off the field full of celebration and laughter.

Johnson's attention, however, was not on the 1890 season but rather on the one to come. He announced that just two days earlier, he and two other backers (E. B. Talcott of New York and Wendell Goodwin of Brooklyn) had met with committees from the National League and American Association. They had decided to explore the possibility of consolidating the three leagues into a single, two-division association. The men would also seek to combine the clubs of all the cities that now included more than one team and keep the most profitable of the rest of the clubs. The players in the room were stunned. Why did the backers meet with the NL and the AA without any player representatives?

Why did they meet with those leagues in the first place? More than anything, it seemed, the players did not want to play alongside the men who had deserted them a year ago. Somehow Johnson actually thought the players would be happy with his news. Somehow he believed that consolidation could work out in terms favorable to the Players League. He was quickly renounced of such ideas by nearly everyone in the room, including Boston backers Julian Hart and Arthur Dixwell.[2]

Some of the Players League's financial backers were apparently unhappy that they lost money in 1890. While the Players League clearly defeated the National League in attendance figures, nearly every team lost more money than it earned. Aggregate attendance across both leagues may have surpassed the total attendance of 1889, but split between two leagues, or in the case of Brooklyn, where clubs from the PL, the NL, and the AA were all present, the numbers for each club definitely fell short.[3] Players League secretary Frank Brunell estimated that the Players League lost a total of $125,000 in 1890, with Pittsburgh, Buffalo, and Philadelphia losing the most at about $20,000 a piece.[4] (The National League, he surmised, lost about $234,000.)[5] At least five of the eight Players League clubs were unable to pay salaries toward the end of the season.[6] Chicago's directors stopped paying salaries at some point in August, according to Brunell. Whether the club's collapse at the end of the month, when it lost eleven of twelve games beginning on August 19, is related to the missing paychecks is debatable. Only Boston, Brunell estimated, made a profit.[7] The detailed accounting books of Frederick Long reveal that Boston did, indeed, make a profit—$138.89 on the year.[8] While this figure is hardly enough to meaningfully split among a group of about twenty-five investors, it is remarkable considering that Long included the cost of construction (an expense the team would not have to pay again for several years). Without that cost Boston would have made a profit of $41,486, a figure on par if not exceeding the profit margins of the most successful clubs of the National League in preceding years.[9] The 1889 National League pennant–winning New York club, for example, made a profit of $45,000.[10]

"Stupidity, Avarice, and Treachery"

Despite this clear potential and the new league's competitive advantage over the National League—with more fans, better players, and now one of the National League's most successful cities—some of the Players League's backers did not have the patience to wait out any additional losses. And even the most faithful among them put their interests ahead of the players. Chief among the self-serving Players League backers were those from New York. And they were not, it was later revealed, acting alone.

The National League owners had met at the Fifth Avenue Hotel in New York on October 9 to discuss their plans for going forward in relation to the Players League and the American Association. Delegates from each of the league's remaining seven cities, plus two from Indianapolis, attended. Rumors had been spreading for months now that some form of peace settlement would arise between the leagues, but the NL delegates could not reach consensus on any form of potential truce. Instead the league appointed Spalding, Byrne, and John Day as a committee to formally meet with committees from the Players League and the American Association. The NL committee immediately sent invitations for a meeting to Allen Thurman, William Barnie, and Chris Von der Ahe, who were staying in the same hotel and representing the American Association, and to a small group of Players League directors, who were unofficially meeting in a hotel down the street. Albert Johnson, Edward Talcott, Wendell Goodwin, James Wagner, George Wagner, and John Ward (the only player present) had gathered at the St. James Hotel in anticipation of potential conferences with the National League. Upon receiving the NL's invitation, the Players League men delegated Johnson, Talcott, and Goodwin to meet with the NL and the AA at the Fifth Avenue Hotel that evening.[11]

As Johnson would recall to the stunned Boston and New York players two days later, the committees agreed in principle to consolidate all three leagues, collapsing many of the competing clubs of the same city into single, amalgamated clubs. The only debate that evening in the posh Parlor F of the Fifth Avenue Hotel seemed to revolve around what this new baseball association would be called. The National League wanted to keep its well-brandished moniker, but the AA and PL delegates hoped for a name that would reflect the confluence of the three associations. "After several whispered consultations among the National League delegates, Mr. Spalding inquired if the United National League would do for a name."[12] Johnson suggested "United League" instead, but the NL men were noncommittal. The Players League directors agreed that an official name could be established in consultation with the rest of the Players League. The committees agreed to meet again on an official basis on October 22 in the same place. After the meeting adjourned, Johnson said to a reporter, "If the National League is willing to change the name, I think there is no question but that there will be a full settlement of the fight."[13]

Questioned about his decision to allow the Players League's capitalists to meet with the NL and the AA without any players present, Ward replied, "I have implicit confidence in our financial backers." Showing sympathy for the financially troubled investors, Ward added, "The gentlemen back of the Players League have been forced to expend many thousands of dollars and now they are entitled to some consideration. . . . I believe every player in our league will be well satisfied with any arrangements they may make."[14]

Ward's faith in the capitalists and assessment of the players would prove naive. The following week, while Ward and his Brooklyn teammates were playing an exhibition game in Bellefonte, Pennsylvania, Players League stockholders of the New York, Brooklyn, Pittsburgh, Chicago, and Cleveland clubs each met with their National League counterparts to discuss terms of consolidation.[15] On no occasion were any players present. No deals were made, as the moneyed men agreed to wait for the scheduled October 22 meeting of the AA, the NL, and the PL committees.

But New York's capitalists appeared to have already made a handshake agreement. "We're all very happy," Edward Talcott said of the Players League and National League stockholders after they met on

October 14. "We have had no trouble at all in understanding one another, and in a very short time a definite arrangement will be made whereby New York will be represented by one first class club."[16]

Negotiations in Cleveland and Brooklyn each hinged on which ballpark the consolidated club would use, as nearly all the directors in those cities had invested in the adjacent trolley lines or properties.[17] The location of the new ball club for these investors was the difference between two wholly separate investments or two investments that would feed off each other.

The directors of Pittsburgh's two clubs met twice during the same week but could not agree on the relative value of each club.[18] The Players League men wanted 70 percent of the consolidated team's stock, a proposal with which the National League directors disagreed so strenuously that "the meeting [first] nearly broke up in a wrangle."[19] Nevertheless, the Pittsburgh Players League backers concluded, "We are perfectly willing to consolidate, and think it would be a good idea, but the National League will have to shade their figures very materially before we can meet them."[20]

Chicago Players League president John Addison met with Chicago NL secretary Jim Hart, in Frank Brunell's office on October 17. "The session was short, but not sweet," as Addison refused to meet with Spalding to discuss consolidation. But after arriving in New York on the morning of the twentieth, Chicago PL president John Addison was walking down Broadway with Edward Talcott, and they just happened to run into J. Walter Spalding in front of the Spalding sporting-goods store. Walter asked Addison if he wanted to meet his brother, Albert. Mentioning that he had seen him in person only when Spalding was a player in Chicago, Addison agreed to meet him. They exchanged pleasantries, and Addison said to him, "I have a friend in Chicago, Mr. Spalding, who says you are one of the ablest men in the city . . . and I may add that he will say the same thing about me."[21] No business was discussed that day, but the Addison-Spalding meeting (almost certainly prearranged by Talcott and Spalding) was the icebreaker that would eventually lead to consolidation of the Chicago clubs.

The brotherhood, which was still a separate entity from the Players League, met later that day on October 20 and 21 at the St. James Hotel in New York. Having read about some of the consolidation meetings in the press, "a number of the players had expressed themselves rather forcibly concerning the policy of the capitalists of the Players League in conducting peace negotiations with the National League without the aid of the players."[22] The brotherhood asserted that the capitalists never should have discussed consolidation at all, as that would mean the end of the Players League.[23] Ward argued that players should be present at the October 22 "tripartite" meeting of the Players League, the National League, and the American Association:

> It is true that the players want to be represented on Wednesday. They have interests to be considered and are anxious to have a hand in settling up this trouble. Take my own case, for instance. I have just as much money invested in the Brooklyn Players Club, proportionately, as Messrs. Goodwin and Wallace. In fact, I have all my money— $3,800—invested in the club and I think I ought to have some say in the general settlement that is to come. There are a number of other players who have invested their all, too, and they want to be heard, and I think our capitalists should show us some recognition.[24]

Now, Ward seemed to be arguing, it is "the men who invest the money," not "the men who do the work," who should take part in the governance of the game.

Despite its members' grumblings the brotherhood offered an official endorsement of their financial backers. Perhaps following the lead of Ward or perhaps because the backers had not yet actually made any decisions without them, the players sent the following letter of support to the Central Board of Directors of the Players League: "In view of the many rumors current, the members of the Brotherhood of Ball Players feel it due both to you and themselves to extend to you the assurance of their entire confidence in your ability to safely conduct the affairs of the Players League."[25] The letter was signed by James L.

White, Arthur A. Irwin, James H. O'Rourke, N. F. Pfeffer, George E. Andrews, George A. Wood, Edward Hanlon, Paul Radford (by proxy), T. J. Keefe (secretary), and John M. Ward (president).

The following day at the Fifth Avenue Hotel, the Players League Central Board of Directors (which still included as many players as nonplayer delegates) responded to the brotherhood's letter: "Your valuable favor of this morning, expressing your confidence in this body, is received. We desire to express to you, in return, our appreciation of the compliment contained therein, and beg you to accept our thanks for its proffer at the present time. Without the support you have given us during the past season, the success of the Players League would have been impossible. Your action now stimulates us to a still stronger effort for your interests in the future."[26] More importantly, Chicago backer, John Addison, made a motion to include three players on the league's committee in charge of meeting with the NL and the AA. His motion was seconded, but a long debate followed. New York investor Edwin McAlpin spoke for a half hour against the motion, arguing that consolidation was absolutely necessary, and in order to continue the process, the Players League should not make any moves that would provoke the National League into backing away. Philadelphia delegate John Vanderslice disagreed, contending it was morally and legally necessary to grant the players representation. Ward then "made a manly and eloquent appeal in behalf of the players," according to a reporter from *Sporting Life*.[27]

"Gentleman," Ward said, "do I understand that it is a crime to be a ball player? On the committee appointed by the League ... you will find the name of A. G Spalding and William Barnie, both retired ball players. Are they any better than the men who take part in the game?"[28] The delegates voted; all but McAlpin voted in favor of the motion. The committee would now include Ward, Ned Hanlon, and Arthur Irwin, in addition to Johnson, Goodwin, and Talcott.

After a break for lunch, each set of delegates reported on what, if any, consolidation plans had taken place. Despite the stories already in the press, everyone, except for the delegates from New York, responded that consolidation would be impossible, and they were not working toward it. McAlpin countered that only one team could exist in New York, and consolidation was a necessity. The central board passed a motion "that the committee be instructed to confine its deliberations in the joint conference committee to an effort to compromise and not consolidate," with the amendment "except when it is found to be for the good of the Players League."[29] Before the central board adjourned, a unanimous decision was made to not make any further moves without first conferring back to the board of directors.

On his way out of the meeting, New York backer Edward Talcott appeared very unhappy. Asked for his sentiments on the meeting, Talcott replied, "I decline to say a word. I am a member of the conference committee and cannot talk."[30] Frank Robinson, the treasurer of the New York Players League, suggested that only Talcott and Spalding should meet to decide the fate of the two leagues, as little could be done with more than a dozen men in the room at one time. New York's position on the future of the Players League was clear: consolidate with the National League.

Nevertheless, Talcott was tasked with representing the Players League, despite his club's differences. Accordingly Talcott joined Johnson, Goodwin, Hanlon, Irwin, and Ward shortly after midnight that same evening, now October 23, at the Fifth Avenue Hotel, where they were to meet with the committees from the National League and the American Association. Upon the Players League's arrival in Parlor F, however, Allen Thurman refused to call the meeting to order. The Players League committee consisted of Johnson, Talcott, and Goodwin, he argued, not anyone else. The addition of three players violated the terms of their agreement to meet in equal numbers on an official basis. The players were livid. "I am trying to appreciate the extreme delicacy displayed by the chairman of your joint committee," Ward said to the men assembled there,

his remarkable unwillingness to assume any responsibility in calling to order a meeting not constituted precisely of the same persons who composed the original joint committee, but I confess the objection seems to me purely technical, and, in view of the interests at stake, decidedly trivial. The reason for making the membership of our committee six was: First, because there are six of you gentlemen here acting together, and we felt that we were entitled at least to an equal numerical representation with you; the second reason, and I wish to be frank, was because one of the fundamental principles of the Players League recognizes an equal representation of players in its central board, and therefore the three new members are players.[31]

Ward was referring, in his first reason, to the alliance the American Association and the National League still held through the National Agreement. The Players League expected the AA to vote in lockstep with the NL. As for his second reason, Ward was once again attempting to elevate the status of baseball players as "men who do the work" and thus rightfully as equal partners in shaping the industry. He was, in short, maintaining the premise of the Players League.

But Thurman and his allies refused to call the meeting to order, insisting on maintaining strict class divisions both for this meeting and for the future of baseball. "It was mutually decided that the question of a compromise," Spalding said afterward, "should be settled between the moneyed men of both organizations on a purely business basis."[32]

The Players League committee left the meeting at 1:00 a.m. and briefly gathered at the Hoffman House across the street, before returning to Parlor F of the Fifth Avenue Hotel fifteen minutes later. But Ward, Hanlon, and Irwin, upon returning, exited through a side door, leaving their capitalist backers to confer with the National League and the American Association while they waited outside. The Players League investors made a motion to include the players, but this motion was voted down by the six AA and NL delegates. The PL committee therefore left the room, and the meeting was adjourned.[33]

Hanlon and Irwin retired to their rooms for the evening, Ward to his home on Park Avenue, Goodwin to his home somewhere uptown. But Talcott convinced Johnson to stay behind. Joined by New York Players League treasurer Frank Robinson, Talcott led Johnson to Room 214 of the Hoffman House. Inside were Albert Spalding and Charles Byrne, part owner of Brooklyn's National League franchise.[34] "What can we do?" an unidentified man from the Players League asked, according to Spalding. "You, gentlemen, and you alone, can best answer that question," Spalding replied.[35] Byrne said afterward of the impromptu meeting, "The gentlemen of the other side present are as fine, honorable, and upright men as I ever met. They realize at last the ingratitude of the players. They desire to bring this war to a close. There is no reason for further negotiations of a compromise committee. The clubs in the different cities may try to arrange matters between themselves."[36]

And indeed they did. Not surprisingly New York was the first to consolidate. Frank Robinson announced just days after the meeting, "We will certainly consolidate in New York. There exists no reason for our not doing so. It would be to the best interests of the game, the players and ourselves to bring about harmony. . . . The talk that the players will be injured in case of consolidation is the veriest [sic] nonsense."[37] It would take some time to finalize the legal technicalities of consolidation, but the consolidation of the New York clubs, Robinson declared in a circular sent to all PL clubs, was, for all intents and purposes, a done deal.[38] The new consolidated New York club would play its games in the National League and in Brotherhood Park, which it would rename the Polo Grounds.[39]

John Addison rode the train back to Chicago along with his new friend Albert Spalding. No one but the pair knows what was discussed, but the players were growing suspicious. "It is no secret among a select circle of Players League folks," the *Chicago Herald* reported, "that Addison seeks a conference with Spalding, the hoped result being a consolidation of the two local clubs, but the primary object a method of evening up on the losses incurred by Addison and his association."[40] An anonymous source from Chicago claimed, "The Chicago Brotherhood men have lost confidence in Mr. Addison."[41]

Some of Brooklyn's Players League stockholders "had several secret conferences" with their National League counterparts during the final week of October, but they had yet to reach any formal agreement.[42] Wendell Goodwin informed the Brooklyn PL backers at an October 29 meeting "that the National League men were sincere in their efforts to reach a settlement, and that he was in favor of the club's doing its share toward such a settlement."[43] No players were present at the meeting.

An increasingly testy Ward commented, "I don't like the way certain capitalists of the Players League have been acting of late. They are not treating the players in good faith." And then in his most explosive attack so far on the men he had befriended one year earlier, Ward said, "The Players League had the call when the season closed, but the ridiculous and needless weakening by the local backers has placed it in an embarrassing position, while the National League magnates have been benefited."[44]

New York pitcher Tim Keefe agreed: "It doesn't pay to fool with a buzz saw and the capitalists in this city ought to know this. The National League is very shrewd. The various club presidents sit back in the chairs and certain Players League backers run all over the country to see them about a compromise. Why, the Players League had the old organization 'killed' three weeks ago. Now everything has changed."[45]

In an attempt to stop the bleeding, Boston PL president Charles Prince called for an official meeting of "loyal clubs in the Players League."[46] Delegates from each of the league's teams, except for Buffalo, met at the Monongahela House in Pittsburgh on November 11 and 12.[47] As expected New York officially resigned from the league, though not before offering to sell its franchise for $50,000, contending that this was "a price lower than we'll sell to anybody else."[48] No one was able to pay that sum, and the club withdrew from the Players League.

Then, to the shock of most of the men gathered there, the Pittsburgh club announced that it was consolidating with the National League club on a fifty-fifty basis. The consolidation announcement "was denounced in the severest terms by the delegates."[49] "We had no idea they would attempt to put the knife into us so quick," Arthur Irwin said.[50] Ned Hanlon, without whom Pittsburgh would never have had a Players League club, was "despondent over the Pittsburg Club's break."[51]

The meeting's second day "was a short and stormy one."[52] The league appointed a new conference committee of Prince, Ward, and Johnson, who traveled immediately to New York so that they could meet with the National League owners.

As the conference committee's train rolled across Pennsylvania en route to New York, John Addison sold the Chicago Players League franchise to a group of National League magnates. "When in Pittsburg," Addison explained, "I was approached by J. P. O'Neill [of the NL Pittsburgh club] and [former PL president and New York stockholder Edwin] McAlpin, who made an offer of $20,000 cash and $15,000 worth of stock in the New York Club for my club here. I held off, and the cash bonus was raised to $25,000. This I accepted, and the club passed out of my possession into that of the National League."[53] Frank Robinson concluded the deal by wire from New York. In a nod to the players, Addison insisted that as part of the sale all unpaid salaries must be paid. Player stockholders, unwanted in the National League, were given 50 percent of the value of their stock.[54]

Brooklyn's backers continued to negotiate a consolidation, which still rested only on where the club would play. Cincinnati's status was up in the air, as the National League announced it was going to place a new club in that city. Cleveland's position was so dire that Johnson could not get anyone to even entertain an offer for consolidation or sale, despite his best efforts. Boston and Philadelphia were thus effectively the only clubs left in the Players League. Both sets of stockholders sought admission into the American Association.

Ward, in a deep despair, went to Bellefonte to stay with his family. "He has little to say on the situation," a telegram from Bellefonte read, and he "regards the Players League as a thing of the past."[55] A week later Ward released the following statement: "The cause of the Players League trouble can be summed up in three words: stupidity, avarice and treachery."[56]

Collapse

In a near-tragic accident that nonetheless symbolized the Players League's fate, the grandstand at Eastern Park collapsed on Thanksgiving Day. At the time 1,800 people were on the grandstand waiting for the start of the Yale-Princeton football game, and many of them had been "hopping from one foot to the other all that time in an effort to keep warm in the frosty morning air."[57] The stand collapsed gradually, enabling many of the people to flee for safety before it finally came crashing down all at once. Several people were injured, but no one was killed.[58]

Although the Players League was still officially in business, Spalding was not far off the mark when he wrote, "The Players League is deader than the proverbial doornail. It is now undergoing the embalming process, and when this has been done it will be respectfully buried. In about two weeks we will strew immortelles upon its grave and build a nice new monument sacred to the memory of the revolution of 1890. Then when the spring comes and the grass is green upon the last resting place of anarchy, the National Agreement will rise again in all its might and restore to America in all its purity its national pastime—the great game of base ball."[59]

Shortly before Christmas Tim Keefe sued the Players League to recover the money his company lost in its contract to supply the official league ball and for profits he expected to gain in subsequent years.[60]

The collapsed grandstand notwithstanding, it is possible that none of these dominoes would have fallen if not for the New York stockholders' eagerness to get out of the Players League. After all, before the October meeting between Spalding, Day, Johnson, and Talcott, the Players League appeared in relatively good shape. But once New York left the league, its backers worked tirelessly, and effectively, to convince the other clubs to follow suit. But from where was this eagerness among New York's backers to consolidate coming?

Buck Ewing, it turned out, played a major role in New York's withdrawal from the Players League. Confirming rumors that had been circulating for months, the *New York Clipper* reported in early January that the New York catcher and founding brotherhood member had secretly met with John Day, Cap Anson, and Albert Spalding the previous summer in order to bring down the Players League.[61] Ewing was a good friend of Day's, and it pained him to see his former boss, the man with whom he had won the 1889 National League pennant, so financially broken by the baseball war.

The meetings began one evening in early July. Anson and Spalding headed uptown in their carriage from the Fifth Avenue Hotel, at Fifth Avenue and Twenty-Fourth Street. After they picked up Day, "a long tedious drive began." Near High Bridge, at 173rd Street in Manhattan, the carriage stopped. Anson got out for a moment before climbing back in. Another carriage then began to follow them. After crossing the river they got out at 155th Street in the Bronx, where Anson led Day and Spalding through a "dimly lighted cigar shop" named Keffler's and into a private room at the back of the shop.[62] Anson then stepped outside, where he greeted the occupants of the second carriage, whom he led into the same back room. Anson and Day were startled to see before their eyes Players League stalwarts Buck Ewing and Danny Richardson. Ewing said the PL was not in good financial shape and that it could not last. The men spoke past two in the morning; during the discussion the players allegedly informed the magnates of the inner workings of their league.

Ewing continued to meet with Spalding, Anson, and Day for the rest of the summer and agreed to persuade Players League players to jump back to the National League. (Richardson, who may or may not have been aware of the nature of the late-night meeting at Keffler's before he agreed to attend, did not appear to collude with the National League again.) Ewing was unsuccessful at convincing the players (not a single player switched from the PL to the NL during the season), but he did find willing turncoats among his club's backers.

Already suspicious of Ewing throughout the summer of 1890, the players now openly expressed their hatred for the man. "Ewing is worse than any of the deserters," one player told the *New York Clipper*.[63] "He claimed to be a friend of the new movement, while in reality he was its bitterest opponent. All last summer he was in consultation with John B. Day, A. G. Spalding and others, for the purpose of selling the Players League. He succeeded in grand style, and it behooves every member of the Brotherhood to shun Ewing and men of his class. Glasscock and Denny deserted us, but they did it openly, while Ewing acted the part of the cunning traitor."[64]

The Players League held one final meeting, on January 16, at the St. James Hotel. Loyal delegates from clubs that had already left the league met to formally disband the organization. Ward showed up but left after a few minutes. At 7:30 in the evening, the Players League was quietly declared dead, and the meeting adjourned.[65]

The National League, which was holding its annual meeting at the Fifth Avenue Hotel that same week, wasted no time restoring order to the baseball world. The day after the Players League's meeting, the National League ordered all its clubs to "send to the chairman of the National Board, a list of players then under contract with or reservation by it, whom it may wish to continue in its service," noting, "All players not included in this list shall be placed in the hands of the National Board, which shall have full power to make such disposition of unclaimed players as may seem to it fair and equitable to all interests."[66] Consisting of a representative from each of the three leagues--the National League, the American Association, and the Western Association—the National Board was the National Agreement's decision-making body. Its reinforced reserve rule claimed that any player whom a club held under reservation in 1889 was still rightfully the club's in 1891.

In addition to reinforcing the reserve rule, the National Board announced the following month that players' salaries would be based, in part, on "the private or personal character of the ball players." Allen Thurman, the American Association representative on the National Board, explained: "Every month each manager of a club files with our board a private report containing a full personal history of every player in his club. The history shall detail his habits, temperate or the reverse; his obedience, tractability, etc.; his deportment and action on the diamond; his age, height, weight, physique, etc. These reports are filed with us every month."[67]

That same week, Ward signed with the newly consolidated Brooklyn National League club. Immediately after signing his contract, he boarded the *Umbria*, a steamer headed for Europe, where he stayed until April 1.[68]

The draconian plans of the National League and the American Association, however, would have to wait another year for their implementation. Just after the war with the Players League officially ended, the American Association withdrew from the National Agreement in protest over the National Board's ruling that Lou Bierbauer, whom Philadelphia's AA club claimed was under its reservation, could be signed by Pittsburgh.[69] The subsequent battle over players increased salaries from their $3,000 average in 1890 to $3,500 in 1891. Emblematic of the utter lack of a reserve rule in 1891, Mike Kelly was expected during the off-season to stay with his teammates on the Boston American Association club in 1891. But he ended up signing a contract with the Cincinnati club, which had finally been sold by Albert Johnson to John Day. After eighty-two games Kelly jumped back to the Boston AA club only to then move just four games later to the Boston National League team.

The competition for players proved too expensive for most American Association clubs. The National League absorbed four of the more successful clubs—Baltimore, Washington, St. Louis, and Louisville—and the American Association folded. The following year, in 1892, with the reserve rule firmly back in place and the National League the only game in town, average player salaries dropped to $2,400. They fell to $1,700 in 1893.[70]

Looking back on the 1890 season in his autobiography, Spalding placed blame for the Players League's failure not on Buck Ewing, as many of the players did, but on the very notion "that professional ball players can at the same time direct both the business and the playing ends of the game."[71] The collapse of the league, he argued, was the result of the players' refusal to follow the social division of labor that governed capitalism more generally: "Like every other form of business enterprise, Base Ball depends for results upon two interdependent divisions, the one to have absolute control and direction of the system, and the other to engage—always under the executive branch—in the actual work of production. The theory is as true in the production of the game of Base Ball as in the making of base balls or bats."[72]

But Ewing's treachery notwithstanding, it was the self-centered, shortsighted, and often stupid actions of those men who in Spalding's eyes were better suited to run "the executive branch" that killed the Players League. The players' fatal mistake—and this was Ward's fault as much as it was anyone else's—was that they trusted their financial backers. They believed that capital would act in the interests of labor. But building a league—constructing any industry—amid a political economy in which property does not come for free, is nearly impossible without an enormous initial sum of money, something the players did not have. Unable or unwilling to fight back, the players would not overturn the reserve rule again until 1975.

In certain respects the carpenters who built the Players League's ballparks were more successful in their labor struggle than were the players. In the case of Chicago, the carpenters' strike that had interrupted the construction of Brotherhood Park was still going on in January 1891, when the Players League folded. A group of apparently sympathetic contractors offered to settle with the UCC, but the carpenters ultimately refused. Finally, with the 1893 World's Fair in the offing, the city's principal group of contractors caved. They signed a contract on March 21, 1891, that guaranteed the carpenters eight-hour days, thirty-five cents an hour, and binding arbitration. It was a landmark contract that, although periodically renegotiated, would end up staying in place for nine years. More significantly, the carpenters' successful campaign for an eight-hour workday spearheaded similar victories in not just their own profession but for working men and women across the industrialized landscapes of North America.[73]

But the 1890 Players League is nonetheless relevant to the contemporary sports industry. Today's professional sports and entertainment industry has developed and expanded into an internationally scaled, multibillion-dollar business. The growth of the sports industry, in particular, and the reason that it has continued to flourish despite the end of the reserve rule in 1975, can be attributed to the monopolization of each sport's league, new forms of territorial rights, and the explosion of secondary markets, such as multimedia broadcasting, advertising, merchandise, and various other licensed products. The revenue earned from these sources, in addition to the money saved by forcing taxpayers to cover the costs of stadium construction, has allowed Major League Baseball, the NFL, the NBA, and to a lesser degree, the NHL, to remain increasingly profitable despite the escalating salaries of its now-unreserved players.

So where does that leave organized professional sports today? And what difference does the history of the Players League make? Are professional sports leagues and other similarly profitable facets of the culture industry, now invincible? Is there no room, and given the incredible power and paychecks of the players, no reason, for meaningful intervention? To the extent that organizations such as Major League Baseball now increasingly earn its billions on the backs of sweatshop seamstresses, underpaid custodians, and a vast array of other thoroughly exploited and de-skilled workers from around the world, there is certainly reason for intervention. And given the spotlight shone on professional sports and other facets of the entertainment industry, there is room. The off-the-field workers on the back end of this industry can discursively connect their labor to those on the front end in order to shed light on their material connections and lay claim to at least a greater proportion of the profits therein created. In other words, the ushers, garment makers, carpenters, concession-stand saleswomen, and all other underpaid workers of the sports, arts, and entertainment industry can and must convince the general public, their employers, and, indeed, the players that they, too, are the men—and women—who "do the work." And they too deserve to share in the profits of the game.

NOTES

Introduction

1. "The Players Aims," *Sporting Life*, November 27, 1889.
2. "A Short Stop," *Brooklyn Daily Eagle*, January 9, 1890.
3. "Ward Wins His Fight," *New York Times*, January 29, 1890.
4. Green, *Death in the Haymarket*.

1. Professionalization of Baseball

1. Block, *Baseball before We Knew It*. Block's landmark study includes an annotated bibliography of early references to baseball and its antecedents. Most significantly, Block's book pushed the origins of baseball back (from 1823) to at least 1796 with his discovery of a German book that describes "Ball mit Freystaten (oder das englische Base-ball)," or, "ball with free station, or English base-ball" (J. C. F. Gutsmuths, *Games for the Exercise and Recreation of Body and Spirit for the Youth and His Educator and All Friends of Innocent Joys of Youth* [1796], 67, quoted in Block, *Baseball before We Knew It*, 67). With this and other primary sources, Block convincingly argues that baseball emerged *before* the English game of rounders, which, until the publication of *Baseball before We Knew It*, was largely considered the principal progenitor of American baseball. It is important to note here in relation to the role of baseball's press that even Gutsmuths's early reference to baseball was prescriptive in tone. Base-Ball was a spiritually and physically healthy activity, Gutsmuths suggested to the parents who were to read his book. Alas, the game never caught on in Germany.
2. Spalding, *America's National Game*, 4.
3. Block, *Baseball before We Knew It*.
4. Burk, *Never Just a Game*, 3.

5. Seymour, *Baseball*, 15.

6. Burk, *Never Just a Game*, 8–9.

7. Burk, *Never Just a Game*, 8–9

8. Burk, *Never Just a Game*, 15–16.

9. Block, *Baseball before We Knew It*.

10. Henry Chadwick, *Beadle's Dime Base Ball Player*, quoted in Block, *Baseball before We Knew It*, 221.

11. Seymour, *Baseball*.

12. Burk, *Never Just a Game*.

13. Seymour, *Baseball*; Burk, *Never Just a Game*.

14. Seymour, *Baseball*.

15. Seymour, *Baseball*.

16. Block, *Baseball before We Knew It*; Burk, *Never Just a Game*.

17. Seymour, *Baseball*, 70.

18. Seymour, *Baseball*, 75.

19. Quoted in Seymour, *Baseball*, 81.

20. Quoted in Seymour, *Baseball*, 91.

21. Seymour, *Baseball*.

22. Seymour, *Baseball*, 92.

23. Seymour, *Baseball*, 88.

24. Seymour, *Baseball*, 89.

25. Levine, *A. G. Spalding and the Rise of Baseball*.

26. Albert Spalding, *Spalding's Base Ball Book and Official League Guide for 1884*, quoted in Gelzheiser, *Labor and Capital*, 24.

27. See Kimmel, "Baseball and the Reconstruction"; Blewett, "Deference and Defiance"; Bederman, *Manliness & Civilization*; Roper, "Between Manliness and Masculinity."

28. Spalding, *Spalding's Base Ball Guide and Official League Book for 1889*, 56.

29. Nemec, *Beer and Whisky League*; Achorn, *Summer of Beer and Whiskey*.

30. Ward, *Base-ball*.

31. Ward, *Base-ball*, 18.

32. Ward, *Base-ball*, 20.

33. See Block (*Baseball before We Knew It*) for a more detailed analysis of Ward's thoughts on baseball's origins. While it is true that Ward's conclusion was utterly baseless, he did devote considerable research at least to debunking Henry Chadwick's baseball-from-rounders theory, which Block confirmed more than a century later.

34. Ward, *Base-ball*, 26.

35. Ward, *Base-ball*, 27.

36. The extent to which women used that inclusion as a space for resistance remains dependent on further research. Most research on women and baseball has focused on women's baseball leagues.

37. Some popular baseball songs of the period include "The Base Ball Polka," "The Base Ball Fever," "The Live Oak Polka," "The Base Ball Quadrille," "Home Run Quick Step," "Slide, Kelly! Slide!" (dedicated to the eventual Players League star Mike "King" Kelly), and "Casey at the Bat" to name just a few (Seymour, *Baseball*). Articles about baseball occasionally appeared in the *Nation, Cosmopolitan,* and *Lippincotts,* among other magazines.

38. Quoted in Seymour, *Baseball,* 45.

39. Burk, *Never Just a Game.*

40. Burk, *Never Just a Game*; Goldstein, *Playing for Keeps.*

41. Burk, *Never Just a Game.*

42. Burk, *Never Just a Game,* 20.

43. Burk, *Never Just a Game,* 19

44. Burk, *Never Just a Game,* 44–45.

45. See Marx, *Capital,* vol. 1; Smith, *Uneven Development*; Harvey, "Body as an Accumulation Strategy"; and Orzeck, "What Does Not Kill You"

46. Voigt, *American Baseball.*

47. That said, Steven Riess's study of NAPBBP players reveals that 43 percent were born in Philadelphia, Brooklyn, Baltimore, or New York (*Touching Base*). Many of these players, however, may have lived elsewhere by the time they were signed, especially in this period of massive westward migration.

48. Burk, *Never Just a Game,* 47.

49. Burk, *Never Just a Game.*

50. Burk, *Never Just a Game.*

51. Burk, *Never Just a Game.*

52. Burk, *Never Just a Game.*

53. Ribowsky, *Complete History of the Negro Leagues*; Lomax, *Black Baseball Entrepreneurs*; Ruck, *Raceball.*

54. Seymour, *Baseball,* 42.

55. Moses Walker's brother, Welday Walker, joined Toledo for six games later in the 1884 season (Lomax, *Black Baseball Entrepreneurs*).

56. Letter dated April 11, 1884, Chicago Base Ball Club Records, Chicago Historical Society, quoted in Levine, *A. G. Spalding and the Rise of Baseball,* 47.

57. Bowman, "Baseball Mascots."

58. Quoted in Di Salvatore, *Clever Base-ballist,* 220.

59. Di Salvatore, *Clever Base-ballist*

60. Seymour, *Baseball.*

61. The connections between nineteenth-century theater and professional baseball are legion and in need of further study. Nineteenth-century accounts of baseball in the press were peppered with comparisons to the stage and with gossip regarding actor-player romances, friendships, and social gatherings. A good number of baseball players also enjoyed acting careers (usually after their baseball days were over), and troupes of actors often played amateur baseball (see Rosenberg, *Cap Anson 2*).

62. Gelzheiser, *Labor and Capital.*

2. Rise of the National League

1. Burk, *Never Just a Game.*

2. National League of Professional Base Ball Clubs, *Constitution.*

3. National League of Professional Base Ball Clubs, *Constitution.*

4. National League of Professional Base Ball Clubs, *Constitution.*

5. The 1876 National League included Philadelphia, Boston, Hartford, Brooklyn, Chicago, Cincinnati, Louisville, and St. Louis.

6. John Ward, unidentified newspaper clipping, John Ward File, National Baseball Hall of Fame Library, Cooperstown, New York, hereafter referenced as National Baseball Hall of Fame Library.

7. As the sport and industry developed, however, intra- and interclass struggles over the profits produced by these secondary markets have proliferated. The profits garnered by, say, the sale of a New York Knicks jersey with Carmello Anthony's name on the back are split between Anthony, the Knicks, the NBA, Nike, and probably several other factions as well. Even more interesting are the struggles that Anthony engaged in over the sale of his Syracuse University jerseys. Because of NCAA rules that forbid college athletes from earning money, Anthony did not receive a dime from any of the number 15 jerseys bought by so many basketball fans except those sold after Anthony's university days were over. The NCAA claimed that he was not entitled to any revenue from the sales, as the jerseys only included his number, not his name.

8. Seymour, *Baseball.*

9. February 2, 1878, quoted in Levine, *A. G. Spalding and the Rise of Baseball*, 72.

10. Albert Spalding, advertisement for Spalding & Brothers Sporting Goods, *Sporting Life*, March 13, 1889.

11. Levine, *A. G. Spalding and the Rise of Baseball.*

12. Burk, *Never Just a Game*, 57.

13. Spalding, advertisement.

14. Spalding, advertisement.

15. Seymour, *Baseball*, 194.

16. Seymour, *Baseball*, 194.

17. Seymour, *Baseball*, 194.

18. Seymour, *Baseball*, 125.

19. Seymour, *Baseball*, 125.

20. Seymour, *Baseball*, 126.

21. Seymour, *Baseball*.

22. Seymour, *Baseball*.

23. Kelly, *"Play Ball,"* 71.

24. *Boston Daily Globe*, October 3, 1889.

25. *Chicago Daily Tribune*, October 3, 1889.

26. *Chicago Daily Tribune*, October 3.

27. Burk, *Never Just a Game*.

28. Gelzheiser, *Labor and Capital*.

29. Seymour, *Baseball*, 111.

30. Seymour, *Baseball*, 111 and 106.

31. Seymour, *Baseball*, 108.

32. Burk, *Never Just a Game*.

33. Quoted in Gelzheiser, *Labor and Capital*, 38.

34. Gelzheiser, *Labor and Capital*, 38.

35. Gelzheiser, *Labor and Capital*, 38.

36. Burk (*Never Just a Game*, 243) puts that proportion closer to a third.

37. Quoted in Seymour, *Baseball*, 101.

38. The National League Board of Directors voted down a proposal to establish a system wherein the top IA clubs and worst NL clubs would each year be promoted or relegated from one league to the other (a system similar to most contemporary international soccer leagues).

39. Burk, *Never Just a Game*.

40. Burk, *Never Just a Game*.

41. Seymour, *Baseball*, 102.

42. Burk, *Never Just a Game*.

43. Quoted in Seymour, *Baseball*, 136.

44. Burk, *Never Just a Game*.

3. Brotherhood of Professional Base Ball Players

1. Ward, "Players National League," 3.

2. Ward, "Players National League," 3.

3. Tim Keefe, Brotherhood of Professional Base Ball Players Meeting Minutes, unpublished, viewed online at *Hunt Auctions*, http://huntauctions.com/live/imageviewer_online.cfm?auction_num=19&lot_num=1149&lot_qual=. The descendants of brotherhood secretary Tim Keefe privately held the union's meeting minutes until 2005, at which time they auctioned them to a private collector for $90,000. The price reflects the growing market for baseball signatures, of which the minutes contain several. Thus, despite the rotting cadavers, the secondary market for trading upon the bodies of nineteenth-century baseball players is alive and well. The auction house that facilitated the sale provided photographed excerpts of the minutes, but despite my efforts and those of the National Baseball Hall of Fame to track down the minutes, the precise content and whereabouts are now unknown. Tim Wiles, the director of research at the Hall of Fame, believes that the signatures have probably been cut out of the minutes and pasted next to framed and readily salable photographs of the players (personal communication).
4. Lewis, *Structure to Last Forever*; Burk, *Never Just a Game*.
5. Burk, *Never Just a Game*.
6. Burk, *Never Just a Game*, 42.
7. Gelzheiser, *Labor and Capital*.
8. Kelly, *"Play Ball,"* 9.
9. Kelly, *"Play Ball,"* 9.
10. Kelly, *"Play Ball,"* 13.
11. Kelly, *"Play Ball,"* 12.
12. Burk, *Never Just a Game*; Gelzheiser, *Labor and Capital*.
13. Spalding gave Anson extraordinary power over his Chicago club. While Spalding managed the business end of the team, Anson issued the fines for the disciplinary infractions of his teammates. Generally, a team's captain was its best and most respected player. He was in charge, ostensibly at least, of the players' on-field performance. He was sometimes at odds, however, with a club's manager (who supervised captains and players from the bench and also often ran the economic affairs of a team) and owners (who were generally off the field but nonetheless kept a close eye on the players and managers). For this reason, among others, captains joined (or formed, in the case of Ward) the brotherhood as much as anyone else.
14. Burk, *Never Just a Game*, 94.
15. Quoted in Di Salvatore, *Clever Base-Ballist*, 31.
16. Di Salvatore, *Clever Base-Ballist*, 31.
17. Quoted in Di Salvatore, *Clever Base-Ballist*, 39.

18. Di Salvatore, *Clever Base-Ballist*.

19. Ward, "Notes of a Base-Ballist," 213.

20. Burk, *Never Just a Game*.

21. Ward, "Notes of a Base-Ballist," 211.

22. Di Salvatore, *Clever Base-Ballist*.

23. Ward, "Notes of a Base-Ballist," 211.

24. Ward, "Notes of a Base-Ballist," 212–13.

25. Ward, "Notes of a Base-Ballist," 213.

26. Ward, "Notes of a Base-Ballist," 214.

27. Ward, "Notes of a Base-Ballist," 214.

28. Ward, "Notes of a Base-Ballist," 214.

29. Quoted in Di Salvatore, *Clever Base-Ballist*, 108.

30. Since 1871 only twenty-three Major League pitchers, including Ward, have thrown a perfect game. Ward was one of only two pitchers in the nineteenth century to throw a perfect game (the other was Lee Richmond, in 1880).

31. The National League, as well as most other baseball associations, awarded the team with the most wins at the end of each season with a pennant to be flown majestically over the club's ballpark. At the time the actual pennant itself was as important as that which it represented. The *New York Clipper*, for instance, noted, "The Newark people are disappointed in the Eastern League Championship pennant, which was received in that city October 22 [1886]. Instead of a silk pennant of the value of $100 it is a large bunting flag valued at about $30" ("Baseball," October 30, 1886). While the value and material of the pennant are no longer a concern, many contemporary baseball teams still fly pennants from their flagpoles (others merely paint a pennant onto the facade of their stadium), and "the pennant" still indicates any sort of baseball championship.

32. Di Salvatore, *Clever Base-Ballist*.

33. Di Salvatore, *Clever Base-Ballist*.

34. Di Salvatore, *Clever Base-Ballist*; Gelzheiser, *Labor and Capital*.

35. Di Salvatore, *Clever Base-Ballist*.

36. Ward, "Notes of a Base-Ballist," 214.

37. Di Salvatore, *Clever Base-Ballist*.

38. It is unclear exactly how Dauvray became so wealthy. While she was successful on the stage, the wealth she enjoyed at such a relatively young age suggests that she was the beneficiary of a large inheritance.

39. Quoted in Di Salvatore, *Clever Base-Ballist*, 208.

40. Di Salvatore, *Clever Base-Ballist*.

41. Travis, "Rise and Fall"; Sante, *Low Life*.

42. Bernheim, *Business of the Theatre*; Saraceni, "Herne and the Single Tax." A relatively militant group of actors organized the "Actors' Order of Friendship" in 1849 in Philadelphia in response to encroaching managerial control. The group, however, quickly lost its antagonistic stance and became a social and benevolent association. In 1882 the Actors' Fund of America formed, which likewise served as a social and benevolent association but did not engage in labor politics (Saraceni, "Herne and the Single Tax").

43. Di Salvatore, *Clever Base-Ballist*, 327.

44. Di Salvatore, *Clever Base-Ballist*, 327.

45. "Unknown Philadelphia Paper," quoted in Di Salvatore, *Clever Base-Ballist*, 330.

46. Upon moving to the West Dermot changed her name to Maxine Elliot and enjoyed a successful career as an actress and theater owner (Di Salvatore, *Clever Base-Ballist*; Forbes-Robertson, *My Aunt Maxine*).

47. Tim Keefe, Brotherhood of Professional Base Ball Players Meeting Minutes.

48. Di Salvatore, *Clever Base-Ballist*, 183.

49. Di Salvatore, *Clever Base-Ballist*, 183.

50. Law and political science curricula shared a lot of territory in those days. It was not uncommon for a student to earn both degrees. They were often sought simultaneously, but Ward, perhaps because of his baseball schedule (there were a few weeks of overlap), chose to earn them in succession (Di Salvatore, *Clever Base-Ballist*).

51. Ward, "Notes of a Base-Ballist," 219.

52. John Ward, "The Reserve-Rule and Contract Breakers," *New York Clipper*, February 14, 1885.

53. Ward, "Reserve-Rule and Contract Breakers."

54. Ward, "Reserve-Rule and Contract Breakers."

55. Ward, "Reserve-Rule and Contract Breakers."

56. Ward, "Reserve-Rule and Contract Breakers."

57. Ward, "Reserve-Rule and Contract Breakers."

58. Seymour, *Baseball*, 149.

59. Ward, "Reserve-Rule and Contract Breakers."

60. Quoted in Seymour, *Baseball*, 164.

61. Di Salvatore, *Clever Base-Ballist*; Stevens, *Baseball's Radical for All Seasons*.

62. Kelly, *"Play Ball,"* 32.

63. Ward, "Reserve-Rule and Contract Breakers."

64. Di Salvatore, *Clever Base-Ballist*.

65. Ward, "Notes of a Base-Ballist," 217.

66. Ward, "Notes of a Base-Ballist," 217. "Mr. Ingersoll" was Robert Ingersoll, a well-known agnostic, who wrote and spoke critically about religion and politics between the 1860s and 1890s. In addition to denouncing the irrationality and authoritarianism of organized religion, Ingersoll championed the rights of immigrants, African Americans, women, and the working class (Ingersoll, *What's God Got to Do with It?*; Jacoby, *Great Agnostic*). Ward's reference to him here indicates, at the very least, a basic understanding of his work. Ingersoll was also familiar with Ward's work. Ingersoll is paraphrased in November 1889 by the *Chicago Tribune* ("Ball-Players Meeting," November 5, 1889) as saying that the National League contracts "are not worth the paper they are printed on."

67. Ward, "Notes of a Base-Ballist," 216–17.

68. Ward, "Notes of a Base-Ballist," 217.

69. Ward, "Notes of a Base-Ballist," 217.

70. Ward, "Notes of a Base-Ballist," 216.

71. Ward, "Notes of a Base-Ballist," 216, emphasis in the original.

72. Ward, "Notes of a Base-Ballist," 216.

73. Ward, "Notes of a Base-Ballist," 216.

74. Francis Richter, "Base Ball," *Sporting Life*, November 17, 1886.

75. John Ward, "As to Contracts: The Question from a Players Standpoint," *Sporting Life*, July 20, 1887.

76. Ward, "Is the Base Ball Player a Chattel?"

77. Ward, "As to Contracts."

78. Ward, "As to Contracts."

79. "Dry Weather Signs," *Sporting Life*, July 20, 1887.

80. "Dry Weather Signs," *Sporting Life*.

81. "Ward's Letter," *Sporting Life*, July 20, 1887.

82. "Ward's Letter," Sporting Life. This "ex-New York correspondent 'layman'" was later identified as Jas. F. Blackhurst, a lawyer hired by the brotherhood in September 1887, who understood "base ball thoroughly" ("What They Want," *Sporting Life*, September 21, 1887).

83. John Ward, "A Conference Asked," *Sporting Life*, August 24, 1887.

84. Ward, "Conference Asked."

85. Ward, "Conference Asked."

86. Ward, "Conference Asked."

87. Ward, "Conference Asked."

88. Ward, "Conference Asked."

89. Ward, "Conference Asked."

90. Ward, "Conference Asked."

91. See Lowenfish, and Lupien, *Imperfect Diamond*; Zimbalist, *Baseball and Billions*; and Burk, *Never Just a Game*.

92. "The League's Position Defined," *Sporting Life*, September 28, 1887.

93. "League's Position Defined."

94. "The Brotherhood's Side," *Sporting Life*, September 28, 1887.

95. "Brotherhood's Side."

96. "Brotherhood's Side."

97. "Brotherhood's Side."

98. Ward, "Conference Asked."

99. Burk, *Never Just a Game*.

100. Spalding, quoted in Lamster, *Spalding's World Tour*, 40.

101. *Sporting Life*, March 28, 1888, quoted in Lamster, *Spalding's World Tour*, 35.

102. Lamster, *Spalding's World Tour*; Levine, *A. G. Spalding and the Rise of Baseball*.

103. Lamster, *Spalding's World Tour*, 2.

104. Levine, *A. G. Spalding and the Rise of Baseball*.

105. The trip utilized six different luxury steamers. In addition to the S.S. *Adriatic*, the travelers rode the S.S. *Alameda* (from San Francisco to Australia), the S.S. *Salier* (Australia to Egypt), the S.S. *Stettin* (through the Mediterranean Sea), the S.S. *Normandie* (across the English Channel), and the S.S. *Prince of Wales* (across the Irish Sea) (Lamster, *Spalding's World Tour*).

106. Quoted in Lamster, *Spalding's World Tour*.

107. Anderson, "Cultural Hegemony"; Anderson, "Idea of Chinatown."

108. Lamster, *Spalding's World Tour*.

109. Quoted in Lamster, *Spalding's World Tour*, 113.

110. Quoted in Lamster, *Spalding's World Tour*, 160.

111. Lamster, *Spalding's World Tour*, 160.

112. Lamster, *Spalding's World Tour*, 160.

113. Lamster, *Spalding's World Tour*, 163.

114. Palmer, quoted in Lamster, *Spalding's World Tour*, 166.

115. Lamster, *Spalding's World Tour*, 166.

116. Lamster, *Spalding's World Tour*, 166.

117. Anson, *Ball Player's Career*.

118. Lamster, *Spalding's World Tour*, 155.

119. Quoted in Di Salvatore, *Clever Base-Ballist*, 238.

120. National League, 1889, quoted in Seymour, *Baseball*, 129.

121. Quoted in Lamster, *Spalding's World Tour*, 172.

122. Di Salvatore, *Clever Base-Ballist*.

123. Di Salvatore, *Clever Base-Ballist*; Burk, *Never Just a Game*.

124. Gelzheiser, *Labor and Capital*.

125. Burk, *Never Just a Game*.

126. Di Salvatore, *Clever Base-Ballist*.

127. Ward, "Players National League," 4.

128. Quoted in Di Salvatore, *Clever Base-Ballist*, 261.

129. Ward, "Players National League," 4.

130. Ward, "Players National League," 4.

131. Ward, "Players National League," 4.

132. Quoted in Seymour, *Baseball*, 225.

133. Seymour, *Baseball*, 225.

134. Baseball, *New York Clipper*, July 6, 1889.

135. Baseball, *New York Clipper*, July 13, 1889.

136. Baseball, *New York Clipper*, July 13, 1889.

137. Ward, "Players National League." 4. As Di Salvatore (*Clever Base-Ballist*) suggests, the timing of the meeting—on Bastille Day—may be more coincidental than significant. July 14 happened to be a Sunday, when the league had the day off. All the teams were scheduled, both immediately before and after the fourteenth, to be in Washington, Philadelphia, New York, or Boston, thus putting everyone within a relatively short train trip of the meeting ("Correct Official National League Schedule," *Sporting Life*, April 13, 1889).

4. Preparing for the Players League

1. "The Brotherhood's Side," *Sporting Life*, September 28, 1887.

2. "Die Is Cast," *Boston Daily Globe*, November 5, 1889; the *Sporting Life* ("In Hostile Territory," November 13, 1889) wrote "to be consummated Wednesday," the following day, November 5, when the players were to meet with the financial backers.

3. "Die Is Cast."

4. Quoted in "In Hostile Territory."

5. Ward, "Players National League," 4.

6. "In Hostile Territory."

7. Ward, "Players National League," 4.

8. "In Hostile Territory."

9. Ward, "Players National League," 4.

10. Quoted in "How It Started," *Sporting Life*, November 6, 1889.

11. "How It Started."

12. "How It Started."

13. Di Salvatore, *Clever Base-Ballist*.

14. "The Rumored Trust," *Sporting Life*, September 18, 1889.

15. "Cleveland Budget," *Sporting Life*, September 18, 1889.

16. "Rumored Trust."

17. "Rumored Trust."

18. O'Connell, *Tom Johnson*; Lorenz, *Tom L. Johnson*.

19. "Magnates Telling Experiences," *Sporting Life*, November 1, 1890.

20. "Magnates Telling Experiences."

21. "How It Started."

22. Cleveland Chips, *Sporting Life*, November 6, 1889.

23. Rose, *Cleveland*.

24. Cleveland Chips, *Sporting Life*, November 6, 1889; "Base Ball Rebellion," *Philadelphia Inquirer*, November 4, 1889.

25. "Players League Meeting," *New York Clipper*, March 22, 1890.

26. St. Louis was explored as an alternate location in case one of the clubs could not raise enough capital or had to move midseason (as clubs sometimes did in the nineteenth century). Although it never was home to a Players League club, it did host some preseason exhibition contests.

27. "A Great Ball Trust," *Chicago Daily Tribune*, September 22, 1889.

28. Johnson's reversal compelled *Sporting Life* to write this paragraph about his honesty: "Mr. Johnson may consider that deliberate infractions of the biblical law relating to statements of a communicative character are permissible, if not commendable, in business transactions, but a good many persons with whom he has conversed on the subject during the past few weeks will find it difficult to appreciate the situation, or to reconcile his past and present utterances. I should dislike to say that either Mr. Johnson, [Cleveland pitcher Jay] Faatz, or one or two other Cleveland players have dallied with the virgin truth in conversing on the subject of the Brotherhood's plans, but it must be admitted that they evinced talents in that direction that, if backed with literary ability, would place them in the front ranks of our modern romancists [*sic*]" ("Cleveland Chips," November 6, 1889).

29. The Brooklyn, Cleveland, and Chicago clubs followed suit, reincorporating themselves.

30. "The Schemers," *Sporting Life*, October 16, 1889.

31. News, Notes, and Gossip, *Sporting Life*, October 16, 1889.

32. Ad hoc World Series had been taking place since 1884 (though in that year it was more appropriately called the "Championship of the United States" [Ivor-Campbell and Pietrusza, "Postseason Play"]). By all accounts these

games were not considered nearly as significant as today's World Series. The NL's pennant winner was considered the champion of professional baseball, regardless of how it fared in the games with the American Association leader. But the series, whose format changed year by year and was arranged by the clubs themselves and not sanctioned by the leagues, were, nonetheless, an easy way for owners to earn additional revenue after the season ended. That players often received a small portion of the gate receipts was said to induce some of them to throw games so that the series would last longer. And in certain years the team owners scheduled a set number of games, regardless of the outcome (1887's World Series, for example, featured fifteen games played in ten different cities; the NL Detroit Wolverines defeated the AA St. Louis Browns ten games to five). Moreover, various teams played games in the off-season against clubs from other leagues, thus further diluting the importance of the AA-NL series. The first modern World Series between the American League and the National League pennant winners occurred in 1903, two years after the inception of the "junior circuit," and coincidentally for four of the games, in Pittsburgh's Exposition Park, which the Players League had built (Ivor-Campbell and Pietrusza, "Postseason Play"; Seymour, *Baseball*).

33. "The Brotherhood Plans," *New York Times*, November 2, 1889.

34. "With the Ball-Players," *Chicago Daily Tribune*. November 8, 1889.

35. "The Ball Players Meet," *New York Times*. December 17, 1889.

36. It was Connor's lifetime homerun record of 138, set in 1895, which Babe Ruth broke in 1921 (Thorn, *Total Baseball*). Ward (who was also elected to the Hall of Fame) initially bought stock in the New York club but then shifted his investment to Brooklyn once he learned he would be playing there. As Ward explained, "When I subscribed for stock in the New York Club it was intended that Jack Glasscock would captain and manage the Brooklyn team. His desertion [discussed later] changed our plans and, as I want to own stock in the club where I play, I took a block in the Brooklyn Club" (quoted in News, Notes, and Comment, *Sporting Life*, December 18, 1889).

37. James B. Billings, letter from James Billings to Charles Porter, 1888, Frederick Long Papers, box 1, folder 7, National Baseball Hall of Fame Library.

38. Frederick Long, financial report issued to the Boston directors, May 16, 1888, Frederick Long Papers, box 1, folder 17, National Baseball Hall of Fame Library.

39. Seymour, *Baseball*.

40. Di Salvatore, *Clever Base-Ballist.*

41. Morrill and Wright were retired ballplayers. Both spent the majority of their careers in Boston. Morrill, however, despite announcing the end of his fourteen-year career after the 1889 season, ended up playing in two games for Boston in 1890 (Thorn, *Total Baseball*).

42. Frederick Long, list of Boston Players League stockholders, 1890, Frederick Long Papers, box 2, folder 10, National Baseball Hall of Fame Library.

43. John Haynes, letter to Frederick Long, December 13, 1889, Frederick Long Papers, box 2, folder 15, National Baseball Hall of Fame Library.

44. Hub Happenings, *Sporting Life*, November 20, 1889.

45. Haynes, letter to Frederick Long; James Hart, letter to Frederick Long, August 11, 1890, Frederick Long Papers, box 2, folder 15, National Baseball Hall of Fame Library; Long, list of Boston Players League stockholders.

46. Hub Happenings," *Sporting Life*, November 20, 1889.

47. Haynes, letter to Frederick Long; Long, list of Boston Players League stockholders.

48. News, Notes, and Comment, *Sporting Life*, November 27, 1889; News, Notes, and Gossip, *Sporting Life*, December 4, 1889.

49. Pittsburg Pencillings, *Sporting Life*, November 20, 1889.

50. "Brotherhood News," *Sporting Life*, November 27, 1889.

51. "Clubs Organized," *Sporting Life*, December 18, 1889; Stray Sparks from the Diamond, *New York Clipper*, January 25, 1890.

52. Ginsberg, "John Kinley Tener."

53. Pittsburg Pencillings, *Sporting Life*, November 6, 1889.

54. The Pittsburgh correspondent for *Sporting Life*, for example, remarked earlier in the month, "As for a Brotherhood club in Pittsburg I hardly see where anything can be gained. Here is a town which can't pay a dividend on the stock of one club, and what is the use of trying to do it with two" (Pittsburg Pencillings, *Sporting Life*, November 6, 1889).

55. Pittsburg Pencillings, *Sporting Life*, October 23, 1889.

56. News, Notes, and Comment, *Sporting Life*, November 27, 1889.

57. Pittsburg Pencillings, *Sporting Life*, November 27, 1889.

58. "And He Can Spare It," *Sporting Life*, December 11, 1889.

59. "More of the Big Scheme," *Philadelphia Inquirer*, October 8, 1889.

60. Philadelphia Pointers, *Sporting Life*, November 13, 1889.

61. "The Big Ball Scheme," *Philadelphia Inquirer*, November 6, 1889.

62. That said, the one other instance where a Philadelphia hotel is mentioned in connection with the Players League is when Boston player-owner Arthur Irwin arranged to meet Matt Kilroy at the city's Continental Hotel to discuss

Kilroy's potential Players League contract ("After Barnie's Men," *Sporting Life*, November 27, 1889). At this point, however, in mid-November 1889, the clubs were still organizing themselves and had not drawn up any agreements regarding the exclusive rights over hotels or other businesses.

63. "Philadelphia Pointers," November 20, 1889; "Big Ball Scheme." Whitall and Taggart, who were described by *Sporting Life* as "smaller stockholders," sold their shares to Vanderslice, Wagner, and Love at the end of December 1889 (Philadelphia Pointers, *Sporting Life*, January 1, 1890). "I have come to the conclusion that it does not promise to be a profitable investment," said Taggart, adding, "it is a good thing for the players but not for the stockholders" (Philadelphia Pointers). Speaking to the *New York Clipper*, Taggart added, "There was no trouble among us, and the report that Mr. Whitall and I withdrew owing to a 'split' is untrue" (Stray Sparks from the Diamond, *New York Clipper*, January 4, 1890). Whitall, Taggart said, "withdrew for business reasons," and as for himself, he claimed, "I cannot spare the time and attention that is required from a director of such an enterprise" (Stray Sparks).

64. Philadelphia Pointers, *Sporting Life*, November 13, 1889; "More of the Big Scheme," *Philadelphia Inquirer*, November 6, 1889.

65. "More of the Big Scheme."

66. "More of the Big Scheme."

67. Ballzell, *Philadelphia Gentlemen*.

68. "Big Ball Scheme"; Philadelphia Pointers, *Sporting Life*, November 20, 1889.

69. "Players Clubs Organized," *Sporting Life*, December 4, 1889; Thorn, *Total Baseball*.

70. Philadelphia Pointers, *Sporting Life*, November 13, 1889.

71. "Players Clubs Organized."

72. The *Chicago Inter-Ocean* did not cover the Players League in much detail.

73. Brunell would become a correspondent for *Sporting Life* after the 1890 season.

74. The *Tribune* story ("Great Ball Trust"), like most newspaper articles of the time, does not feature a byline, but Brunell later took credit for the story.

75. Di Salvatore, *Clever Base-Ballist*.

76. "Great Ball Trust"; "More of the Big Scheme," *Philadelphia Inquirer*, October 8, 1889.

77. "Chicago in Line," *Sporting Life*, December 4, 1889.

78. News, Notes, and Comment, *Sporting Life*, December 18, 1889.

79. News, Notes and Comment, *Sporting Life*, December 18, 1889.

80. "Chicago in Line"; Stray Sparks from the Diamond, *New York Clipper*, January 4, 1890.

81. News, Notes, and Comment, *Sporting Life*, November 20, 1889; Stray Sparks from the Diamond, *New York Clipper*, January 10, 1890.

82. "The New Brooklyn Club," *Sporting Life*, December 11, 1889.

83. "Brooklyn Budget," *Sporting Life*, December 18, 1889.

84. "Brooklyn Budget."

85. "Brooklyn Budget"; Gelzheiser, *Labor and Capital*.

86. "League Magnates Meet," *Chicago Daily Tribune*, November 14, 1889.

87. Stray Sparks from the Diamond, *New York Clipper*, February 8, 1890; 1893 editions of the *Street Railway Journal* and the *Electrical Engineer* list George H. Wirth, of Brooklyn (and Wendell Goodwin), as one of the directors of the Buffalo & Niagara Falls Electric Railway Company, which had just that year been incorporated ("Street Railway News," *Street Railway Journal* 9, no. 5 [1893]: 273–346; "From Buffalo to Niagara by Electric Car," *Electrical Engineer* 15 [1893]: 248). There is no available evidence that Wirth was involved in the railway business before then. But his partnership with Goodwin, who had been involved with the railway industry by at least 1889, when he joined Wirth in the Brooklyn PL club, suggests the possibility that Wirth had invested in the railway business, perhaps with Goodwin, sooner as well.

88. Lowry, *Green Cathedrals*).

89. "An Injunction," *New York Clipper,* January 17, 1890; "To Prevent Consolidation," *New York Times*, January 7, 1891.

90. Stray Sparks from the Diamond, *New York Clipper*, December 28, 1889; Stray Sparks from the Diamond, *New York Clipper*, October 18, 1890.

91. Macht, *Connie Mack*; Stray Sparks from the Diamond, *New York Clipper*, October 18, 1890.

92. Macht, *Connie Mack*; Stray Sparks from the Diamond, *New York Clipper*, October 18, 1890.

93. Stray Sparks from the Diamond, *New York Clipper*, December 28, 1889; Oronhyatekha. *History of the Independent Order*.

94. Stray Sparks from the Diamond, *New York Clipper*, December 28, 1889; Stray Sparks from the Diamond, *New York Clipper*, October 18, 1890; W. Harrison, *The Political Blue Book: An Official Manual of Buffalo and Erie County, New York* (Buffalo: Dau, 1905).

95. "Buffalo Budget," *Sporting Life*, November 20, 1889.

96. As with the July 14 meeting, it is not clear whether the date of the occasion was chosen for symbolic purposes. But given the fact that twice, now, the brotherhood's meetings fell on historic dates that were metaphorically related to the players' struggle, there is a chance that the occurrences were

beyond coincidence. Either way Henry Chadwick, in an uncharacteristically caustic rebuke to the players, was quick to ascribe significance to the date of the brotherhood's meeting: "This is the anniversary of the day known in English history as 'Guy Fawkes' Day,' an event singularly appropriate for the culmination of the conspiracy in this city, by means of which the Guy Fawkes of the base ball world intend to blow up the League House of Parliament of the national game" ("The Situation," *Sporting Life*, November 13, 1889).

97. "Big Ball Scheme."

98. "Big Ball Scheme."

99. "In Hostile Array," *Sporting Life*, November 13, 1889.

100. Seymour, *Baseball*.

101. "With the Ball-Players," *Chicago Daily Tribune*, November 8, 1889. After a March PL meeting, these figures changed to $6,250 for the first place team; second place, $4,800; third, $3,500; fourth, $2,500; fifth, $1,750; sixth, $800; seventh, $400 ("Players League Meeting," *New York Clipper*, March 22, 1890).

102. Arthur Irwin's younger brother, John, was also a member of the Players League but was not active in its governance.

103. "In Hostile Array."

104. Quoted in "Players League Launched Successfully at Last," *Sporting Life*, December 25, 1889.

105. National League of Professional Base Ball Clubs. *Constitution*.

106. Frederick Long, Standard Players League Contract, 1890, Frederick Long Papers, box 2, folder 15, National Baseball Hall of Fame Library.

107. "Meeting of the Players," *Chicago Daily Tribune*, December 17, 1889.

108. "Players League Launched Successfully at Last," *Sporting Life*, December 25, 1889.

109. News, Notes, and Comment, *Sporting Life*, November 13, 1889.

110. Gelzheiser, *Labor and Capital*; Di Salvatore, *Clever Base-Ballist*.

111. Burk, *Never Just a Game*.

112. Quoted in "In Hostile Array."

113. Quoted in "Players Will Not Sign," *Chicago Daily Tribune*, October 22, 1889.

114. "The Situation," *Sporting Life*, October 30, 1889.

115. "That Notice," *Sporting Life*. October 30, 1889.

116. "The Players to Meet," *Sporting Life*, October 30, 1889.

117. "Denny Will Stay with the League," *Chicago Daily Tribune*. November 9, 1889.

118. "Kelly's Home Run," *Boston Daily Globe*, November 5, 1889.

119. "Kelly's Home Run."

120. "Chasing after Players," *Sporting Life*, December 4, 1889.

121. "Chasing after Players."

122. "Chasing after Players."

123. That Lake Erie does not have significant tides—certainly none that could require a piggyback ride—suggests the exaggerations with which Andrews sprinkled his stories.

124. "Chasing after Players."

125. Joseph Andrews Sommers was known as "Andy" in his day but is erroneously listed as "Pete Sommers" in *Total Baseball*'s (Thorn) otherwise definitive player register.

126. "Chasing after Players."

127. John Morrill, letter to Frederick Long, December 8, 1889, Frederick Long Papers, box 2, folder 7, National Baseball Hall of Fame Library.

128. John Morrill, letter to Frederick Long.

129. Arthur Dixwell, letter to Frederick Long, December 8, 1889, Frederick Long Papers, box 2, folder 7, National Baseball Hall of Fame Library.

130. Arthur Dixwell, telegram to Frederick Long, December 7, 1889, Frederick Long Papers, box 2, folder 8, National Baseball Hall of Fame Library.

131. Frederick Long, personal note to Arthur Dixwell, undated but on or shortly after December 7, 1889, Frederick Long Papers, box 2, folder 8, National Baseball Hall of Fame. Long's message was written on the back of the telegram sent to him by Dixwell regarding Clarkson's request. Given the reports in the papers in the following weeks (e.g., "Not Disturbed, *Sporting Life*, December 18, 1889), one can conclude that Long did convey this message, in one form or another, to Dixwell.

132. Stray Sparks from the Diamond, *New York Clipper,* January 18, 1890.

133. Arthur Dixwell, letter to Frederick Long, December 13, 1889, Frederick Long Papers, box 2, folder 7, National Baseball Hall of Fame Library.

134. The Players League, *Sporting Life*, December 11, 1889.

135. "News and Gossip Gleaned Here and There," *Sporting Life*, October 9, 1889.

136. "Spalding Undisturbed," *Sporting Life*, November 13, 1889.

137. News, Notes, and Comment, *Sporting Life*, November 13, 1889.

138. "The Law Suit," *Sporting Life*. December 25, 1889.

139. Clark, "Implications of Lumley v. Wagner."

140. Clark, "Implications of Lumley v. Wagner," 702.

141. "A Precedent," *Sporting Life*, October 30, 1889. The plaintiff, John T. Ford,

also owned the infamous Ford's Theatre, in which President Lincoln was shot (Barnett, "Proper Scope of the Police Power").

142. "The Law Suit," *Sporting Life*, December 25, 1889.

143. "Ward Wins His Fight," *New York Times*, January 29, 1890.

144. "Ward Wins His Fight."

145. "Ward Wins His Fight."

146. "Ward Wins His Fight."

147. News, Notes, and Comment, *Sporting Life*, December 18, 1889.

148. Lowry, *Green Cathedrals*.

149. "After a Philadelphia Ground," *Sporting Life*, October 9, 1889.

150. "After a Philadelphia Ground."

151. *Sporting Life*'s description of Forepaugh Park is odd given that by opening day, in May 1890, the field seemed just as shoddy as that of its crosstown rival; as the *Philadelphia Record* (1890) noted "the grounds were very soft and uneven, and errors were easy to make."

152. Lowry, *Green Cathedrals*.

153. When teams folded or ballparks otherwise shuttered their front gates, the clubs usually dismantled their ballparks and sold the folding chairs, much of the "bleaching boards" and other wood, leaving just the ground itself in their wake. The point is that had the Players League leased the Athletics' ground, it would have had to either build its ballpark from scratch or buy the grandstand from the Athletics. Aside from its location, the only economic advantage, then, was that the field would have already been leveled.

154. Later the home ballpark of Willie Mays, among other New York Giants, Brotherhood Park was renamed the Polo Grounds in 1891 after the NL club moved in. This ballpark was the third version of the Polo Grounds, the first at 110th Street and Fifth Avenue and the second, adjacent to the third. The grandstand of the new Polo Grounds was rebuilt after a fire partially destroyed it in 1911, but Major League Baseball was otherwise played there continuously from 1890 until it was finally demolished after the 1963 season. The Polo Grounds was the last Major League ballpark to be located in Manhattan.

155. "The Brotherhood Plans," *New York Times*, November 2, 1889; "An Alleged Foothold in New York," *Sporting Life*, October 9, 1889.

156. New York News, *Sporting Life*, October 9, 1889.

157. According to ballpark historian Phil Lowry, the Polo Grounds featured the "steepest and largest embankment ever in a major league park" (*Green Cathedrals*, 150). In a game against Chicago in September 1889, center

fielder George Gore was unable to climb the muddy embankment to fetch a ball that Cap Anson hit. Anson rounded the bases with an inside-the-park home run. Brotherhood Park, in contrast, featured "a gentle fall" from "the pitcher's box toward the outfield" (Stray Sparks from the Diamond, *New York Clipper*, April 19, 1890).

158. News, Notes, and Comment, *Sporting Life*, November 13, 1889; Stray Sparks from the Diamond, *New York Clipper*, April 19, 1890.

159. Stray Sparks from the Diamond," *New York Clipper*, April 19, 1890; Burrows and Wallace, *Gotham*.

160. "From Byrne's Bailiwick," *Sporting Life*, November 6, 1889.

161. Stray Sparks from the Diamond, *New York Clipper*, February 1, 1890.

162. Stray Sparks from the Diamond, *New York Clipper*, February 1, 1890.

163. "Stray Sparks from the Diamond, *New York Clipper*, February 8, 1890.

164. "The New Brooklyn Club," *Sporting Life*, December 11, 1889.

165. News, Notes, and Comment, *Sporting Life*, November 20, 1889.

166. Bromley, *Atlas*.

167. Diamond Gossip, *Chicago Daily Tribune*, November 24, 1889.

168. Hub Happenings, *Sporting Life*, December 18, 1889.

169. "Working to Perfect the Organization," *Sporting Life*, November 20, 1889.

170. "Die Is Cast," *Boston Daily Globe*, November 5, 1889.

171. "Brotherhood News," *Sporting Life*, November 27, 1889.

172. "Cleveland's Advance," *Sporting Life*, October 30, 1889.

173. "Cleveland's Advance"; Lowry, *Green Cathedrals*.

174. "Cleveland's Advance." It is important to note that these measurements, when referring to the size of the grounds, were not the dimensions of the playing field. The grounds included both the playing field and the grandstand. However, the length and width of the grounds were indicative of the relative size of the playing field.

175. "Cleveland's Advance"; News, Notes, and Comment, *Sporting Life*, November 13, 1889.

176. "More Johnsonian Views," *Sporting Life*, November 27, 1889.

177. Lowry, *Green Cathedrals*.

178. Lowry, *Green Cathedrals*.

179. Pittsburg Pencillings, *Sporting Life*, November 20, 1889.

180. "It's All Nonsense," *Boston Daily Globe*, November 17, 1889.

181. "Will the Players Sign?," *Chicago Daily Tribune*, October 21, 1889; "News and Gossip Gleaned Here and There," *Sporting Life*, October 9, 1889.

182. "Grounds for the Players League," *Chicago Daily Tribune*, December 17, 1889.

183. "Object to the Ballpark," *Chicago Daily Tribune*, December 19, 1889.
184. "Object to the Ballpark."

5. The Men Who Do the Work

1. W. H. Keyes & Co. Contractors and Builders, receipts from construction of Boston's Congress Street Grounds, 1890, Frederick Long Papers, box 2, folders 14–15, National Baseball Hall of Fame Library.
2. This calculation is based on 3,433.64 "days" of labor, according to Keyes's (1890) figures, divided by the 70 days on which work actually took place.
3. Keyes, receipts from construction.
4. Frederick Long, "Receipts and Expenses Boston Ball Club Season of 1890," financial report most likely submitted to Boston Players League stockholders, 1890, Frederick Long Papers, box 2, folder 10, National Baseball Hall of Fame Library.
5. Keyes, receipts from construction.
6. Keyes, receipts from construction.
7. Long, "Receipts and Expenses."
8. "In Hostile Array," *Sporting Life*, November 13, 1889.
9. "Sympathy from Organized Labor," *Sporting Life*, November 13, 1889.
10. "Sympathy from Organized Labor."
11. "Sympathy from Organized Labor."
12. "Labor Men Take a Hand," *Sporting Life*, December 18, 1889.
13. News, Notes, and Comment, *Sporting Life*, December 11, 1889.
14. *Carpenter* 4, November 15, 1889.
15. Gelzheiser, *Labor and Capital*.
16. Stray Sparks form the Diamond, *New York Clipper*, January 25, 1890.
17. Stray Sparks form the Diamond, *New York Clipper*, January 25, 1890.
18. *Carpenter*, 1, February 15, 1890.
19. United Carpenters' Council, Minutes of the Chicago United Carpenters' Council Meeting, January 31, 1890, Records of the United Brotherhood of Carpenters and Joiners of America, Chicago District Council of Carpenters. Chicago Historical Museum.
20. United Carpenters' Council, Minutes.
21. The April 15, 1980, *Carpenter* reported that PL clubs in "Philadelphia, Boston, Washington DC, and Brooklyn NY" did not hire union carpenters ("Base Ball and Carpenters,"). That Washington was not ever a Players League city and Chicago was omitted from this list forces one to take the publication's claims (in this and perhaps other matters) with a grain of salt. Research into the construction of ballparks in Philadelphia, Brooklyn, and

the other Players League cities did not elucidate any serious conflicts or extraordinary circumstances.

22. Reckman, "Carpentry."

23. Reckman, "Carpentry."

24. Reckman, "Carpentry."

25. Montgomery, *Fall of the House of Labor*.

26. Christie, *Empire in Wood*; Reckman, "Carpentry."

27. Reckman, "Carpentry."

28. Schneirov and Suhrbur, *Union Brotherhood, Union Town*, 5.

29. The Chicago City Council nearly passed an ordinance after the Great Fire of 1871 that would have prohibited any new construction with wood. Charging that brick and stone buildings would be too expensive for the common workingman to afford, ten thousand workers, including several hundred carpenters, forced their way into city hall to demand that the government reconsider. After hiding in the cloakroom for several hours, Mayor Joseph Medill led the city council toward the passage of a compromise resolution that prohibited the use of wood only in the city center (Schneirov and Suhrbur, *Union Brotherhood, Union Town*).

30. Agnew, *The United States in the World-Economy*.

31. *Chicago Daily Inter-Ocean*, quoted in Schneirov and Suhrbur, *Union Brotherhood, Union Town*, 7.

32. Frank Duffy, "The Birth of 'The Brotherhood'" (1941), manuscript, Records of the United Brotherhood of Carpenters and Joiners of America, Chicago District Council of Carpenters. Chicago Historical Museum.

33. "Want the Strike Ended," *Chicago Daily Tribune*, April 12, 1890.

34. Schneirov and Suhrbur, *Union Brotherhood, Union Town*.

35. Duffy, "Birth of 'The Brotherhood,'" 1.

36. "Carpenters' Win," *Boston Daily Globe*, March 25, 1890. According to the receipt of the contractor, W. H. Keyes, he was charging the Boston club three dollars per day for most workers and two dollars for some others. The difference between the two wage figures may have related to differing skill levels (Keyes, receipts from construction).

37. "Carpenters' Win."

38. "Carpenters' Win."

39. "Carpenters' Win."

40. Keyes, receipts from construction. This particular concession was not reported in the newspapers but is evident in Keyes's record of construction. Between March 25 and April 30, days are measured in ninths; after May 1, they are in eighths.

41. "They Marched Anyway," *Boston Daily Globe*, May 9, 1890.
42. "Plumbers Again at Work," *Chicago Daily Tribune*, April 9, 1890.
43. United Carpenters' Council, Minutes of the Chicago United Carpenters' Council Meeting. March 27, 1890, Records of the United Brotherhood of Carpenters and Joiners of America, Chicago District Council of Carpenters, Chicago Historical Museum.
44. James Brennock, "History: The Carpenters of Chicago, Ill.," manuscript, Records of the United Brotherhood of Carpenters and Joiners of America, Chicago District Council of Carpenters, Chicago Historical Museum, 2.
45. "Carpenters Still Out," *Chicago Daily Tribune*, April 10, 1890.
46. "Intercepting Arrivals," *Chicago Daily Tribune*, April 16, 1890.
47. "To Remain in the League," *Chicago Daily Tribune*, April 22, 1890.
48. "Settlement in Sight," *Chicago Daily Tribune*, April 19, 1890.
49. "Players League Launched Successfully at Last," *Sporting Life*, December 25, 1889.
50. "There was a great deal of competition for the privilege of furnishing the [PL's] ball," according to the *New York Clipper* ("Baseball, the Players National League," December 28, 1889). In addition to Keefe & Becannon, Kiffe, Wright & Ditson, Shibe Brothers, and A. J. Reach bid for the ball contract. That George Wright, of Wright & Ditson, was a Boston PL stockholder suggests that the Keefe & Becannon ball was not a shoe-in simply because of Keefe's ties with the league. Reach was the president of Philadelphia's National League club.
51. "Players League Meeting," *New York Clipper*, March 22, 1890.
52. Boston Base Ball Club, contract between the Boston Base Ball Club and A. Bronson Cooper, 1890, Frederick Long Papers, box 2, folder 13, National Baseball Hall of Fame Library.
53. Boston Base Ball Club, contract.
54. John Patterson, letter to Frederick Long, December 2, 1889, Frederick Long Papers, box 2, folder 13, National Baseball Hall of Fame Library.
55. Boston Base Ball Club, contract between the Boston Base Ball Club and Hyneman & Bryant, 1890, Frederick Long Papers, box 2, folder 13, National Baseball Hall of Fame Library.

6. 1890 Players League

1. Stray Sparks from the Diamond, *New York Clipper*, April 19, 1890.
2. "Slide Kelly, Slide!" sheet music, composed by J. W. Kelly (1889), Mike Kelly File, National Baseball Hall of Fame Library. (There was no relation between J. W. Kelly and Mike Kelly.)

3. The applause may have been directed primarily at Barnes, who played for Boston's National Association of Professional Base Ball Players (NAPBBP) team from 1871 to 1875 and with its National League club in 1881. Barnes was one of the best hitters in the history of the NAPBBP, holding the records for most career runs, hits, doubles, walks, and stolen bases and the highest batting average, and on-base percentage (Thorn, *Total Baseball*).

4. "'Twas a Beauty," *Boston Daily Globe*, April 20, 1890.

5. "'Twas a Beauty."

6. "'Twas a Beauty."

7. "'Twas a Beauty."

8. The *Boston Daily Globe* ("'Twas a Beauty") puts the figure at 10,000; *Sporting Life* (The Players League, April 26, 1890) insists that "exactly 8,333" entered the grounds.

9. "'Twas a Beauty."

10. "'Twas a Beauty."

11. The Players League, *Sporting Life*, April 26, 1890.

12. Stray Sparks from the Diamond, *New York Clipper,* May 3, 1890.

13. "A Labor Boycott," *Sporting Life*, April 19, 1890.

14. Pittsburg Pencillings, *Sporting Life*, April 12, 1890.

15. Quoted in Britcher, "1890 Burghers and Alleghenys."

16. "A King in the Box," *Pittsburgh Press*, April 20, 1890.

17. Stray Sparks from the Diamond, *New York Clipper*, April 19, 1890.

18. The Players League, *Sporting Life*, April 26, 1890; The Players League, *New York Clipper*, April 26, 1890.

19. The *Sporting Life* (The Players League) reported 5,000 fans in attendance at the National League opener in New York, a figure that was most likely provided for the newspaper by Philadelphia officials. But according to the personal account book of Philadelphia team president Harry Wright, in which he recorded not just attendance figures but every penny he spent and received, including each lunch, dinner, hat, and shoeshine he bought, 3,524 people attended, but only 1,520 paid for tickets (Harry Wright's Personal Account Book, Harry Wright Papers, box 14, Spalding Collection, New York Public Library).

20. Stray Sparks from the Diamond, *New York Clipper*, May 17, 1890; The Players League, *Sporting Life*, May 3, 1890.

21. Stray Sparks from the Diamond, *New York Clipper*, May 17, 1890.

22. Stray Sparks from the Diamond, *New York Clipper*, May 17, 1890.

23. "First Game at the Players Park," *Chicago Daily Tribune*, May 6, 1890.

24. "To Open Next Saturday," *Chicago Daily Tribune*, April 27, 1890; "Won as They Pleased," *Chicago Daily Tribune*, April 20, 1890.

25. "Won as They Pleased."

26. The Players League, *Sporting Life*, April 26, 1890.

27. The Players League, *Sporting Life*, April 26, 1890.

28. The Players League," *New York Clipper*, April 26, 1890.

29. Chas. D. Blake & Co., "Hurrah for the Brotherhood Boys," advertisement, *New York Clipper*, May 10, 1890.

30. Stray Sparks from the Diamond, *New York Clipper*, May 3, 1890.

31. Stray Sparks from the Diamond, *New York Clipper*, May 17, 1890.

32. Julian Hart, letter to Frederick Long, March 10, 1890, Frederick Long Papers, box 2, folder 9, National Baseball Hall of Fame Library.

33. John M. Ward, "John Ward's Missive," *Sporting Life*, April 19, 1890.

34. Ward, "John Ward's Missive."

35. Ward, "John Ward's Missive."

36. Stray Sparks from the Diamond, *New York Clipper*, May 3, 1890.

37. Ward, "John Ward's Missive."

38. Stray Sparks from the Diamond, *New York Clipper*, May 3, 1890.

39. "Conflicting Dates," *Sporting Life*, May 3, 1890.

40. Stray Sparks from the Diamond, *New York Clipper*, June 7, 1890.

41. "1890 National League Standard Batting," *Baseball-Reference.com*, available at http://www.baseball-reference.com/leagues/nl/1890-standard-batting .shtml; "1890 Players League Standard Batting," *Baseball-Reference.com*, available at http://www.baseball-reference.com/leagues/pl/1890-standard -batting.shtml; "1889 National League Standard Batting," available *Baseball-Reference.com*, http://www.baseball-reference.com/leagues/nl /1889-standard-batting.shtml.

42. A native of Rochester, New York, Coots moved to Brooklyn in the 1880s, where he designed several row houses in the Park Slope and Crown Heights neighborhoods of Brooklyn, in addition to the PL park, a shoe factory, and a steam laundry (Harrison, *Alice and Agate Courts*).

43. Stray Sparks from the Diamond, *New York Clipper*, March 29, 1890.

44. Stray Sparks from the Diamond, *New York Clipper*, March 29, 1890.

45. Stray Sparks from the Diamond, *New York Clipper*, March 29, 1890.

46. Stray Sparks from the Diamond, *New York Clipper*, May 31, 1890.

47. Stray Sparks from the Diamond, *New York Clipper*, April 19, 1890.

48. Stray Sparks from the Diamond, *New York Clipper*, May 24, 1890.

49. Much of the grandstand was rebuilt in 1911, before Mays started playing, as a fire burned all but the left- and right-field grandstands and center-field bleachers (Lowry, *Green Cathedrals*).

50. "A King in the Box," *Pittsburg Press*, April 20, 1890.

51. "King in the Box."

52. Stray Sparks from the Diamond, *New York Clipper*, May 31, 1890.

53. Stray Sparks from the Diamond, *New York Clipper*, May 17, 1890.

54. "First Game at the Players Park," *Chicago Daily Tribune*, May 6, 1890.

55. News, Notes, and Comments, *Sporting Life*, July 5, 1890.

56. "To Open Next Saturday," *Chicago Daily Tribune*, April 27, 1890.

57. "To Open Next Saturday."

58. "To Open Next Saturday."

59. "To Open Next Saturday."

60. Stray Sparks from the Diamond, *New York Clipper*, May 17, 1890.

61. The National League, *New York Clipper*, May 17, 1890.

62. The Players League, *New York Clipper*, May 24, 1890.

63. Stray Sparks from the Diamond, *New York Clipper,* June 14, 1890.

64. Stray Sparks from the Diamond, *New York Clipper,* June 14, 1890.

65. Stray Sparks from the Diamond, *New York Clipper,* June 21, 1890.

66. Stray Sparks from the Diamond, *New York Clipper*, June 14, 1890.

67. "Shut out by Ward's Team," *Brooklyn Daily Eagle,* June 22, 1890.

68. "Shut out by Ward's Team."

69. "Shut out by Ward's Team."

70. "Shut out by Ward's Team."

71. The Players League, *New York Clipper*, June 28, 1890; "Broke Tie Base-Ball Record," *Chicago Daily Tribune*, June 22, 1890.

72. Thorn, *Total Baseball*.

73. Stray Sparks from the Diamond, *New York Clipper*, August 30, 1890.

74. "1890 Players League Standard Pitching," *Baseball-Reference.com*, available at http://www.baseball-reference.com/leagues/pl/1890-standard-pitching .shtml.

75. Quoted in Stray Sparks from the Diamond, *New York Clippe*r, July 5, 1890.

76. The Players League, *New York Clipper*, July 5, 1890.

77. The Players League, *New York Clipper*, July 5, 1890.

78. The Players League, *New York Clipper*, June 14, 1890.

79. Stray Sparks from the Diamond, *New York Clipper*, May 10, 1890.

80. The Players League, *New York Clipper*, June 21, 1890.

81. The Players League, *New York Clipper*, June 21, 1890.

82. See, for example, Stray Sparks from the Diamond, *New York Clipper*, June 14, 1890.

83. Stray Sparks from the Diamond, *New York Clipper*, May 24, 1890.

84. Stray Sparks from the Diamond, *New York Clipper*, May 24, 1890.

85. "1890 Players League Standard Batting," *Baseball-Reference.com*, available at http://www.baseball-reference.com/leagues/pl/1890-standard-batting .shtml; "1890 National League Standard Batting," *Baseball-Reference.com*, available at http://www.baseball-reference.com/leagues/nl/1890 -standard-batting.shtml; "1889 National League Standard Batting," *Baseball-Reference.com*, available at http://www.baseball-reference .com/leagues/nl/1889-standard-batting.shtml.

86. "1890 Players League Standard Batting," *Baseball-Reference.com*.

87. "1890 National League Standard Batting," *Baseball-Reference.com*.

88. Stray Sparks from the Diamond, *New York Clipper*, May 24, 1890.

89. The Players League, *New York Clipper*, July 26, 1890.

90. The American Association, *New York Clipper*, July 12, 1890.

91. "Twenty-Three Thousand People," *Chicago Daily Tribune*, July 5, 1890.

92. "Twenty-Three Thousand People."

93. "Twenty-Three Thousand People."

94. Stray Sparks from the Diamond, *New York Clipper*, August 2.

95. "Pittsburg, 20; Cleveland, 12," *Boston Daily Globe*, April 24, 1890. One history of the team claims that only 17 people attended this game (McCollister, *Good, the Bad, and the Ugly*, 95). But there is no other evidence of such a low figure. The *Pittsburg Press* does not mention the attendance for that game; the *Chicago Daily Tribune* claims "not more than 150" people were in attendance; and the *Boston Daily Globe* has 162 fans in the ballpark (Sporting, *Pittsburg Press*, April 24, 1890; "Pittsburgh, 20; Cleveland, 12," *Chicago Daily Tribune*, April 24, 1890; "Pittsburgh, 20; Cleveland, 12," *Boston Daily Globe*, April 24, 1890).

96. "Pittsburgh, 20; Cleveland, 12."

97. Sporting, *Pittsburg Press*, April 24, 1890; The Players League, *New York Clipper*, May 10, 1890.

98. "Pirates Single Game Records," MLB Advanced Media, available at http:// pittsburgh.pirates.mlb.com/pit/history/single_game_records.jsp.

99. Stray Sparks from the Diamond, *New York Clipper*, May 10, 1890.

100. Stray Sparks from the Diamond, *New York Clipper*, May 17, 1890.

101. Stray Sparks from the Diamond, *New York Clipper*, July 12.

102. Quoted in Stray Sparks from the Diamond, *New York Clipper*, July 5, 1890.

103. The National League, *New York Clipper*, June 28, 1890.

104. Sporting, *Pittsburg Press*, June 20, 1890.

105. "Billy Gumbert Statistics and History," *Baseball-Reference.com*, available at http://www.baseball-reference.com/players/g/gumbebi01.shtml.

106. "Billy Gumbert Minor League Statistics and History," *Baseball-Reference.com*, available at http://www.baseball-reference.com/minors/player.cgi?id=gumber001bil; "Billy Gumbert Statistics and History."

107. "George Ziegler Minor League Statistics and History." *Baseball-Reference.com*, available at http://www.baseball-reference.com/minors/player.cgi?id=ziegle001geo.

108. Regarding Ziegler's compensation, see Nemec, *Rank and File*, 86; quotation from Sporting, *Pittsburg Press*, June 20, 1890.

109. "George Ziegler Minor League Statistics and History."

110. Burton and Benita Boxerman's *Jews and American Baseball* claims that Leo Fishel, who debuted with the New York Giants on May 3, 1899 (and also just pitched in one game), was the first Jewish pitcher in the major leagues. But Ziegler, who was buried in a Jewish cemetery in Kankakee, Illinois, should be considered the first ("George Ziegler Minor League Statistics and History"). The first Jewish position player to appear in a major league game was Lipman Pike. After five years in the National Association of Professional Base Ball Players, Pike played in the National League between 1876 and 1881 for St. Louis, Cincinnati, Providence (with John Ward), and Worcester between 1876 and 1881 (Boxerman and Boxerman, *Jews and American Baseball*). Including Fishel and Pike, Boxerman and Boxerman list only six Jewish players who played major league baseball during the nineteenth century.

111. "1890 Pittsburgh Alleghenys Batting, Pitching, & Fielding Statistics," *Baseball-Reference.com*, available at http://www.baseball-reference.com/teams/pit/1890.shtml. Only three players on Pittsburgh's Players League team, in contrast, appeared in fewer than eighteen games ("1890 Pittsburgh Burghers Batting, Pitching, & Fielding Statistics," *Baseball-Reference.com* available at http://www.baseball-reference.com/teams/pbb/1890.shtml).

112. "Games to Be Played," *New York Clipper*, August 2, 1890.

113. Stray Sparks from the Diamond, *New York Clipper*, August 2, 1890.

114. Stray Sparks from the Diamond, *New York Clipper*, August 2, 1890.

115. "Fred Dunlap," *Retrosheet.org*, available at http://www.retrosheet.org/boxesetc/D/Pdunlf101.htm.

116. "Henry Youngman," *Retrosheet.org*, available at http://www.retrosheet.org/boxesetc/Y/Pyounh102.htm.

117. "Billy Sunday," *Retrosheet.org*, available at http://www.retrosheet.org/boxesetc/S/Psundb101.htm; Britcher, "1890 Burghers and Alleghenys."

118. "1890 Pittsburgh Alleghenys Batting, Pitching, & Fielding Statistics"; the 1899 Cleveland Spiders won 20 games and lost 134.

119. Stray Sparks from the Diamond, *New York Clipper*, August 2, 1890; Britcher, "1890 Burghers and Alleghenys."

120. Browning, *Cy Young*.

121. "A Close Finish," *Brooklyn Daily Eagle*, August 7, 1890; Browning, *Cy Young*.

122. Browning, *Cy Young*, 12.

123. Browning, *Cy Young*, 12.

124. The National League, *New York Clipper*, August 16, 1890.

125. Browning, *Cy Young*.

126. Browning, *Cy Young*, 12–13.

127. Ward, "Is the Base Ball Player a Chattel?"

128. Stray Sparks from the Diamond, *New York Clipper*, September 20, 1890.

129. "Players League Meeting," *New York Clipper*, July 26, 1890.

130. "Players League Meeting."

131. *New York Clipper*, August 2, 1890.

132. *New York Clipper*, August 2, 1890.

133. *New York Clipper*, August 2, 1890.

134. Stray Sparks from the Diamond, *New York Clipper*, August 30, 1890.

135. "Players League Meeting," *New York Clipper*, August 16, 1890.

136. The Players League, *New York Clipper*, July 26, 1890.

137. Thorn, *Total Baseball*.

138. The Players League, *New York Clipper*, August 16, 1890.

139. The Players League, *New York Clipper*, August 16, 1890.

140. The Players League, *New York Clipper*, August 23, 1890.

141. The Players League, *New York Clipper*, August 23, 1890.

142. The Players League, *New York Clipper*, August 23, 1890.

143. "1890 Chicago Pirates Batting, Pitching, & Fielding Statistics," *Baseball-Reference.com*, available at http://www.baseball-reference.com/teams/chi/1890.shtml; "Events of Monday, August 18, 1890," *Retrosheet.org*, http://www.retrosheet.org/boxesetc/1890/08181890.htm#1.

144. "1890 New York Giants Batting, Pitching, & Fielding Statistics," *Baseball-Reference.com*, available at http://www.baseball-reference.com/teams/nyi/1890.shtml.

145. "1890 Chicago Pirates Batting, Pitching, & Fielding Statistics."

146. "Events of Thursday, September 4, 1890," *Retrosheet.org*, available at http://www.retrosheet.org/boxesetc/1890/09041890.htm#1.

147. Cited in "Figures Can't Lie," *Sporting Life*, October 11, 1890.

148. Quoted in "Baseball: The Cincinnati Club," *New York Clipper*, October 11, 1890.

149. "Figures Can't Lie."

150. "Figures Can't Lie."

151. "Figures Can't Lie." *Reach's 1891 Official American Association Base Ball Guide* published these same figures. Incidentally, both Burk's (*Never Just a Game*) account of the Players League and Di Salvatore's (*Clever Base-Ballist*) argue that *Reach's* are the most reliable numbers available, positing that they come from a somewhat independent source. Neither author recognizes that *Sporting Life* and the *Boston Globe* printed these same figures five months earlier.

152. "Champions Honored," *Sporting Life*, October 18, 1890.

153. "Champions Honored."

154. "Champions Honored."

155. The idea behind "1891" rather than "1890" was that a team was the champion for a full year *after* it had won the pennant, not for the season leading up to its league title.

7. Fall of the 1890 Players League

1. "Champions Honored," *Sporting Life*, October 18, 1890.

2. "Anxious and Indignant Players," *Sporting Life*, October 18, 1890.

3. "Figures Can't Lie," *Sporting Life*, October 11, 1890.

4. "Brunell's Budget," *Sporting Life*, November 22, 1890.

5. "Brunell's Budget."

6. Stray Sparks from the Diamond, *New York Clipper*, January 3, 1891.

7. That Brunell's figures were only estimates is reinforced by a private letter that Boston Players League president Charles Prince sent to club treasurer Frederick Long: "My Dear Long:—When can we see your books, as treasurer, all completed and closed? Some three months have gone by; and we are now with no knowledge of our exact condition: which we should have. Will you do me a personal favor by hurrying the matter as fast as you can?" (January 2, 1891, Frederick Long Papers, box 2, folder 17, National Baseball Hall of Fame Library). Not even all the directors of the clubs themselves were sure of their financial condition. Exactly why Long had not shared these figures, since he did have them, is unknown. It is quite possible that everyone in the club, including Prince, knew of the general financial condition but had not yet seen the precise figures.

8. Receipts and Expenses Boston Base Ball Club Season 1890, Frederick Long Papers, box 2, folder 10, National Baseball Hall of Fame Library.

9. Receipts and Expenses; Burk, *Never Just a Game*.

10. Burk, *Never Just a Game*.

11. "Baseball: A Noted Gathering," *New York Clipper*, October 18, 1890.

12. "Baseball: A Noted Gathering."

13. "Baseball: A Noted Gathering."

14. "Baseball: A Noted Gathering."

15. Stray Sparks from the Diamond, *New York Clipper*, October 25, 1890; "Baseball: The Purposed New League," *New York Clipper*, October 25, 1890; "What Mr. Abell Says," *New York Clipper*, October 25, 1890; "Agreeing to Disagree," *Sporting Life*, October 25, 1890.

16. "Players' League: Sudden Tumble into a Deep and Wide Pitfall," *Sporting Life*, October 18, 1890.

17. "Agreeing to Disagree."

18. "Agreeing to Disagree."

19. "Agreeing to Disagree"; "Baseball: The Purposed New League," *New York Clipper*, October 25, 1890.

20. "Baseball: The Purposed New League."

21. "Agreeing to Disagree."

22. Baseball, *New York Clipper*, November 1, 1890.

23. "The Brotherhood," *Sporting Life*, October 25, 1890.

24. "Agreeing to Disagree."

25. Baseball, *New York Clipper*, November 1, 1890.

26. "Players League in Session," *New York Clipper*, November 1, 1890.

27. "Players League Meeting," *Sporting Life*, October 25, 1890.

28. "Players League Meeting."

29. "Players League Meeting."

30. "Players League Meeting."

31. "The Tripartite Committee Meets," *New York Clipper*, November 1, 1890.

32. "Tripartite Committee Meets."

33. "Tripartite Committee Meets."

34. "Conference Talk," *Sporting Life*, November 1, 1890.

35. "To Divide Capitalists and Players," *Sporting Life*, October 25, 1890.

36. "The First Meeting," *Sporting Life*, November 1, 1890.

37. "Robinson, of New York, Talks," *Sporting Life*, November 1, 1890.

38. Stray Sparks from the Diamond, *New York Clipper*, November 15, 1890.

39. The decision to use Brotherhood Park did not come until about a month and a half later, when Day and Spalding toured the former Players League grounds for the first time. "When they saw the field and the grand stand, they expressed themselves as very much in favor of those grounds for the future home of the New Yorks" (Stray Sparks from the Diamond, *New York Clipper*, December 13, 1890).

40. Quoted in "Addison Turns Up," *Sporting Life*, November 8, 1890.

41. "Suspicion's Finger," *Sporting Life*, November 1, 1890.

42. Stray Sparks from the Diamond, *New York Clipper*, November 8, 1890.

43. Stray Sparks from the Diamond, *New York Clipper*, November 8, 1890.

44. Stray Sparks from the Diamond, *New York Clipper*, November 8, 1890.

45. "The First Meeting," *Sporting Life*, November 1, 1890.

46. Stray Sparks from the Diamond, *New York Clipper*, November 15, 1890.

47. Pittsburgh's Monongahela House, located on the corner of Smithfield and Water Streets, along the banks of the Monongahela River, was considered one of the most luxurious and modern hotels west of New York. It had previously served as a safe house on the Underground Railroad and was the site in 1856 where a band of abolitionists formed the Republican Party. Between 1839 and 1935, when it was razed to make way for a bus depot, it hosted eleven U.S. presidents, including Abraham Lincoln in 1861, when he and his family were on their way to Washington for his inauguration (John W. Jordon, *A Century and a Half of Pittsburg and Her People*, vol. 4 [New York: Lewis, 1908]; Breanna Smith, "Let's Learn from the Past: The Monongahela House," *Pittsburgh Post Gazette*, January 17, 2013).

48. "Baseball: The Players League," *New York Clipper*, November 22, 1890.

49. "Baseball: The Players League."

50. "Baseball: The Players League."

51. "Baseball: The Players League."

52. "Baseball: The Players League."

53. Stray Sparks from the Diamond, *New York Clipper*, November 22, 1890.

54. Stray Sparks from the Diamond, *New York Clipper*, January 10, 1891.

55. *New York Clipper*, November 29, 1890.

56. Stray Sparks from the Diamond, *New York Clipper*, December 6, 1890.

57. "Collapse of a Crowded Stand at Eastern Park," *Brooklyn Daily Eagle*, November 28, 1890.

58. This section of the grandstand was actually on loan from the Players League's Forepaugh Park for the purpose of putting on the football game. No structural damage to Eastern Park's baseball grandstand occurred ("Collapse of a Crowded Stand at Eastern Park").

59. Albert Spalding, Spalding's Review, *Sporting Life*, November 29, 1890.

60. Stray Sparks from the Diamond, *New York Clipper*, December 20, 1890.

61. Reprinted in Stray Sparks from the Diamond, *New York Clipper*, January 10, 1891.

62. Stray Sparks from the Diamond, *New York Clipper*, January 10, 1891.

63. Stray Sparks from the Diamond, *New York Clipper*, January 17, 1891.

64. Stray Sparks from the Diamond, *New York Clipper*, January 17, 1891.
65. "The Players League Meeting," *New York Clipper*, January 24, 1891.
66. "National League Meeting," *New York Clipper*, January 24, 1891.
67. Stray Sparks from the Diamond, *New York Clipper*, February 14, 1891.
68. Stray Sparks from the Diamond, *New York Clipper*, February 14, 1891.
69. The AA's withdrawal is complicated, but it rested on the legal interpretation of the post-1890 reserve rule. The AA and the NL each had a club in Boston and Philadelphia in 1891, and in both cities the AA team had been in the Players League the previous year. To complicate things further the Philadelphia club, still owned by the Wagner brothers, had legally purchased Philadelphia's American Association club, the Athletics, which literally had no other assets at this point other than its name. Immediately after the NL's meeting in January, Pittsburgh's consolidated National League club signed second baseman Lou Bierbauer. The Philadelphia American Association, however, club claimed that it held Bierbauer under reservation, on the grounds that Bierbauer had played for the 1889 Philadelphia AA club. Pittsburgh argued that Philadelphia had failed to submit its reserve list before the mandated deadline, a mistake the AA club claims was due merely to a clerical error. Bierbauer was one of the best second basemen in the game, and his presence in the National League with Pittsburgh or the American Association with Philadelphia would make a significant impact in the drawing capacity of every opposing club. The National Board agreed to adjudicate the situation. Inexplicably American Association representative Allen Thurman voted along with Albert Spalding to allow Pittsburgh to sign Bierbauer. The AA clubs immediately fired Thurman. At their meeting the following week, the American Association unanimously voted to withdraw from the National Agreement. Pittsburgh also signed Connie Mack via similar technicalities, and the club was soon dubbed the "Pirates" for allegedly "pirating" these players (Britcher, "1890 Burghers and Alleghenys").
70. Burk, *Never Just a Game*.
71. Spalding, *America's National Game*, 281.
72. Spalding, *America's National Game*, 271.
73. Ross, "Scales and Skills of Monopoly Power"; Schneirov and Suhrbur, *Union Brotherhood, Union Town*.

BIBLIOGRAPHY

Achorn, Edward. *The Summer of Beer and Whiskey: How Brewers, Barkeeps, Rowdies, Immigrants, and a Wild Pennant Fight Made Baseball America's Game*. New York: Public Affairs, 2013.

Agnew, John A. *The United States in the World-Economy: A Regional Geography*. Cambridge: Cambridge University Press, 1987.

Anderson, Kay J. "Cultural Hegemony and the Race-Definition Process in Chinatown, Vancouver: 1880–1980." *Environment and Planning D: Society and Space* 6, no. 2 (1988): 127–49.

———. "The Idea of Chinatown: The Power of Place and Institutional Practice in the Making of a Racial Category." *Annals of the Association of American Geographers* 77, no. 4 (1987): 580–98.

Anson, Adrian C. *A Ball Player's Career, Being the Personal Experiences and Reminiscences of Adrian C. Anson*. Chicago: Era, 1900. Available at http://www.gutenberg.org/files/19652/19652-h/19652-h.htm.

Ballzell, E. Digby. *Philadelphia Gentlemen: The Making of a National Upper Class*. Philadelphia: University of Pennsylvania Press, 1979.

Barnett, R. "The Proper Scope of the Police Power." *Notre Dame Law Review* 79 (2003): 2–60.

Bederman, Gail. *Manliness & Civilization: A Cultural History of Gender and Race in the United States, 1880–1917*. Chicago: University of Chicago Press, 1995.

Bernheim, Alfred L. *The Business of the Theatre: An Economic History of the American Theatre, 1750–1932*. New York: B. Blom, 1964.

Blewett, Mary H. "Deference and Defiance: Labor Politics and the Meanings of Masculinity in the Mid-Nineteenth-Century New England Textile Industry." *Gender & History* 5, no. 3 (1993): 398–415.

Block, David. *Baseball before We Knew It: A Search for the Roots of the Game.* Lincoln: University of Nebraska Press, 2005.

Boucher, John Newton, and John W. Jordan. *A Century and a Half of Pittsburg and Her People.* New York: Lewis, 1908.

Bowman, Larry G. "Baseball Mascots in the Nineteenth Century." *National Pastime*, no. 19 (1999): 107-10.

Boxerman, Burton Alan, and Benita W. Boxerman. *Jews and American Baseball.* Jefferson NC: McFarland, 2007.

Britcher, Craig. "The 1890 Burghers and Alleghenys: Why 'We Are Pirates!'" *Western Pennsylvania History*, forthcoming.

Bromley, George. *Atlas for the City of Boston.* Philadelphia: G. W. Bromley, 1891.

Browning, Reed. *Cy Young: A Baseball Life.* Amherst: University of Massachusetts Press, 2000.

Burk, Robert Fredrick. *Never Just a Game: Players, Owners, and American Baseball to 1920.* Chapel Hill: University of North Carolina Press, 1994.

Burrows, Edwin G., and Mike Wallace. *Gotham: A History of New York City to 1898.* New York: Oxford University Press, 1999.

Chadwick, Henry. *The American Game of Base Ball, How It Is Played; A Manual.* Philadelphia: T. Holland, 1888.

Chadwick, Henry. *The Art of Base Ball Batting.* New York: A. G. Spalding & Bros., 1885.

———. *How to Play Base Ball.* New York: A. G. Spalding & Bros., 1889.

Christie, Robert A. *Empire in Wood: A History of the Carpenters' Union.* Ithaca NY: Cornell University, 1956.

Clark, George. "Implications of Lumley v. Wagner." *Columbia Law Review* 17, no. 8 (1917): 687-702.

Di Salvatore, Bryan. *A Clever Base-Ballist: The Life and Times of John Montgomery Ward.* New York: Pantheon Books, 1999.

Forbes-Robertson, Diana. *My Aunt Maxine: The Story of Maxine Elliott.* New York: Viking Press, 1964.

"From Buffalo to Niagara by Electric Car." *Electrical Engineer* 15 (1893): 248.

Gelzheiser, Robert P. *Labor and Capital in 19th Century Baseball.* Jefferson NC: McFarland, 2006.

Ginsberg, Daniel. "John Kinley Tener." In *Deadball Stars of the National League*, edited by Tom Simon, 26-28. Washington DC: Brassey's, 2004.

Goldstein, Warren. *Playing for Keeps: A History of Early Baseball.* Ithaca NY: Cornell University Press, 1989.

Green, James R. *Death in the Haymarket: A Story of Chicago, the First Labor Movement, and the Bombing That Divided Gilded Age America*. New York: Pantheon Books, 2006.

Harrison, Tara. *Alice and Agate Courts Historic District Designation Report*. Edited by Mary Beth Betts. New York: New York City Landmarks Preservation Commission, 2009.

Harvey, David. "The Body as an Accumulation Strategy." *Environment and Planning D: Society and Space* 16, no. 4 (1998): 401–21.

Ingersoll, Robert Green. *What's God Got to Do with It? Robert G. Ingersoll on Free Thought, Honest Talk, and the Separation of Church and State*. Edited by Tim Page. Hanover NH: Steerforth Press, 2005.

Ivor-Campbell, F., and D. Pietrusza. "Postseason Play." In Thorn, *Total Baseball*, 319–540.

Jacoby, Susan. *The Great Agnostic: Robert Ingersoll and American Freethought*. New Haven CT: Yale University Press, 2013.

Keefe, Tim. Brotherhood of Professional Base Ball Players Meeting Minutes. Hunt Auctions, 1885. doi: http://huntauctions.com/live/imageviewer _online.cfm?auction_num=19&lot_num=1149&lot_qual=.

Kelly, Michael J. *"Play Ball": Stories of the Diamond Field*. Jefferson NC: McFarland, 2006.

Kimmel, Michael. "Baseball and the Reconstruction of American Masculinity." In *Cooperstown Symposium on Baseball and American Culture*, edited by Alvin Hall, 281–97. Westport CT: Meckler, 1989.

Lamster, Mark. *Spalding's World Tour: The Epic Adventure That Took Baseball around the Globe—and Made It America's Game*. New York: Public Affairs, 2006.

Levine, Peter. *A. G. Spalding and the Rise of Baseball: The Promise of American Sport*. New York: Oxford University Press, 1985.

Lewis, Ethan M. *A Structure to Last Forever: The Players League and the Brotherhood War of 1890*. 2001. Available at http://www.ethanlewis.org/pl/ch1.html.

Lomax, Michael E. *Black Baseball Entrepreneurs, 1860–1901: Operating by Any Means Necessary*. Syracuse NY: Syracuse University Press, 2003.

Lorenz, Carl. *Tom L. Johnson, Mayor of Cleveland*. New York: A. S. Barnes, 1911.

Lowenfish, Lee, and Tony Lupien. *The Imperfect Diamond: The Story of Baseball's Reserve System and the Men Who Fought to Change It*. New York: Stein & Day, 1980.

Lowry, Philip J. *Green Cathedrals: The Ultimate Celebration of Major League and Negro League Ballparks*. New York: Walker, 2006.

Macht, Norman L. *Connie Mack and the Early Years of Baseball*. Lincoln: University of Nebraska Press, 2007.

Marx, Karl. *Capital*. Vol. 1, *A Critique of Political Economy*. New York: International, 1977.

McCollister, John. *The Good, the Bad, and the Ugly Pittsburgh Pirates: Heart-Pounding, Jaw-Dropping, and Gut-Wrenching Moments from Pittsburgh Pirates History*. Chicago: Triumph Books, 2008.

MLB Advanced Media. "Pirates Single Game Records | Pirates.com: History." Pittsburgh Pirates. Available at http://pittsburgh.pirates.mlb.com/pit /history/single_game_records.jsp.

Montgomery, David. *The Fall of the House of Labor: The Workplace, the State, and American Labor Activism, 1865-1925*. Cambridge: Cambridge University Press, 1987.

National League of Professional Base Ball Clubs. *Constitution and Playing Rules of the National League of Professional Base Ball Clubs: Official, 1876*. St. Louis: Horton, 1988.

Nemec, David. *The Beer and Whisky League: The Illustrated History of the American Association—Baseball's Renegade Major League*. Guilford CT: Lyons Press, 2004.

———. *The Rank and File of 19th Century Major League Baseball: Biographies of 1,084 Players, Owners, Managers and Umpires*. Jefferson NC: McFarland, 2012.

O'Connell, Kevin. *Tom Johnson: The Life and Times of Cleveland's Greatest Mayor*. Cleveland: Green Road Press, 2001.

Oronhyatekha. *History of the Independent Order of Foresters*. Toronto: Hunter, Rose, 1894.

Orzeck, Reecia. "What Does Not Kill You: Historical Materialism and the Body." *Environment and Planning D: Society and Space* 25, no. 3 (2007): 496–514.

Reach, A. J. *Reach's 1891 Official American Association Base Ball Guide*. Philadelphia: A. J. Reach, 1891.

Reckman, Bob. "Carpentry: The Craft and Trade." In *Case Studies on the Labor Process*, edited by Andrew S. Zimbalist, 73–102. New York: Monthly Review Press, 1979.

Ribowsky, Mark. *A Complete History of the Negro Leagues, 1884 to 1955*. Secaucus NJ: Carol Publishing Group, 1995.

Riess, Steven A. *Touching Base: Professional Baseball and American Culture in the Progressive Era*. Westport CT: Greenwood Press, 1980.

Roper, Michael. "Between Manliness and Masculinity: The 'War Generation' and the Psychology of Fear in Britain, 1914-1950." *Journal of British Studies* 44, no. 2 (2005): 343-62.

Rose, William Ganson. *Cleveland: The Making of a City*. Cleveland: World, 1950.

Rosenberg, Howard W. *Cap Anson 2: The Theatrical and Kingly Mike Kelly: U.S. Team Sport's First Media Sensation and Baseball's Original Casey at the Bat*. Arlington VA: Tile Books, 2004.

Ross, Robert B. "Scales and Skills of Monopoly Power: Labor Geographies of the 1890-1891 Chicago Carpenters' Strike." *Antipode* 43, no. 4 (2011): 1281-304.

Ruck, Rob. *Raceball: How the Major Leagues Colonized the Black and Latin Game*. Boston: Beacon Press, 2011.

Sante, Luc. *Low Life: Lures and Snares of Old New York*. New York: Farrar, Straus, & Giroux, 1991.

Saraceni, Gene Adam. "Herne and the Single Tax: An Early Plea for an Actors' Union." *Educational Theatre Journal* 26, no. 3 (1974): 315-25.

Schneirov, Richard, and Thomas J. Suhrbur. *Union Brotherhood, Union Town: The History of the Carpenters' Union of Chicago, 1863-1987*. Carbondale: Southern Illinois University Press, 1988.

Seymour, Harold. *Baseball: The Early Years*. New York: Oxford University Press, 1989.

Smith, Neil. *Uneven Development: Nature, Capital and the Production of Space*. Oxford: Basil Blackwell, 1990.

Spalding, A. G. *America's National Game: Historic Facts concerning the Beginning, Evolution, Development, and Popularity of Base Ball, with Personal Reminiscences of Its Vicissitudes, Its Victories, and Its Votaries*. Lincoln: University of Nebraska Press, 1992.

———. *Spalding's Base Ball Guide and Official League Book for 1889*. St. Louis: Horton, 1988.

Stevens, David. *Baseball's Radical for All Seasons: A Biography of John Montgomery Ward*. Lanham MD: Scarecrow Press, 1998.

"Street Railway News." *Street Railway Journal* 9, no. 5 (1893): 273-346.

Thorn, John. *Total Baseball: The Ultimate Baseball Encyclopedia*. Wilmington DE: Sport Media, 2004.

Travis, Steve. "The Rise and Fall of the Theatrical Syndicate." *Educational Theatre Journal* 10, no. 1 (1958): 35-40.

Voigt, David Quentin. *American Baseball: From Gentleman's Sport to the Commissioner System*. Norman: University of Oklahoma Press, 1966.

Ward, John M. *Base-ball: How to Become a Player, with the Origin, History, and Explanation of the Game.* Philadelphia: Athletic, 1888.

———. "Is the Base Ball Player a Chattel?" *Lippincott's*, August 1887, 310–19.

———. "Notes of a Base-Ballist." *Lippincott's*, August 1886, 212–20.

———. "The Players National League." In *1890 Players National League Base Ball Guide: All the Official Figures.*, edited by Frank Brunell, 3–6. Chicago: F. H. Brunell, 1890.

Zimbalist, Andrew S. *Baseball and Billions: A Probing Look inside the Big Business of Our National Pastime.* New York: Basic Books, 1992.

INDEX

Page numbers in italic indicate illustrations.

ballparks: accessibility of, 126–27; admission prices to, 10, 48, 114; in Boston, 129–30, 137, 150–51, *154*; in Brooklyn, 12–13, 129, 157, 163, 195, 232n58; in Buffalo, 131; carpenters and, 36–37, 140–50; in Chicago, 36, 37, 132–33, 165–66; in Cleveland, 130–31, 220n174; concessions at, 30, 33–37, 150–51, 200, 204n7; construction of, 77, 135–40; design and structure of, 36, 163, 165–66; gambling at, 7, 9, 11, 114; in New York, 97, 128–29, 157, 163, *164*, 165, 192, 219n154, 219–20n157, 231n39; in Philadelphia, 127–28, 219nn151–53; in Pittsburgh, 131–32, 165; Players League securing of, 126–33; sale of alcohol at, 10–11, 46–47, 114; and urban expansion, 107. *See also* attendance, ballpark

The Ball Player's Book of Reference, 7

Barnes, Ross, 154, 224n3

Barnie, William, 185, 189

baseball books, 6, 7, 11, 12, 14–15

baseball image, 2, 3–4, 9–10, 16, 18; class conflict over, 4–5, 12–13; of player celebrities, 23–24

baseball origins, 2–3, 201n1; Ward on, 15, 202n33

baseball players: African American, 13, 24–26, 56, 203n55; buying and selling of, 59–60, 72, 73, 87, 175; celebrity image of, 23–24; disciplining of, 30, 37–43, 55; health of, 39; Jewish, 172–73, 228n110; as labor force, xvi–xvii, 1, 16, 22, 27; as main fan attraction, xvii, 16, 77; residency of, 20–21, 203n47; skill levels of, 17–18, 19–20, 53; unpleasant aspects of profession, 69; working-class identity of, 53–54, 67, 71–72. *See also* Brotherhood of Professional Base Ball Players; reserve rule; salaries

baseball popularity, 2, 26–27, 32–33; and Civil War, 6, 7; and profitability, 84, 200

baseball rules, 6, 16–18, 21–23, 113–14

baseballs, 13, 21; mass production of, 34; in Players League, 113–14, *115*, 150, 169, 223n50

baseball statistics, 6, 17

baseball terminology, 6–7

batting averages, 6, 22, 169

Beadle's Dime Base Ball Player, 6, 7, 12

Beaman, Charles, xv

Beckley, Jake, 156, 170

Beeman, E. E., 93

Beemer, John, 100

bidding wars, 48, 76, 106; and increased salaries, 9, 20, 22, 45, 47, 74, 116–17

Bierbauer, Lou, 120, 167, 178, 233n69

Billings, James B., 98

Binghamton Crickets, 58

Binghamton Morning Republican, 58

Blackhurst, James F., 74, 209n82

blacklisting, 38, 41, 47, 60, 65–66, 67

black ballplayers, 13, 24–26, 56, 203n55

Blake, Charles D., 159

Block, David, 201n1

Boston MA: carpenters in, 140, 144–46, 222n36

Boston Globe, 38, 155–56, 168, 171, 180, 181

Boston National League franchise, 33, 45, 155

Boston Players League franchise: ballpark in, 129–30, 137, 150–51, *154*; during 1890 season, 153–56, 168–69, 177–79, 180–81, 184; investors in, 97–100; signing of players for, 120, 121

Boyle, Henry, 119

McAlpin, Edwin, 97, 109, 110, 189–90, 194

McCallin, William, 100

McDermott, George, 63–64

McGuire, Peter J., 139, 142

McGunnigle, William, 103–4

Meakin, Alexander, 97

Medill, Joseph, 222n29

Meyers, George, 100

Miller "Cash," 174

Mills, A. G., 44, 47, 48

Morrill, John, 78, 99, 121, 129–30, 214n41

Murdough, James, 105

Murnan, Tim, 168

Mutrie, Jim, 95

Myers, Al, 104

Myers, George, 108

Nash, Billy, 83, 99, 121, 155

National Agreement (Tripartite Pact), 48, 191, 198, 233n69

National Association of Amateur Base Ball Players (NAABBP), 8

National Association of Base Ball Players (NABBP), 6, 7, 18, 20, 21; birth and death of, 5, 8; exclusion of black players from, 25

National Association of Professional Base Ball Players (NAPBBP), 8, 9, 20, 21

National Flint Glass Workers' Association, 100

National League (NL): and American Association, 13, 22, 45–47, 123–24, 191, 198; and ballpark concessions, 30, 33–37; baseball image wanted by, 9–11; and baseball rules, 21–23; and Cincinnati franchise, 10, 179–80, 194; defections of brotherhood members to, 118–20, 122–23; disciplining of players' behavior by,

30, 37–43; 1890 season of, 171–74, 184, 227n95; exclusion of black players from, 24; fan attendance for, 155, 156, 157–59, 171, 174, 176, 224n19, 227n95; formation of, 9; geographic spread of, 31, 204n5; and International Association, 43–45, 205n38; legal action against Players League by, xiii–xvi, 117–18, 124–26; as monopoly, xvii, 51; pennant of, 58, 207n31; Players League competition with, xix–xx, 77, 87–88, 116, 159–81; Players League consolidation with, 185–94; after Players League demise, 197–98; profitability of, 29–30, 32, 33, 43; relations with brotherhood by, 73–74, 75–76, 78, 83–84; replacement players of, 123–24, 162, 173, 174–75; and reserve rule, xv–xvi, 39, 41, 48, 52, 70–71, 117–18, 124–26, 197–98; salary control efforts of, 22, 37–38, 41–42, 82; schedule competition by Players League with, xix, 160–62; stated purpose of, 111; territorial rights in, 29–33, 160; and Union Association, 65–67

National Police Gazette, 61

newspapers, 5, 13–14

New York Clipper, 32, 54, 163, 171; about, 5–6; on brotherhood, 83, 84; on Players League, 150, 157, 170, 178, 196–97; Ward and, 65–66, 68

New York Knickerbockers, 3, 5

New York Mercury, 5

New York National League franchise, 192, 231n39; expulsion and readmittance of, 31–32, 47–48; incorporation of, 94; and NL profitability, 32, 33; and Players League, xiii–xv, 94–96, 157